T0314743

TWENTIETH-CENTURY DRAMA
DIALOGUE AS ORDINARY TALK

For Eirian and Saskia

Twentieth-Century Drama Dialogue as Ordinary Talk
Speaking Between the Lines

SUSAN MANDALA
University of Sunderland

ASHGATE

Published by
Ashgate Publishing Limited
Wey Court East
Union Road
Farnham
Surrey, GU9 7PT
England

Ashgate Publishing Company
110 Cherry Street
Suite 3-1
Burlington
VT 05401-3818
USA

Ashgate website: http://www.ashgate.com

British Library Cataloguing in Publication Data
Mandala, Susan
Twentieth-century drama dialogue as ordinary talk : speaking between the lines
   1. Pinter, Harold, 1930-. Homecoming 2. Pinter, Harold, 1930- – Literary style 3. Wesker, Arnold, 1932-. Roots 4. Wesker, Arnold, 1932- – Literary style 5. Rattigan, Terence. In praise of love 6. Rattigan, Terence – Literary style 7. Ayckbourn, Alan, 1939-. Just between ourselves 8. Ayckbourn, Alan, 1939- – Literary style 9. Dialogue analysis 10. Conversation analysis
   I. Title
   401.4'1

Library of Congress Cataloging-in-Publication Data
Mandala, Susan, 1968-
   Twentieth-century drama dialogue as ordinary talk : speaking between the lines / by Susan Mandala.
      p. cm.
   Includes bibliographical references and index.
   ISBN-13: 978-0-7546-5105-5 (alk. paper)
   1. English drama—20th century—History and criticism. 2. Dialogue. 3. Pinter, Harold, 1930- Homecoming. 4. Wesker, Arnold, 1932- Roots. 5. Rattigan, Terence. In praise of love. 6. Ayckbourn, Alan, 1939- Just between ourselves. 7. Discourse analysis, Literary. 8. Conversation analysis. I. Title.

PR736.M35 2007
822'.91409—dc22

2007010453

ISBN: 978-0-7546-5105-5

Transferred to Digital Printing in 2014

MIX
Paper from responsible sources
FSC
www.fsc.org   FSC® C004959

Printed and bound in Great Britain
by Printondemand-worldwide.com

Contents

List of Tables

Acknowledgements

Much of the work on this book was done while I was on research leave at the University of Sunderland, and I am grateful to the Culture Area and Media Area Research Committees of the School of Arts, Design, Media and Culture for granting me the time to work on this project. I am blessed with a particularly supportive group of colleagues at Sunderland who were a constant source of support while I was writing this book. Very special thanks, however, go to Stuart Sim, who took a sincere interest in the project and was never too tired or too busy to read drafts or answer questions. All young academics should have a colleague like Stuart. I would also like to thank Richard Terry and John Strachan, colleagues who were also generous with their time and their expertise, and who encouraged me every step of the way with kindness, unfailingly good advice, and coffee. Grateful thanks are also extended to Richard Steadman-Jones for reading a draft of the manuscript, to Saskia Barker and Eirian Davies for listening to most of it, and to Sue Cottam and Hazel Holt for their help with printing out drafts. I would also like to thank the anonymous reader located by my editor, whose very valuable comments were a great help as I was finishing the book. Thanks are also due to a group of friends at my local café, who always made me feel welcome when I needed a break. Last but certainly not least, heartfelt thanks go to my students, past and present, who never fail to inspire me.

Preface

Why this Book?

This book offers a linguistic study of selected dialogue from four modern plays – Harold Pinter's *The Homecoming*, Arnold Wesker's *Roots*, Terence Rattigan's *In Praise of Love* and Alan Ayckbourn's *Just Between Ourselves*. It aims to demonstrate that the application of methods, perspectives, and findings from the linguistic investigation of ordinary talk can deepen our understanding of the art form that is drama dialogue. While the approaches used here can be applied to drama texts from any age (e.g., see Hermann 1995), I have chosen to look at four well known plays from playwrights writing at a critical juncture in the history of British theatre, a time when traditional themes and practices in playwrighting (as evidenced by Rattigan and, some have said, Ayckbourn) were being challenged by new forms and concerns, the so-called 'new wave' in British drama (as evidenced by Pinter and Wesker).

Why is a book like this of interest? One reason is that the stylistics of drama is still relatively uncharted territory. In her ground-breaking work on drama dialogue and discourse published in 1980, Deirdre Burton claimed that stylisticians typically did not deal with drama texts (1980: 3). Apparently, very little has changed since then. Culpeper et al. (1998: 3), writing 18 years after Burton, echo her observation by noting that in comparison to poetry and fiction, drama texts are a 'neglected child' and 'have received relatively little attention from both twentieth century literary critics and stylisticians'.

Culpeper et al. (1998) are not exaggerating. Toolan's (1990) *The Stylistics of Fiction* addresses itself, as the title indicates, to prose fiction, primarily Faulkner, and his 1988 work on narrative has a similar focus. Leech and Short (1981) similarly constrain themselves to prose fiction, and Babb's (1972) collection is devoted primarily to articles on poetry and prose. In like fashion, Widdowson's (1975) exploration of stylistics foregrounds analyses of fiction and poetry. Carter and Nash (1990) deal with both literary and non-literary texts in their exploration of style, but drama texts do not feature heavily in their account. Their section on dialogic structure is limited to dialogue in fiction, and the entry for 'dialogue' in their glossarial index is similarly demarcated 'in fiction'. Their entry on 'speech' follows suit in being limited to indirect and free indirect speech in fiction. Recent journals seem to be following the same trend. Of the four issues of *Language and Literature* published in 2002, for example, none contained articles on drama. Course books tend to follow the same pattern. Wright and Hope's (1996) textbook on stylistics concerns itself with prose, primarily prose fiction, and Toolan's (1998) introduction to the subject is similarly unconcerned with drama texts. Short's (1996) work on poems, plays and prose is by no means dismissive of drama texts in stylistics, but even he devotes only two chapters of his book-length treatment to the study of drama.

If the stylistic study of drama is rare, the stylistic study of drama dialogue as talk is even rarer. Nine years after Burton's (1980) work, Carter and Simpson (1989: 5) were still characterizing her discourse analytic approach to drama dialogue as somewhat out of the ordinary. Herman (1995: 3), writing six years after Carter and Simpson, still cites a lack of interest in drama dialogue as talk among stylisticians, noting that 'studies of dramatic dialogue as discourse – as a speech exchange system – are hardly in evidence, even in investigations of "the language of drama"'. Culpeper et al.'s collection of articles on how the study of conversation can be applied to drama dialogue did not appear until 1998, and they point out in their introduction that the only book-length treatment of drama dialogue as talk to have joined Burton's was Herman's (1995) *Dramatic Discourse* (Culpeper et al. 1998: 4). More recent work also bears evidence of the dearth of material on the study of drama dialogue as talk. Piazza's 1999 analysis of *The Caretaker* and other modern plays lists Burton (1980) as its only reference for previous work on drama dialogue as discourse, and Toolan (2000) cites only a handful of scholars working in this tradition, many of whom are also cited in Culpeper et al.'s 1998 collection. As Culpeper et al. (1998: 4) note, the paucity of studies in this area is particularly surprising given the availability of theoretical approaches to talk that have appeared since the publication of Sinclair and Coulthard's *Towards an Analysis of Discourse* in 1975.

A second reason for writing this book is to demonstrate that it is time for linguists to stop apologizing for daring to work on literary texts. Since Jakobson's declaration that it was the 'right and duty of linguistics to direct the investigation of verbal art in all its compass' (1960/1996: 33), the role of linguistics in the study of literature has been fiercely debated (Fowler 1986/1996: 196; Carter and Simpson 1989: 1; Attridge 1987/1996: 37; Carter 1982: 1). While many linguists have been keen to turn their hand to the study of literature, literary critics have not, on the whole, welcomed this attention (Fowler 1986/1996: 196). As Carter (1982: 7) has pointed out, it is the linguists who have often felt the need 'to play the game according to literary rules'. Malcolm Coulthard (1977/1985: 179), for example, declares 'it is reasonable to suggest that a detailed analysis of authorial technique and stylistic features can be more successfully achieved within a rigorous linguistic framework', but not without first noting that 'evaluation and interpretation is the province of the literary critic'. While Carter (1982: 8) has called for adjustment and accommodation on both sides of the literary/linguistic divide, I argue here that linguists who turn their attention to literature and literary language have no need to make excuses for their discipline, its sub-disciplines, and their methods. In fact, many of the arguments levelled against the use of linguistic methods in the study of literature and drama appear to be based on only a partial understanding of how linguists proceed in their work.

It has been claimed, for example, that linguistic analysis, because it employs scientific methods, is near-robotic, an automatic process divorced from human agency (see Fish 1973/1996). Fowler very aptly summarises this view as follows:

there is a common misconception that linguistics – any linguistics – is a kind of automatic analyzing device which, fed a text, will output a description without human intervention. The critics of course regard this as a soullessly destructive process, a cruelty to poems … (Fowler 1986/1996: 197).

A similar stance is taken by the critic Evans (1977), even in a book on dramatic language. For him, work in linguistics means only two things, either 'fastidious ministrations to language' or 'immense and often fierce lab-work' (Evans 1977: viii). As Fowler (1986/1996: 197) notes, however, these are misconceptions based on rather stereotypic notions of what the science of linguistics actually involves. Procedures in linguistics are not best described as robotic or fastidious or fierce. Rather, they are *systematic*. As Burton (1980: 119) explains, there is a commitment in linguistics to analytical rigour such that the theoretical and descriptive frameworks proposed seek to account for all of the data collected. In addition, methods of analysis are described in detail so that procedures are replicable, and criteria for judgements made are transparent and retrievable (Carter and Simpson 1989: 14; Carter 1982: 5–6). And while certain kinds of linguistic analysis may appear to be independently mechanical to those unfamiliar with the nature of linguistic enquiry, the analytical procedures adopted are conceived of, directed, *and interpreted* by a person, as Fowler (1986/1996: 197) points out. The analyst is every bit as involved as the critic even if the observations of the former have a tendency to be reported in the passive voice (Simpson 1997: 3).

It has also been claimed (see Fish 1973/1996) that linguists aspire to provide objective accounts of the texts they are studying. This, according to some critics, makes their methods inappropriate to the study of literature, which necessarily involves subjective value judgements (Fowler 1986/1996). While linguists do call for specificity, precision, and the provision of evidence in support of claims made, aspirations to objectivity are no longer widely invoked. As Carter and Simpson (1989: 6, see also Toolan 1990/1996: 131) have noted,

> it is naïve to pretend that any application of linguistic knowledge, whether modelled or otherwise, and however dedicatedly and rigorously formalized the model, can result in an 'objective', value-free interpretation of data.

It is now widely accepted that both texts and readers are culturally, socially, politically and economically situated. The call made by Sarah Mills (1992/1996: 12) for a 'Marxist feminist contextualised stylistics' that proposes 'a move away from text immanent criticism to a more theoretical concern with the factors outside the text that may determine or interact with elements which appear in the text' is certainly an indication of this acceptance. And while work in stylistics does tend to make the case for a relationship between form and meaning, structure and effect, it is now generally recognised that this relationship can be problematic, and cannot be posited without reflection (see Toolan 1990/1996: 12). Carter and Simpson (1989: 4), for example, caution against 'too narrow a focus on linguistic form' in the study of literary texts. What will be of interest, they go on to point out, is how these forms '*implicate aspects of context*' or 'signal, directly or indirectly, *the many functions* they *can be made* to perform' (Carter and Simpson 1989: 4, italics mine). Work in stylistics has clearly come a long way from its formalist roots, and the commitment to analytical rigour is a strength, not an embarrassment. As the studies in this book will demonstrate, Jakobson in one respect, at least, was right – it is the prerogative, even the duty, of the linguist to contribute to the study of literature.

Books such as mine do not generally receive a warm welcome from critics. In their review of Adrian Beard's *Texts and Contexts* (2001), for example, Doumont and van Noppen (2002) are relieved to discover that it 'is not, thank heavens, the umpteenth attempt at making linguistics relevant to literary critics' (248), and they go on to point out that critics are in the main 'quite happy with the instruments in their toolkit' (Doumont and van Noppen 2002: 248). While my book may indeed be the 'umpteenth attempt' to demonstrate that linguistics is relevant to criticism, I have gone a step further than many other studies in stylistics. Instead of mentioning a few critical responses and citing the corresponding sources (as do Toolan 2000; Herman 1995; and Burton 1980, for example), I have taken an in-depth look at how drama critics have dealt with the language of the plays in which I am interested. I have been able to show that when it comes to analyzing the language of drama, methods and findings from linguistics are beneficial tools to have at hand. I have found that when critical accounts explicitly engage issues of language without reference to work in linguistics they are not as persuasive as they could be. This does not mean that I think critics who want to look at issues of language must retrain and become linguists. Rather, my claim is that work in linguistics is relevant to their enterprise and worthy of their consideration even if it is (at first) unfamiliar to them or outside their ordinary domain of study.

While my approach may engage me in a stance that some might find combative, I have taken special care to be fair. I have not sought out 'fringe' authors in questionable publications for an easy fight. I look at formative voices in the debate, acknowledged keystones in the edifice of modern drama criticism such as J.R. Taylor, Martin Esslin, Ronald Hayman, Andrew Kennedy, and J.L. Styan. Many of these critics remain influential in the field through reprints and new editions of their work that still appear on university drama course reading lists (Short 1998: 7). Similarly, I have searched for the descendants of these pioneers in respected academic journals (e.g. *Modern Drama, Tulane Drama Review*) and mainstream scholarly presses (e.g. Cambridge University Press, Methuen, Heinemann, Routledge), and many of the recent critics I deal with are multiply cited in the critical literature.

It should also be borne in mind that I am not claiming that all other approaches be discontinued in favour of linguistic ones. Feminist, Freudian, postmodern, historical and political approaches have all added much to our understanding of drama, and where critics have made convincing arguments from within their own frameworks of study I have said so. Nor do I take the view that work in linguistics is 'perfect' or free from variant interpretations. Herman (1995), for example, draws on Goffman (1979) and Levinson (1988) to suggest that Beatie, the main character in *Roots*, does not own her own utterances until the end of the play. In contrast, my interpretation of *Roots*, which draws on variation in English, is very different.

What Coulthard (1977/1985: 179) has said of literature can also be said of drama: it is an art form crafted entirely in and through language. It is surprising that linguistics, the study of language, is so routinely ignored or resisted in modern drama criticism. As the studies in this book clearly demonstrate, applying methods and findings from linguistics to the study language in drama allows us to shed new light on the plays investigated.

Chapter 1

Drama Dialogue and Talk

This book is about drama dialogue, and its aim is to look at how the linguistic study of natural conversation can inform our understanding of represented conversations in plays. It seeks to achieve this aim by offering a series of in-depth investigations into how the dialogue of four modern plays (Harold Pinter's *The Homecoming*, Arnold Wesker's *Roots*, Terence Rattigan's *In Praise of Love* and Alan Ayckbourn's *Just Between Ourselves*) works with respect to the pragmatic and discoursal norms postulated for ordinary conversation. Given such a focus, this study falls under what is known as the stylistics of drama, which is itself part of the discipline of literary stylistics: the use of theories in linguistics to study the language of literature. As Carter and Simpson (1989) have pointed out, the analyst in this field will typically want to

> draw eclectically on linguistic insights and to use them in the service of what is generally claimed to be fuller interpretation of language effects than is possible without the benefit of linguistics (7).

This orientation, however, is not uncontroversial, and a number of issues need to be discussed before the analyses of the chosen play texts begin.

Text and Performance

One of the first questions that needs to be asked is whether play texts can legitimately be studied apart from their performances. The stylistic study of drama assumes that a rigorous study of the play text is sufficient for analysis (Culpeper et al. 1998: 6). Is this in fact the case? For a number of critics and drama theorists, divorcing text from performance is problematic. It has been said that drama 'is not a thing but a happening' (Beckerman 1970: 18); that the text consists of 'mere words' (Brown 1967: 133) which are only fully actualized by actors in a performance (Patterson 1996: 52; Beckerman 1970; Brown 1967; Esslin 1968); and that 'no script can ever record the complete play' (Beckerman 1970: 63). Some have even gone so far as to question the ontological status of the play text. According to this view, the play text might not actually exist in its own right, but come into being only upon performance for an audience (Lennard and Luckhurst 2002).

Conceptualizing drama in this way clearly privileges performance over text. What then of those who wish to foreground the text? Mick Short, a specialist in the stylistics of drama, has made the case for the study of play texts apart from their performances very eloquently, and a number of his points are relevant here. If we take the performance-as-primary position to its logical conclusion, it would mean, as Short (1998: 8) notes, that a play could only be intelligently discussed not just by people who had seen it performed, but only by those people who had seen *the same* performance. Clearly, such a strict interpretation of the primacy of performance is rarely upheld. Indeed, performance in most cases starts with the text, as this must be read, understood, and interpreted before the play can be presented to an audience (Short 1998: 7). In addition, the necessity of 'holding constant the object under critical discussion' means that some textual record of the performance is required for critical study and analysis (Short 1998: 7–8).

While the importance of performance is not to be denied, it must also be recognized that scrutiny of the play text itself has a place in the study of drama. Short (1998) notes that each performance can be considered a version of the text, variations on the same theme. While every performance will be different, none of them will be so different as to constitute the telling of an entirely new story (Short 1998: 8). From this point of view, the text is not so much a 'blue print' for performance (Lennard and Luckhurst 2002) as an anchor.

Short (1998: 9) also notes that the play text itself contains a wealth of performance information that is available for readers to access. While it may be tempting to dismiss Short's argument here as radically divergent from the consensus view regarding performance within drama studies, there is evidence to suggest that he is not alone. In his study of Arden, Osborne, Pinter and Wesker, Brown (1972) acknowledges that he proceeds largely by 'imagin[ing] the plays as in performance' (14). Wallis and Shepherd (1998: 2–3) have similarly noted that since the words in the text of the play have been written with performance in mind, the text 'contains an implied production' that the reader can enter into.

While it is well known that an utterance or a line of dialogue in isolation can be interpreted in a number of different ways, we do not in the main encounter in play texts isolated lines of dialogue. Written plays provide contexts for their dialogue, and as Short (1998: 16) has pointed out, these contexts reduce the potentially vast number of possible interpretations down to a plausible few. As users of language, we can and do, as part of the normal reading process (as it is understood by linguists and psychologists), bring substantial amounts of knowledge, organized into what are known as 'schema' (Shank and Abelson 1977), to bear on the 'mere words' of the text. For example, texts usually provide stage directions that specify a location or a situation for the action. This information activates the relevant schema, which in turn allows the reader to fill in a number of relevant details without having to see the piece performed (Short 1998: 10). In a similar way, Short (1989: 144) notes that we can use the given contexts, including the context of the ongoing dialogue itself, to deduce the intended meaning of the represented speech from the written text alone. This also allows us to infer appropriate gestures, body position, gaze, intonation, loudness, accent, and so on (Short 1998: 16). The text, of course, will not make everything explicit, and this certainly leaves room for interpretation; there is, however, less room for movement here than is perhaps widely recognized (Short 1998: 16). Texts may allow several varying interpretations, but they do not warrant an infinite number of divergent readings. While there can clearly be no drama without performance, the status of the written text, and the cognitive ability of its reader, should not be ignored or underestimated.

The Drama Critic and the Linguist

Having decided that texts can be legitimately analysed in the absence of performance, we still have to ask if the linguist needs to be involved in this endeavour. After all, a number of critics have themselves looked at dramatic dialogue and the language of which it is composed (e.g. Batty 2001; Kermode 2000; Malkin 1992; Dukore 1982; Evans 1977; Quigley 1975; Brown 1972; Esslin 1970), and a recent guide to studying plays includes a chapter on various linguistic aspects of interest to the study of dialogue (see Wallis and Shepherd 1998). Does the enterprise of drama criticism actually need the input of the linguist? To begin answering this question, we can look at how critics have dealt with Pinter, a playwright whose dramatic language has been of particular interest since he was first read and performed. For the purposes of this chapter, I will concentrate on only a handful of critics, and show in later chapters how such treatments of language are not atypical of work in drama criticism. While the critics discussed here have all made lasting and undeniably valuable contributions to our understanding of Pinter's plays, I argue that their treatments of his dramatic language are somewhat limited in scope, often because insights from linguistics are not taken on board. Specifically, I will be demonstrating that: 1) a tendency to concentrate on lexical items limits the potential of the analyses; 2) the use of vague, non-technical terms to describe features identified can confuse the discussion; and 3) a tendency to depend on intuitive and impressionistic views of natural talk can undermine the value of the conclusions presented.

While aspects of language are often explicitly proposed as central features worthy of study in Pinter's plays, many of the analyses offered tend to be heavily dependent on the identification of lexical items (individual words and word-like phrases). A case in point is the work of Jeanette Malkin, who explicitly commits herself to an investigation of the language of Pinter's dialogue in a study entitled *Verbal Violence in Contemporary Drama* (1992). In this work, Malkin makes clear that she views language as a powerful force in the plays she studies. Language assumes the role of dramatic antagonist (Malkin 1992: 38, 40); it 'has an almost magical power to wound and destroy' (41), and it 'wield[s] the characters rather than being wielded by them' (40).

While Malkin (1992) is clearly interested in the role of language in Pinter's work, her analysis leans in places on the identification of words and word-like units. For example, her account of the language used by Goldberg and McCann in *The Birthday Party* depends heavily on lexical categories. The language used by these characters is 'a sophisticated mixture of corporate *jargon*, gangster *slang*, and social pieties' (Malkin 1992: 54) that is 'cluttered with the most hackneyed *idioms* and socially sanctioned aspirations' (1992: 65). They speak 'a language consisting of *terms* and *idioms* culled from a stratum of speech beyond their own experience' (Malkin 1992: 61). They use 'philosophical and theological *jargon*' against Stanley (1992: 59), and 'the assault is … a melting-pot of distorted *idioms* and *cliches*' (1992: 59). Goldberg 'uses Yiddish *idioms*' (1992: 55) and his discourse drips with '*proverbial* wisdom', 'social *clichés*' (1992: 66) and advice 'delivered in a highly *clichéd* style' (1992: 55, italics mine). Malkin's analysis of *The Caretaker* follows suit. We are told that 'Mick's speech … snowballs into the convoluted *jargon* of high finance and insurance' (Malkin 1992: 60), and this is followed by a lengthy list of words and phrases that behave like words cited from the play: 'down payments, back payments, family allowances, bonus schemes, remission of term for good behaviour', and so forth.

What is of concern here is not so much the decision to look at idiom, cliché, jargon, and slang. Indeed, these features are clearly relevant to the discussion and Malkin is justified in pointing out that there is something to notice about their use. What I find problematic is that some of the claims made on the basis of identifying words and word-like units do not stand up well under scrutiny. For example, Malkin points to the many jargon forms in the speeches of Pinter's gangster characters, and suggests that these are notable because readers and audiences do not expect 'such specialized language' (1992: 60) from these characters. She suggests that Pinter has 'immaculate control' of jargon, and 'echoes with precision formulae of specialized speech' (Malkin 1992: 60). While she exemplifies instances of 'specialized speech' and 'recognizable jargon styles' with lists of jargon terms (1922: 59), greater attention could also have been paid to their 'proper contexts' by comparing the represented jargon styles in the dialogue with the actual language of the genres listed – 'the gangster movie, the spy novel, the theological sermon, the philosophy lecture', etc. (Malkin 1992: 59). In Malkin's account, the actual language characteristic of these genres is not given detailed consideration, and this undermines her claim that Pinter 'echoes' any particular jargon style 'with precision'.

While an investigation into the language of a particular text can certainly include an analysis of lexical items, it can also go much further. To many professional analysts of language, i.e. linguists, lexical features of texts tend to be the least interesting. In an introductory textbook on stylistics, for instance, Wright and Hope (1996: xiii) purposefully put their chapter on lexis last because it is 'the most limited area linguistically'. In Sanger's (2001) *The Language of Drama*, another introductory textbook that takes an explicitly linguistic approach, lexis is not even given its own chapter. In the main, linguists who turn their attention to drama dialogue go well beyond the lexical level of analysis. Herman (1998), for example, looks at the significance of turn-taking patterns in Osborne's *Look Back in Anger*, and Simpson (1989) uses politeness theory (Brown and Levinson 1978/1987) to explore the dynamics of power in Ionesco's *The Lesson*. Politeness theory has also been used by Bennison (1993), who looks at how readers and audiences infer character traits from the dialogue with reference to Stoppard's *Professional Foul*. Speech acts and exchange structure have also been applied in the study of dramatic language. Short (1989), for example, demonstrates how the performance of infelicitous speech acts can be related to absurdist themes in Beckett's *Waiting for Godot*; Coulthard (1977/1985) looks at questions and prospected answers in a discussion of why Othello is so easily convinced of his wife's adultery; and Nash (1989) shows how discourse structure patterns in the opening of *Hamlet* serve to establish an atmosphere of confusion and apprehension.

Linguists interested in Pinter's language are similarly wide-ranging with respect to the categories of analysis adopted. Short (1989) uses speech act types and participant role relations in order to explore the comically absurd nature of the sketch *Trouble in the Works*; Burton (1980) looks at phatic communion, shared knowledge, and conversational structure to account for the combination of farce and menace in *Last to Go*; Toolan (2000) employs a framework of initiating moves in discourse to look at the interrogation scene in *The Birthday Party*; and Gautam (1987) explores problematic interactions in *The Caretaker* with respect to teacher-pupil discourse (Sinclair and Coulthard 1975), and the cooperative principle of conversation as proposed by Grice (1975). Piazza (1999), also interested in *The Caretaker*, looks at conversational repair strategies in the dialogue.

In seizing on words and word-like units to the virtual exclusion of the many other possible categories of analysis, Malkin may be following the lead of Esslin (1968, 1970), the undisputed 'big name' in Pinter criticism. As with the many critics who followed him, Esslin (1968, 1970) took a specific interest in Pinter's language. For him, Pinter was a master of ordinary talk (Esslin 1970: 219), a pioneer in the artistic use of the thoroughly mundane (1968: 281). While these observations are initially promising, Esslin's account of Pinter's language tends to concentrate on lexical items and in so doing does not always progress his goal of coming to grips with Pinter's linguistic achievements. Consider, for example, Mick's decorating plans in *The Caretaker*:

> You could have an off-white pile linen rug, a table in … in afromosia teak veneer, sideboard with matt black drawers, curved chairs with cushioned seats, armchairs in oatmeal tweed, a beech frame settee with a woven sea-grass seat, white-topped heat resistant coffee table, white tile surround (Mick in *The Caretaker* 1960/1972: 60).

For Esslin, this description is 'genuine poetry' that 'transmutes the jargon of contemporary brand names into a dreamlike world of wish fulfillment' (1968: 281). In support of this conclusion, however, Esslin concentrates on brand names, words that serve as labels. Of potentially greater interest in Mick's speech, however, are the noun phrases. In English, these typically consist of a determiner, optional premodification, and the head noun (e.g. *a big car*). Modification after the head noun is also possible, and frequently occurs (a big car *with tinted windows*). In ordinary conversation, noun phrases are typically simple in structure (Crystal and Davy 1969; Brown and Yule 1983b: 16). If premodification is used, it is generally limited to one or two items (Wright and Hope 1996: 12; Brown and Yule 1983b: 16), and these will tend to be drawn from the frequent, everyday terms (e.g. a *big red* car; a *pretty* smile) that typically characterize informal talk (Adamson 1989). Mick's description clearly deviates from this norm. A number of noun phrases with two or more premodifiers (*off-white pile linen* rug; *white-topped, heat-resistant coffee* table) are used, and many of them are drawn from the semantic field of interior decorating or meant to sound that way (afromosia teak, off-white pile, matt black, white-topped, heat-resistant, oatmeal, beech frame, woven sea-grass).[1] Thus, it is not simply the use of brand names that is noticeable in Mick's speech. It is the use of these names within a larger syntactic construction that transforms 'the jargon of contemporary brand names into a dreamlike world of wish fulfillment'. While the brand names may at first glance be the most obvious point of entry for analysis, it is the fact that they occur in noun phrases distinctly uncharacteristic of ordinary talk that gives them their 'dreamlike' power.

Esslin's dependence on the lexical item as a unit of analysis in the study of Pinter's dialogue is understandable in the late 1960s and early 1970s. At this time, research into the linguistic nature of ordinary talk had only just begun. Developments include the Survey of English Usage, a project devoted to the collection and study of natural conversational data (see Quirk 1968c for an early account), studies of native speaker linguistic acceptability (e.g. Quirk and Svartvik 1966) and investigations into the grammatical features or educated spoken English (Quirk 1968b). While Esslin (1968, 1970) writes too early to benefit from these and subsequent developments, it is clear that such findings can be very usefully brought to bear on more recent explorations of the language of drama. Consider, for example, Malkin's suggestion that Goldberg (in *The Birthday Party*) tends to use 'evasive bureaucratic terminology' (Malkin 1992: 54). As evidence for her claim, she cites the following speech:

> GOLDBERG: The main issue is a singular issue and quite distinct from your previous work. Certain elements, however, might well approximate in points of procedure to some of your other activities. All is dependent on the attitude of our subject. At all events, McCann, I can assure you that the assignment will be carried out and the mission accomplished with no excessive aggravation to you or myself (Pinter 1958: 30, Malkin 1992: 54–5).

While Malkin's point is instructive, a linguistic analysis can shed more light on *why* this stretch of dialogue strikes us as 'evasive' and 'bureaucratic'. Goldberg's speech makes use of the passive voice (*the assignment will be carried out and the mission accomplished*), deverbal adjectives after copular verbs (*is dependent on* rather than 'depends on'), formal conjuncts (*however*), and dependent clauses (*that the assignment will be carried out ...*). Such features, more typical of written documents than ordinary conversation (Brown and Yule 1983b: 14–16), may be what give this speech its 'bureaucratic' flavour. While Malkin usefully asserts the existence of 'bureaucratic terminology', there was scope to take the analysis of Goldberg's language much further.

Critical accounts of Pinter's language have also been hampered by a reluctance to employ the conventional technical terms widely used in linguistics. In some discussions, explanations are offered for this. Brown (1972) and Evans (1977), for instance, argue that by 'language' they mean anything that communicates, and thereby justify their decision to look more generally at the vocabulary of the theatre in relation to the speech of the characters. Evans (1977: viii) even goes so far as to dismiss contributions from linguistics in his study since he finds the discipline to be 'incomprehensible'. However, examining linguistic features of a text without employing the conventional technical terms of the discipline can be problematic.[2] Malkin (1992: 61), for instance, identifies a number of idioms in her discussion, and characterizes them as 'massive and disjointed'. But what exactly do these terms mean? In the first place, how can an idiom be 'massive'? The confusion arises (at least in part) because 'massive' is not in common use as a technical term in linguistics or, for that matter, in literary criticism or drama studies. Five technical dictionaries were consulted (Crystal 1980/1991, Richards et al. 1985/1992, and Trask 1999 for linguistics; Lennard and Luckhurst 2002 for drama; and Cuddon 1992 for literature), and 'massive' was not listed in any of them. This makes it likely that Malkin is using one of the ordinary senses of the term 'massive' (determined here by definitions of the term given in *The Oxford English Dictionary Online*, consulted 14 February 2003).

Since Malkin is predicating 'massive' of 'idioms', it would, of course, be facile to assume that she is applying the first given definition and making some sort of statement regarding the physical size or mass of the idioms. It is far more likely that 'massive' is being used here to mean that the idioms are 'imposing in scale' or 'far-reaching'. But in what sense are the idioms 'imposing in scale'? And if 'far-reaching' is the sense that is intended, this is also problematic as a technical description. How 'far' exactly do the idioms reach? And towards what?

It is also possible that the term could be used as it is applied to diseases, as in 'affecting a large continuous portion of tissue'. This could apply if we looked at the dialogue metaphorically as tissue, and considered that it was 'diseased' by idioms. However, Malkin does not indicate that she is using 'massive' in this way, nor is this use of the term self-evident in her account. A final possibility, of course, is that Malkin is introducing 'massive' as a technical term. However, there is no indication that this is what is intended. A definition is not offered, and criteria for the use of the term in the analysis are not specified.

Malkin's use of 'disjointed' can be treated in a similar way. Like massive, 'disjointed' is not a term with technical status (according to the five dictionaries consulted), and this can leave the reader at a bit of a loss. Drawing again on the search of the *Oxford English Dictionary Online*, 'disjointed' when applied to words or discourse means 'without proper connection or sequence; disconnected; incoherent'. In what way are the idioms improperly sequenced? In fact, is there a proper sequence of idioms? If we try to look at the idioms as 'disjointed' with reference to the text Malkin discusses as a whole, this also falls apart, as sense can be made of it – it is not incoherent.

Reading further in Malkin, what she appears to mean by 'disjointed' is that the idioms and technical jargon are put in the mouths of characters that would not normally be assumed to have mastery over such vocabulary. It should be noted, however, that this is my best guess as to how the term 'disjointed' has been applied to the identified idioms. The use of 'disjointed' has obscured the point, not clarified it.

Malkin's discussion provides other examples, as when she refers to Goldberg's language as a 'seamless web of sententiousness' (1992: 66). While there are certainly grounds for concluding that Goldberg is pompous and apt to offer advice no one has sought, in what way is his language a 'seamless web'? Here, Malkin (1992) may be drawing on earlier critics such as Brown (1967: 142), who characterized Pinter's dialogue as a 'web of conversation'. While the term may have precedence, it, like 'massive' and 'disjointed', has no technical status. Without further qualification as to its intended use, terms such as 'web' when applied to language offer very little information.

Further examples of this kind are not difficult to find in the literature on Pinter. To Malkin's use of 'massive', 'disjointed', and 'seamless web' we can add Kennedy's '*aggressive* jargon', '*broken* phrases', and '*slangy* language' (1975: 189–90); and El Khalfi's (2000: 175) '*dry*', '*fraught with coarseness*' and '*unfriendly*'. While the critic J.L. Styan (1960/1976) has complained about the use of such ultimately meaningless terms (he calls them 'shovel-words'), he himself has used them in discussions of Pinter's language: Pinter represents 'the *evasive* exchanges of everyday life, and has an 'extraordinary talent for '*obliquity* in his dialogues' (Styan 1981/1998: 135, 134, italics mine).

It could be argued, of course, that making such a detailed critique of the use of these terms is pedantic in the extreme, and that linguists have no right to demand that critics meet technical specifications they are under no obligation to uphold. Such a dismissal, however, might prove hasty. While terms such as *slangy, evasive, massive, aggressive*, and *dry* may express legitimate intuitions that critics have about the speech of certain characters, they are far too subjective to be offered as linguistic analysis. As the account above has shown, critics who avoid the relevant technical terminology in discussions of Pinter's language have not, to paraphrase Ron Carter (1982: 5–6), always made their path from reading to judgement clear, and this should not be waved away as the complaint of an unreasonable pedant. The absence of transparent and retrievable procedures makes it difficult for future scholars to build on or refute previous work, and this is a serious pitfall in scholastic activity.

Ordinary Talk and Drama Dialogue

A further concern in the critical record on Pinter is the tendency to offer analyses of his dialogue that are based on unexplored assumptions concerning the linguistic nature of talk. Such assumptions are especially apparent in discussions of how 'true-to-life' Pinter's dialogue is. As Burton (1980: 69) has pointed out, a primary concern among Pinter critics is his ability to write such 'realistic-sounding dialogue', dialogue that in particular represents the vernacular. It is frequently observed, for instance, that Pinter characters use non-standard forms, stammer, hesitate, repeat themselves and at times do not speak at all. While such features may not raise many eyebrows today, they were nothing short of extraordinary in the early years of Pinter's career, and audiences and critics alike were struck by what Esslin (1970: 193) called 'a new band of colours' in 'the spectrum of English stage dialogue'. As Kennedy (1975: 169) put it, Pinter 'seems to carry no literary 'burden of the past' (see also Brown 1972: 73 and Esslin 1968: 292 for similar conclusions). Instead, he uses his 'uncannily accurate ear' for natural talk (Esslin 1970: 194) and his 'mastery of real-life idiom' (Esslin 1968: 276). Kennedy (1975) goes even further, declaring that

> on the linguistic level proper Pinter's dialogue is precise enough to provide samples for a work on the varieties of contemporary English; and the conversational rhythms alone could be used to train 'aural perception' in foreign students of Spoken English (1975: 166).

Leaving aside the problematically vague 'conversational rhythms', linguists interested in the 'linguistic level proper' have noted that while drama dialogue may resemble what we think of as talk, it differs from it in a number of crucial respects. Abercrombie (1963/1965: 4), for example, suggests that stage and screen dialogue present 'spoken prose', which is 'far more different from conversation than is usually realized' (1963/1965: 3). He goes on to warn us that we must not go to novels, plays and films for examples of natural conversation (1963/1965: 3). While the linguistic investigation of talk can and should inform the study of drama dialogue, drama dialogue is not good evidence for the study of conversation. As Herman (1995: 6) has noted, dramatic dialogue that represents the vernacular is not presented simply for mimetic value, but crafted for a purpose – the dramatist who draws on ordinary speech is not merely imitating for effect, but showing the audience something.

This insight, of course, is not in itself new to drama criticism. Styan (1960/1976: 12) notes that drama dialogue is 'speech that has had a specific pressure put on it'; Esslin (1970: 194) points out that Pinter's dialogue does far more than simply reflect ordinary talk, and Kennedy (1975: 2) acknowledges that dramatic language has to be realistic enough to convince ('a dramatist cannot leave behind the 'living speech' of his age'), but at the same time carefully designed in order to effectively accomplish the playwright's purpose. When it comes to analyzing Pinter's work in relation to the 'living speech of the age', however, and exploring just what kind of 'pressure' is put on it in the dialogue, a number of critics have either worked without the benefit of an appropriate set of analytic tools, or not used the tools available to them. Critical accounts that want to discuss how 'realistic' Pinter's dialogue is and how his language relates to or subverts natural talk norms are, I argue, in a better position to do so when issues of linguistic realism are given greater consideration. Recourse to assumptions about the nature of talk can hinder rather than help an analysis since not all such assumptions stand up under closer inspection.

One of these assumptions, as Herman (1995: 4) points out, is that talk is simply not up to the task of communicating complex emotions. This position is articulated particularly clearly by Nicoll (1968), who claims that ordinary language leaves us '"tongue-tied"' in the face of passion, '"stunned with grief"', and '"spluttering"' incoherently in response to our anger (1968: 341, see also Herman 1995:4). This view is partly driven by a similar misconception, that ordinary talk in English is characterized by 'broken or jumbled-up syntax' (Kennedy 1975: 168). Linguists, however, do not typically devalue the vernacular in these ways. It has been shown time and time again that spoken English, while different to written English, is no less grammatical (Crystal and Davy 1969; Brown and Yule 1983a: 4–6; Richards 1990:

72–3; Carter and McCarthy 1995). In addition, it is widely accepted among linguists that ordinary conversation is the primary means of communication in human society, the form from which all other forms derive. It is the everyday spoken language that is first acquired by children and, as Wright and Hope (1996) point out, the everyday spoken language that springs most spontaneously to the lips, especially during times of high emotion.

Another assumption about ordinary talk that frequently undermines discussions of its representation in Pinter's plays is that talk is random. While Esslin (1968: 276) is clearly impressed with Pinter's 'clinically accurate ear', he describes what Pinter manages to capture so brilliantly as absurd, a 'rambling irrelevancy' (1968: 265). Nicoll (1968: 339, 334–45) is similarly dismissive of ordinary talk, claiming that the dramatist should seek to use language that is carefully patterned (with respect to sound concord, associative imagery, etc.) in order to be truly expressive.

What Nicoll (1968) and Esslin (1968) did not, perhaps could not, consider is that ordinary talk *is* patterned. As is now widely accepted (at least by linguists), talk does not just ramble. Work in conversation and discourse analysis has repeatedly shown that turns at talk are specifically made by speakers (and expected by hearers) to be relevant to the ongoing discourse (for a more detailed discussion of these issues, see Chapter 2). While topics of conversation can vary widely, there are understood procedures for introducing new topics, and it has been shown that we cannot in actual fact say anything we want to. Once an initiating move is made, there are only a limited number of expected responses, and anything that occurs will be interpreted in light of those expectations (Sinclair 1992: 83). While participants in a conversation are not bound by a fixed order of speaking turns, these are nevertheless managed in an orderly fashion (Sacks, Schegloff and Jefferson 1974). Even our verbal conflicts have been found to unfold in predictable ways (Vuchinich 1990; Schiffrin 1985). Tannen (1989) has further observed that speakers spontaneously pattern their talk with forms previously thought to be 'reserved' for literary use. When viewed from a linguistic perspective, Pinter's brilliance may not lie in taking the 'randomness' of talk and giving it shape in his dialogue. Rather, his 'ear for dialogue' may come across as extraordinary because of his ability to manipulate and reorder the normally existent patterns of everyday talk (Herman 1995: 4). As will be shown in Chapter 3, Pinter represents ordinary features of the vernacular in unexpected ways, and it is this exploitation of the raw material of talk that leads audiences and readers to ask questions about characters and their actions.

In fairness, critics such as Esslin (1968, 1970) and Nicoll (1968) cannot be held accountable for subscribing to what were then widely held views on the subject of everyday talk. As noted earlier, linguistic research into the nature of ordinary conversation was still in its infancy when they were first writing on Pinter. More difficult to excuse on this account is Kennedy (1975). While Kennedy (1975: 168) is keen to point out that Pinter does much more than simply present ordinary talk in his dialogue, his analysis does not always support his case very well. Part of the problem seems to be a reluctance to make detailed use of a publication that arose out of work on the Survey of English Usage, Crystal and Davy's (1969) *Investigating*

English Style, one of the earliest empirical investigations into the linguistic nature of ordinary English conversation.

While Kennedy (1975) quotes Crystal and Davy (1969), he does not appear to fully engage their arguments or systematically apply their categories of analysis to the dialogue. The result is an account that is engaging in places, but not as convincing as it could be. For example, Kennedy draws directly on Crystal and Davy (1969) in order to characterize natural spoken English, and he goes on to point out how 'life-like' the narrative of Davies the tramp is in the opening of *The Caretaker*. While he cites lines from the play in support of his claim, these strike the linguist as unanalysed. Just what is it in the dialogue cited that makes it so 'life-like'?

> 'Ten minutes off for tea-break in the middle of the night in that place, and I couldn't find a seat, not one. All them Greeks had it ... (Kennedy 1975: 170, citing Davies in *The Caretaker*, ellipses his).

With Crystal and Davy (1969) under his belt, Kennedy could have pointed to a number of linguistic features in just these two lines that are characteristic of spoken English, such as the use of coordinated, as opposed to subordinated, clauses ('*and* I couldn't find a seat'), and the tendency to load adverbials at the end of a sentence ('Ten minutes off for a tea-break *in the middle of the night in that place*'; 'I couldn't find a seat, *not one*'). Also apparent are features that mark inexplicitness, such as situational ellipsis (*Ten minutes off for a tea-break* v. I had *ten minutes off for a tea-break*), demonstrative pronouns with vague referents (*that place*), and the use of personal pronouns (*I*). In addition, a syntactic form is used that is normal in many spoken dialects of English, but proscribed in formal writing (objective *them* instead of demonstrative *those* in *them Greeks*).

Kennedy could also have used Crystal and Davy's (1969) argument concerning the features identified to further his own hypothesis on linguistic reflection and subversion in Pinter's dialogue. As Crystal and Davy (1969) explain, features of talk such as inexplicitness and the use of non-standard forms tend to occur in the speech of people who know each other well and share a store of background knowledge. While there is no reason to suspect this of Aston and Davies in the opening of *The Caretaker*, the language used by Davies nevertheless implies it. There are interesting questions to ask about why this is, and Kennedy might have used Crystal and Davy to greater effect in his thesis on such issues. Instead, however, he moves on to more traditional territory, contrasting the opening of *The Caretaker* with the opening of Beckett's *Waiting for Godot* (Kennedy 1975: 170). While there is much of interest in his comparison, it does little to advance his argument regarding Pinter's exploitation of conversational language.

Problems with assumption and intuition are no less apparent when critics attempt to deal with Pinter's dialogue as represented interaction. As linguists have repeatedly noted (Toolan 2000; Piazza 1999; Culpeper et al. 1998: 3; Herman 1995; Bennison 1993; Simpson 1989: 145; Carter and Simpson 1989; Nash 1989; Burton 1980; Coulthard 1977/1985), critical frameworks that include explicit knowledge of the way talk is managed between and among interlocutors can enrich our understanding of drama, the genre that is actualized through carefully wrought spoken interactions (Herman 1995: 13). As Herman (1995: 6) points out, dramatic dialogue works by exploiting the norms of conversational behaviour that the audience and the dramatist share. Short (1989: 149) proposes a similar framework, noting that when 'character speaks to character ... this discourse is part of what the playwright 'tells' the audience' (for further discussion on Short's framework, see Chapter 2). As Herman (1995) and Burton (1980: 94) both note, however, there were few comprehensive frameworks of ordinary talk as interaction on which to draw prior to the mid-1970s, which saw the publication of Sinclair and Coulthard's (1975) *Towards an Analysis of Discourse*, and Sacks, Schegloff, and Jefferson's (1974) *A Simplest Systematics for the Organization of Turn-taking for Conversation*.

A look at some of the critical accounts interested in Pinter's dialogue as interaction written at or before this time indicates that the lack of such approaches was problematic for the analysis. For example, Kennedy (1975) has to leave key concepts and processes that relate to interactive talk in inverted commas, such as 'transactions', 'living language', and 'shaping'. Inverted commas used in this way are widely known as scare quotes, and they serve to distance the author from the term or terms enclosed within them (Trask 1997: 107). As Trask (1997: 107–8) points out, authors often employ scare quotes when they use terms they find 'unfamiliar or mysterious'. In Kennedy's account, it is especially telling that the term *shaping*, the very process he is trying to define and illuminate, occurs in scare quotes throughout his Pinter chapter (e.g. see pages 177, 187, 188, 190). This is a term that Kennedy adopts from Pinter himself, who used it in *Writing for the Theatre*:

> I think I can say I pay meticulous attention to the shape of things from the shape of a sentence to the overall structure of the play. This shaping, to put it mildly, is of the first importance. But I think a double thing happens. You arrange *and* you listen, following the clues you leave for yourself, through the characters (Kennedy 1975: 175, quoting Pinter).

Pinter's account of the term, however, is not an analysis of how he shapes language in his work, and Kennedy does not shed much further light on the subject. Rather, he recycles the term and distances himself from it by keeping it within inverted commas. The result is that the process of shaping remains, for the most part, a mystery of Pinter's that Kennedy can only partly engage. When an explanation of this term is attempted, it is made with reference to comparisons of questionable relevance to the analysis:

> It is only in retrospect that the spectator or reader can see that each of those shifts of language has been as precisely coded as traffic signals – green into red and so on – and it is only then that the 'shaping', and with it the meaning of the play, is seen (Kennedy 1975: 187).

Kennedy (1975: 185) seems similarly ill at ease when he wants to talk about abrupt changes of topic in the dialogue. Lacking a theoretical framework that accounts for conversational units such as speaking turns and their organisation between interlocutors, he again leans on comparisons, describing such shifts as 'something like a key-change'. While metaphors such as 'key-change' and 'green into red' may evoke images that seem appropriate, they ultimately tell us nothing about the language of Pinter's dialogue and its power to move audiences (Quigley 1975).

Esslin (1970) runs into similar problems when dealing with Pinter's dialogue as represented talk between interlocutors. His starting point is that

> a true understanding of Pinter's use of language must ... be based on deeper, more fundamental considerations: it must start from an examination of the function of language in stage dialogue generally – and indeed from considerations of the use of language in ordinary human intercourse itself (Esslin 1970: 194).

Towards this end, he devotes a chapter, *Language and Silence*, to examining 'some of Pinter's favourite linguistic and stylistic devices' (1970: 199). Without a comprehensive model of conversational interaction on which to base his analyses, Esslin had to depend on intuition and assumption. In some cases, this takes him reasonably far. For example, he goes straight to the heart of the matter with respect to pauses and silences, noting that 'only if the audience knows the possible alternative answers to a question can the absence of a reply acquire meaning and dramatic impact' (1970: 222). With this statement, he shows an intuitive understanding of what conversation analysts today call preference organisation and attributable silences (for further discussion, see Chapter 2).

However, it is not long before intuition and assumption about the nature of talk lead to weaknesses in his discussion. Instead of a detailed account of how pauses and silences work in tandem with the spoken discourse unfolding between the characters, Esslin talks about Pinter's writing and its 'density of texture' (1970: 222), and suggests that Pinter uses silence to signal the end of one movement and the beginning of another, 'as between the movements of a symphony' (1970: 220). When the music metaphor becomes exhausted, Esslin turns to meteorology and biology – 'pauses and silences are thus often the climaxes of [Pinter's] plays, *the still centres of the storm*, the *nuclei* of tension ...' (Esslin 1970: 220, italics mine). While such metaphor loading gives Esslin's writing a certain verve, it does little to show how Pinter has exploited the phenomenon of silence in talk (Quigley 1975).

That Esslin's work will remain as a landmark contribution in the study of Pinter is beyond doubt. However, he ultimately fails in his central purpose of demonstrating how 'each word [of a Pinter play] is essential to the total structure and decisively contributes to the overall effect aimed at' (1970: 219). Without a 'fully articulated' (Burton 1980: 194) theory of conversational interaction, it is difficult for him to define the 'total structure'. In addition, he is limited to the unit of the word in his discussion of 'the overall effect aimed at', when what he needs is the speaking turn, the speech act or the discourse move (all explained further in Chapter 2). While Esslin's insights into the nature of talk were in many ways incisive, they did little to help him with a systematic analysis of language and silence and Pinter's dialogue.

Other features of interactive talk have created similar difficulties in critical discussions of Pinter that cannot or do not engage work in conversation and discourse analysis. Such features include the hesitations, self-repetitions and stammers so typical of many of Pinter's characters. In the critical record on Pinter, the use of such features is typically taken to indicate that a character is inarticulate or lacking in imagination. For example, Petey in *The Birthday Party* has been described as 'tongue-tied almost to the point of imbecility' (Esslin 1968: 272), and Gus in *The Dumb Waiter* is said to repeat himself because he cannot express his thoughts with clarity (Esslin 1970: 201). In like fashion, Kennedy (1975: 177) suggests that Aston and Davies in *The Caretaker* are prone to mid-utterance hesitations because they are inarticulate (see also Hayman 1977: 65, who makes a similar point). A linguistic account of such hesitations, however, reveals that there is considerably more to be said on the matter. This can be demonstrated with a brief example from *The Caretaker*.

As Crystal and Davy (1969: 104) observed, filled pauses (*er*, *mm*, etc.), self-repetitions, and other non-fluencies are to a certain degree normal in ordinary conversation, so much so that they can be tolerated to the point of being barely, if at all, noticed by participants. Thus, the occurrence of such features in drama dialogue cannot be automatically or even routinely taken to indicate that characters are inarticulate. Non-fluencies can also be positively functional in ordinary talk, and such functions can be represented in drama dialogue. For instance, some of the filled pauses used by Davies, the tramp in *The Caretaker*, are not best described as indicating a lack of verbal dexterity. Consider line 2 in the extract below.

1 Aston.	Sit down.
2 Davies.	Thanks. (*Looking about.*) Uuh …
3 Aston.	Just a minute.
	ASTON looks around for a chair, sees one lying on its side by the rolled carpet at the fireplace, and starts to get it out. (Pinter. *The Caretaker* 1960/1972: 7, Methuen Modern Plays edition.)

In line 2, Davies is represented as just 'tailing off into silence' (Crystal and Davy 1969: 103). This does not necessarily mean, however, that he is inarticulate. As Brown and Levinson (1978/1987: 227) go on to point out, such unfinished clauses can be used to mitigate the force of utterances that may be potentially offensive to the hearer, and this is clearly what is happening in the extract above. Aston has invited Davies to sit down without actually providing a chair, and Davies chooses to leave his complaint unfinished, waiting instead for Aston to notice and fix his own mistake. Debates can certainly be had about whether this is the representation of deferent behaviour or a reflection of one of life's many absurdities, but the fact remains that Davies' hesitation here does not have to be read as an inability to express himself.

Work in conversation analysis demonstrates with even greater clarity how the study of hesitation phenomena in talk can invigorate stalled interpretative work on Pinter's plays. Conversation analysts look at phenomena such as filled pauses, false starts, stammers and hesitations within the framework of what is called *repair*. Repair refers to the various strategies employed by speakers in talk to correct perceived problems in an interaction, such as mis-hearings or misunderstandings of what is said, slips of the tongue, changes of word choice, misspeaking, interruptions, etc. (Hutchby and Wooffitt 1998: 57, 59). Four broad types of repair are typically identified (definitions after Hutchby and Wooffitt 1998: 61). Self-initiated self-repair is when the speaker who has produced the trouble source both initiates and carries out the repair (i.e. the speaker corrects him or herself without prompting from anyone else). Self-initiated other-repair is when the producer of the trouble source solicits help from the recipient in order to repair the trouble. The example typically given for this kind of repair is when a speaker stumbles over an unfamiliar name, and either asks for or allows the hearer to supply the right name. Other-initiated self-repair is when the speaker of the trouble spot carries out the repair, but in response to the recipient (i.e. the recipient prompts the speaker to fix the trouble). Other-initiated other repair is when the recipient initiates and carries out the repair (i.e., the hearer corrects the speaker).

Piazza (1999) applies work on repair mechanisms to their representations in *The Caretaker*, and her investigation demonstrates that a conversation analytic treatment of the dialogue can shed further light on two issues frequently discussed by critics: 1) why Pinter characters often hesitate and repeat themselves; and 2) how Pinter plays come to be pervaded with a sense of menace. Typical of critical comments on issue (2) is Esslin, who notes that a trademark feature of Pinter is 'the commonplace situation that is gradually invested with menace, dread and mystery' (Esslin 1968: 265; see also Brown 1967: 122). While critics have noticed both issues, they have not often considered that they might be related. Piazza's work, on the other hand, provides an interpretation that goes well beyond the 'stammer + hesitation + repetition = inarticulate' equation. While Piazza notes that self-initiated self-repair may sometimes indicate that 'Pinter's characters [in *The Caretaker*] experience difficulty in expressing themselves' (1999: 1020), she realizes that this is only one small part of the story. Self-initiated self-repair (which she abbreviates as SRSI) is, of all the four types of repair, the least concerned with the recipient and negotiated interaction. SRSI is a mechanism that virtually by-passes the recipient in that the speaker neither confers nor responds to the hearer in repairing the trouble spot. Characters using SRSI are not so much inarticulate as isolated.

While critics have noticed mostly self-initiated self-repairs – i.e. the stammers, hesitations and repetitions, they have not taken any especial notice of self-repair that is other initiated (SROI) – instances where recipients notice a trouble spot and bring it to the attention of its producer. As Piazza (1999: 1018) notes, these also play a crucial role in the dialogue of *The Caretaker*: in Aston's speech, they tend to convey not only surprise or incredulity, but also indifference, and many times even threat and hostility (Piazza 1999: 1018). And indeed, a closer look at these other-initiated requests for repair made by Aston reveals that they are integral to the sense of menace that often establishes itself in a Pinter play.

1 Davies.	If only the weather would break! Then I'd be able to get down to
2	Sidcup!
3 Aston.	Sidcup?

4 Davies.	The weather's so blasted bloody awful, how can I get down to Sidcup in these
5	shoes?
6 Aston.	Why do you want to get down to Sidcup?
7 Davies.	I got my papers there!
8	Pause.
9 Aston.	Your what? (*The Caretaker*, 1966: 19–20, cited in Piazza 1999: 1018).

As evident in the dialogue cited above, lines 3, 6 and 9 instance successive requests for repair initiated by Aston. As Piazza (1999: 1020) observes, these other-initiated requests for repair are 'a sign of the malfunctioning of the communication channel' that 'parody the backchanneling function' (Piazza 1999: 1020). That is, they may at first glance seem to be nothing more than Aston showing an interest in Davies and his talk. But this is not, as the text makes clear, a hypothesis that can be sustained. Drawing on Tsui (1994) (who is more fully discussed in Chapter 2), it can be noted that each of these requests realizes a challenging move, a move in which Aston indicates that he either queries or refuses to accept the propositions Davies makes in his assessment (lines 1–2 and 4–5) and reporting moves (line 7). Requests for repair and challenging moves are not in and of themselves abnormal in talk or indicative of aggression. Indeed, they can, as Tannen (1984) points out, function to show recipient interest as part of a 'high involvement style'. However, if made repeatedly, they can also result in conflict talk, discourse in which 'participants oppose the utterances, actions or selves of one another in successive turns at talk' (Vuchinich 1990: 118). Thus, a normal feature of talk that can signal support is over-used in the dialogue until polite interest becomes veiled threat (Piazza 1999). Subversions of patterns in ordinary talk such as these are one means of introducing the air of menace so often commented upon in Pinter's work.

As Piazza further points out, sequences of open disagreement, such as can develop more readily from other-initiated other-repair (when hearers correct speakers), are avoided – this kind of repair is not common in *The Caretaker* (1999: 1006). As Piazza (1999: 1015) notes, the repair mechanisms Pinter presents in *The Caretaker* – a preference for self-repair, in particular other initiated self-repair, is a large part of what makes the tension in the play so 'subtle and indirect' (1014–15). Self-repair in *The Caretaker* is 'the means through which verbal fighting gets done' (Piazza 1999: 1021). In other words, loading of self-repair is what Pinter does instead of open conflict for much of *The Caretaker*, and this kind of feature loading is another means by which a sense of menace 'gradually creeps' into the dialogue. By employing a conversation analytic approach, Piazza (1999) shows that patterns in the use of repair mechanisms are not primarily to do with the ability of characters to express themselves; rather, these patterns are integral to conveying isolation and subtle conflict, and in so doing are the building blocks of the air of menace so often noticed by critics but so rarely explained.

As the discussion above demonstrates, Pinter critics writing prior to the development of detailed and comprehensive theories in conversation and discourse analysis notice a number of relevant features in the dialogue, but do not have a sophisticated means of analyzing them. In the absence of an applicable framework, intuition and assumption have had to be used, but the resulting analyses are clearly problematic. Critics writing after 1975, however, do have access to appropriate frameworks of talk. As Herman (1995: 3) and Short (1989: 143) have both noted, anyone at all familiar with the linguistic study of conversation can instance a number of comprehensive theories of interactive talk that have been developed in the past thirty years or so, as work in conversation analysis, discourse analysis, critical discourse analysis, pragmatics, and sociolinguistics is thriving.

Work from within these frameworks is relevant to Malkin's discussion and can be used to further her treatment of repetition in *The Dwarfs*. Malkin (1992: 71) cites the following dialogue between Len and Mark, noting that Len sees Mark as a kind of spider. The dialogue is given as an example of how Len gets caught in Mark's 'web'. For Malkin, the key piece of evidence here is the occurrence of repetition: 'Len … quickly finds himself repeating Mark's words in almost hypnotic parrotry' (1992: 71).

1 Len:	What's this, a suit? Where's your carnation?	
2 Mark:	What do you think of it?	
3 Len:	It's not a schmutta.	
4 Mark:	It's got a zip at the hips.	
5 Len:	A zip at the hips? What for?	
6 Mark:	Instead of a buckle. It's neat.	
7 Len:	Neat? I should say it's neat. […]	
8 Mark:	I don't want it double-breasted.	
9 Len:	Double-breasted? Of course you couldn't have it double-breasted.	
10 Mark:	What do you think of the cloth?	
11 Len:	The cloth? […] What a piece of cloth. What a piece of cloth. What a piece of cloth.	
12	What a piece of cloth. What a piece of *cloth.*	
13 Mark:	You like the cloth?	
14 Len:	WHAT A PIECE OF CLOTH!	
15 Mark:	What do you think of the cut?	
16 Len:	What do I think of the cut? The cut? The cut? What a cut! What a cut! I've never seen	
17	such a cut! (*Pause. He groans.*) (Pinter, *The Dwarfs*: 88, in Malkin 1992: 71–2, ellipses Malkin's, line numbers mine).	

If we consider the repetition that occurs from a linguistic point of view, we can extend the analysis beyond 'hypnotic parrotry' since repetition has been shown to have multiple functions in talk (Herman 1995; Tannen 1989). As Short (1989: 159) points out, adopting the words of your interlocutor into your own speech can be a sign of respect, an acknowledgement of your interlocutor's superior status. Repetition can also be socially cohesive in talk (Coates 1989/1998; Tannen 1989: 50–51), and repeated material is quite normally used in both agreeing and challenging conversational moves (Tsui 1994). In addition, participants can repeat themselves, or each other.

What is the function of the repeated material in the cited dialogue from *The Dwarfs*? Notice first of all that the initial instance given (*Len: A zip at the hips?*) is not unusual. Len has recycled a phrase from Mark's initiating move and used it in his response. In the second and third instances (lines 7 and 9), it is not necessarily the repetition that is unusual, and there is good evidence to suggest that Len is not simply parroting Mark. We can demonstrate this by looking first at lines 6 and 8, in which Mark makes what have been called informative moves (Tsui 1994: Chapter 7).[3] They provide information, evaluations, factual accounts and expressions of personal belief. As responses, they prospect simple acknowledgements or agreement tokens. Since these are the expected responses, the occurrence of something else will be perceived as unusual, and this will prompt the interlocutor (and the audience) to search for implied meanings (Grice 1975, see Chapter 2 for further discussion). Returning to the dialogue, we see in lines 7 and 9 that Len goes well beyond simple acknowledgements or agreement tokens in his responses. In short, he says too much. In addition, agreements such as these that are far too strenuous in the given situation (see especially the highly presumptive uses of *should* in line 7 and *of course* in line 9) may generate irony, or may give the impression that Len is becoming (increasingly) annoyed by the conversation. While Len's exact purpose in this scene will remain a matter for debate, it is clear that his responses are not instances of simple parrotry, hypnotic or otherwise.

Notice, in addition, that towards the end of the given extract Len is repeating or reformulating material within his own conversational turns (lines 11–12 and 16–17) with increasing signs of agitation (the emphasis on *cloth*, and the exclamation marks). Again, this is not indicative of parrotry, as the salient repetition here is within turns, rather than across them. While Len certainly recycles items from Mark's turns, it is clear that he is doing this for his own ends rather than simply repeating what Mark has said.

Conclusion

I have shown in this chapter that drama texts can be analysed apart from performance, and that critical accounts of these texts are advantaged by input from linguistics. In particular, I have shown that the linguistic study of ordinary talk has much to contribute to our understanding of drama dialogue. However, it is only fair to point out that what I have shown is primarily in reference to a single playwright and a handful of critics, only one of whom writes after 1975. To really make the argument, it is necessary to show that the treatments of language in drama dialogue covered in this chapter are more broadly evident in drama criticism. This will be the concern of the remaining chapters of this book. Chapters 3, 4, 5 and 6 will each focus on a single modern play, Pinter's *The Homecoming*; Wesker's *Roots*; Rattigan's *In Praise of Love*; and Ayckbourn's *Just Between Ourselves*. I draw on a number of approaches to talk in the analysis of each play, and these approaches are explained in the next chapter.

Chapter 2

Approaches to Talk

As Short (1989: 149) has pointed out, drama dialogue is helpfully conceptualized as embedded discourse. On one level, characters speak to each other. At the same time, however, this discourse is 'overheard' by viewers or readers, and thus another level of communication occurs between the playwright (or perhaps more appropriately the text) and the audience. As was demonstrated in Chapter 1, explicit linguistic knowledge of the nature of talk can be very valuably brought to bear on the interpretation of this deeper level of communication. By appealing to models of talk in the study of drama, it is possible to distinguish dialogue that is represented as 'normal' from dialogue that is represented as 'odd'. That is, there is a systematic and explicit basis for identifying conversational patterns in the text that are essentially mimetic, and those that deviate from the norm in some way (Short 1989: 145; Carter 1982: 5). In so doing, it is also possible to investigate why texts provoke the reactions and impressions that they do (Toolan 2000: 186).

The method employed in this book, applying frameworks of natural conversation to dramatic texts in order to account for various effects that are achieved, is in keeping with a growing tradition of work in the stylistics of drama, arguably popularized by Burton (1980) and recently articulated by Toolan (2000: 186). For the benefit of readers who may not be familiar with the linguistic study of talk, this chapter outlines the primary approaches to conversation employed in the study of the plays. It aims to be clear and concise but not exhaustive. Insights from other sub-disciplines within linguistics, such as sociolinguistics, are also employed from time to time and explained as they are used (e.g. see Chapter 4 for an account of dialect variation in English and its relevance to understanding Wesker's *Roots*).

The frameworks outlined here either are, or have grown out of, approaches to communication that have become the defining tenets of pragmatics, a discipline within linguistics devoted to the study of how speakers use and understand language in actual situations. With such a focus, pragmatics differentiates itself from phonology, morphology and syntax which, broadly speaking, tell us how language is structured, and semantics, which investigates how language conveys meaning. Pragmatics, however, is not about what language does, but about what speakers do with language.

The starting point of pragmatics as a discipline is generally taken to be J.L. Austin's development of speech act theory (Thomas 1995: 28). While this approach is not itself used in the analysis of the plays in this book, it is covered here (albeit briefly) because it underlies, either implicitly or explicitly, many of the approaches that are used. As Thomas (1995: 29) points out, Austin, in contrast to many of his contemporaries, noticed that ordinary people in everyday situations used language to communicate without difficulty most of the time, and wanted to investigate how this was accomplished. He put forward his ideas in a series of lectures at Harvard, which were later published under the title *How to do Things with Words* (1962/1975). Austin reasoned that everyday language was not primarily about making statements, but about doing things, performing acts of speech to accomplish goals. He suggested that instances of speech were more than locutionary acts (utterances with sense and reference that conformed to the grammatical and phonological rules of the language). They were also illocutionary acts, acts that conveyed illocutionary force, intended meanings that might not be predictable from form alone.[1]

Illocutionary force is largely bound up with the issue of context. To use one of Austin's own examples, the utterance 'I do' means one thing when performed during a marriage ceremony by the bride and groom to be, but something quite different when performed in other circumstances. Austin made an attempt to formalize contextual constraints on illocutionary force in his felicity conditions, conditions pertaining to various social features of the talk (situation, speaker rights and obligations, etc.) that had to be met in order for the illocutionary act to be performed successfully, or *felicitously*, as Austin termed it.

Austin's ideas were revised and extended by his pupil J.R. Searle (1969, 1976). For Searle, Austin's felicity conditions did not serve well enough to distinguish one act from another, which prompted him, as Levinson (1983: 238) observes, to try and systematize Austin's felicity conditions so that they more clearly and consistently defined and differentiated the different kinds of acts. For example, the act 'promise' must, according to Searle (1969), meet four conditions in order to count as such.

1   A future act must be predicated of the speaker (as Searle 1969: 57 explains, one cannot promise to do 'a past act', nor can one make a promise for someone else).
2   The speaker must believe that the act will benefit the hearer (Searle 1969: 58) (a 'promise' to punch someone in the nose will almost certainly be heard as what it is, a threat).
3   It must not be obvious to either the speaker or the hearer that the act is something the speaker would do anyway 'in the normal course of events' (as Searle 1969: 59 puts it, 'a happily married man who promises his wife he will not desert her in the next week is likely to provide more anxiety than comfort').
4   The speaker believes the act is possible, and intends to carry out the act (Searle 1969: 57–61).

Such conditions not only define particular acts, but allow us to tell how one act differs from another. For example, the act 'advise' is also a future, non-obvious act that benefits the hearer, but it differs from 'promise' in that it is the hearer who undertakes the action, not the speaker. Requests are differentiated from commands in a similar way. While both acts are attempts by the speaker to get the hearer to do a non-obvious act that benefits the speaker, commands entail speaker authority over the hearer, while requests do not. Searle develops and refines these defining conditions and eventually proposes a five-category classification of speech acts consisting of representatives (telling people 'how things are'); directives (getting 'them to do things'); commissives (committing 'ourselves to doing things'); expressives (expressing 'our feelings and attitudes'); and declarations (changing the world with our talk. These encompass Austin's original performatives, such as the naming of ships and other institutional acts) (Searle 1976: 23).

Austin and Searle have often been taken to task for their intuitive, non-empirical approach to communication (Eggins and Slade 1997; Mey 1993; Nofsinger 1991; Taylor and Cameron 1987; Burton 1980), which is said to result in a framework that is only partially applicable to actual talk, and only then most suited to a very narrow range of situations. At the same time, however, many of these same people (Eggins and Slade 1997; Nofsinger 1991; Taylor and Cameron 1987) recognize that nearly all units of conversation used in the empirical study of talk are rooted in the speech act, in particular the illocutionary act, as proposed by Austin (1962/1975) and extended by Searle (1969, 1976). Indeed, Searle's (1969, 1976) taxonomy serves for a time as the standard in studies of speech act realizations in talk (see Flowerdew 1990).

While Austin and Searle looked at the business of communication largely from the speaker's point of view, H.P. Grice, who also worked with Austin, was more interested in the hearer's perspective (Thomas 1995: 51, 56). Starting with the observable fact that people often imply or suggest or mean more than they say, Grice (1975) developed an account of how hearers are able to derive these unsaid meanings. He suggested that such meanings were communicated by the generation of *implicatures*, and delineated two types, conventional and conversational (Grice 1975: 44–5). Conventional implicatures derive solely from the syntax and semantics of the utterance. For example, the use of *but* in the sentence *She was beautiful but not frivolous* implies without directly saying so that beautiful women are typically frivolous. Because of the conventional meaning of the conjunction *but*, this implicature will always be generated, even out of context (Grice 1975: 44). Such relatively straightforward implicatures were not of primary interest to Grice (1975), and are not of especial concern here either.

Of greater import are the conversational implicatures, levels of meaning that are generated and understood during the course of ordinary conversation but not directly derivable from the surface structure of the utterance (Grice 1975: 45). Consider the following much quoted example, discussed with particular clarity by Herman (1995: 175–6).

A   What time is it?
B   Well, the postman's been.

Strictly speaking, B's reply does not appear to address A's question. However, A (and most overhearers of this exchange) would begin interpreting this reply by supposing that there was some relationship between the time and postman. As Herman (1995: 175–6) explains, this interpretation rests on the assumption that B was actually addressing the question. With this assumption as the starting point, a reasonable interpretation of B's reply is that she either does not know the time, or has reasons not to say exactly what time it is, but still wants to answer A's question as helpfully as possible. Therefore, as Herman (1995: 175–6) goes on to point out, B chooses a common point of reference with A (the arrival of the postman at about 8:00 every day), and refers to this in order to answer A's question. Since A and B share the knowledge of when the postman typically arrives, and are mutually aware that this knowledge is shared between them, A is able to infer from B's reply that it is after 8:00 (Herman 1995: 175–6).

Exchanges such as that between A and B above are not extraordinary. They are, in fact, fairly routine in ordinary talk. In order for such exchanges to work, Grice (1975) reasoned that a set of principles based on the assumption of mutual cooperation and jointly held by both speaker and hearer must be in operation whenever people joined together in talk. He articulates this insight as follows:

> Our talk exchanges do not normally consist of a succession of disconnected remarks, and would not be rational if they did. They are characteristically to some degree at least, cooperative efforts; and each participant recognizes in them, to some extent, a common purpose or set of purposes, or at least a mutually accepted direction (Grice 1975: 45);

and proceeds to formulate what he calls the Cooperative Principle (CP):

> Make your conversational contribution such as is required, at the stage at which it occurs, by the accepted purpose or direction of the talk exchange in which you are engaged (Grice 1975: 45).

Grice (1975: 45–6) further proposed that the CP could be broken down into four more specific maxims:

Quantity	Make your contribution as informative as required (for the current purposes of the exchange).
	Do not make your contribution more informative than is required.
Quality	Do not say what you believe to be false.
	Do not say that for which you lack evidence.
Relation	Be relevant.
Manner	Avoid obscurity of expression.
	Avoid ambiguity.
	Be brief (avoid unnecessary prolixity).
	Be orderly (Grice 1975: 45–6).

As Thomas (1995: 62) has noted, Grice's use of the imperative in outlining the CP and its maxims led some readers to the erroneous conclusion that his purpose was to dictate optimal conversational behaviour. This was not the case. Rather, Grice (1975) was suggesting that people in conversation generally proceeded under the assumption that both they themselves and everyone else operated with these principles intact.

> Talkers will in general (ceteris paribus [all other things being equal] and in the absence of indications to the contrary) proceed in the manner that these principles prescribe (Grice 1975: 47–8).

Reference to principles such as those formalized in the CP accounts for how hearers like A above are able to interpret utterances such as B's. While *The postman's been* seems at first glance to be irrelevant, the assumption that B *is* behaving cooperatively, and is therefore making a relevant contribution, prompts A to draw on resources beyond the utterance (e.g. shared knowledge) in order to seek an interpretation that makes sense (it is after 8:00) (Herman 1995: 176).

As Grice (1975: 49) also realized, the commonly and mutually held assumption of cooperation in talk enables people to exploit this assumption. That is, people can and do fail to observe maxims not because they have to (because they do not know the answer to a question, for example), but because they want to (Grice 1975: 49). Thomas (1995: 55, 67) illustrates this with a very colourful example involving a paramedic and a drunken man on Christmas Eve. The paramedic is called to assist the drunken man, who then proceeds to vomit on him. The paramedic exclaims, 'Great! That's really great! That's made my Christmas!' How is it that hearers will routinely understand that the paramedic is annoyed? As Thomas (1995: 67) explains, the paramedic's utterance is what Grice (1975) called a *flout* of the maxim of quality – it is obviously false. Since there is no reason in the given circumstance to suppose the paramedic is failing to observe one maxim in order to fulfil another, unable for some reason to observe the CP, or wilfully trying to deceive, hearers seek another plausible interpretation. In this case, this is that the paramedic is being ironic, and in actual fact means the opposite of what he said (Thomas 1995: 67 and Grice 1975: 49).

In addition to flouting, Grice (1975) outlined a number of other ways that maxims could fail to be observed. Of central importance in the present analysis, however, is the difference between flouting, deliberately and obviously failing to observe a maxim in order to generate an implicature, and violating, quietly and unostentatiously failing to observe a maxim, perhaps with the purpose of misleading the interlocutor (Grice 1975: 49). Grice's CP and the interplay between flouting and violating its maxims are employed here in the analysis of Rattigan's *In Praise of Love* (see Chapter 5).

Like Austin (1962/1975) and Searle (1969, 1976), Grice (1975) encountered criticism for developing his model with reference to hypothetical rather than actual utterances. Brown and Levinson (1978/1987: 59), however, who use 'first-hand, tape-recorded' data in their investigation of linguistic politeness, acknowledge the role of Gricean assumptions in their study. Like Grice, they assume that speakers are rational, capable of means-to-end reasoning, and expectant of cooperation in their talk exchanges (1978/1987: 58). What Brown and Levinson (1978/1987) wanted to know was why speakers from unrelated languages (English, Tzeltal, and South Indian Tamil) could be observed to regularly diverge from maximally efficient communication. For instance, why go to the trouble of saying *If it is at all possible, would you mind terribly shutting the window a bit? It is kind of cold in here*, when *Shut the window* communicates basically the same message in less time with less effort? They propose that it is concerns of politeness that govern how or even whether speakers choose to realize given acts in discourse. *Politeness* means something very specific for Brown and Levinson. Drawing on Goffman (1967), they suggest that speakers possess a socially manifested face that has two aspects: the want to remain free from imposition, which they call *negative face*, and the want to be approved of and socially accepted, which they call *positive face* (Brown and Levinson 1978/1987: 62). Speakers are polite when they structure their speech acts with respect to positive and negative face needs (Brown and Levinson 1978/1987: 61). For example, if a face-threatening act cannot be avoided in order for the speaker to achieve his or her goal, a series of strategies can then be used to address speaker and hearer face concerns. This allows the achievement of the interactive goal with least cost in terms of face damage, and maximal benefit in terms of clarity (see Brown and Levinson 1978/1987: 60 for a summary of the argument).

As Brown and Levinson (1978/1987: 74) further point out, the strategy chosen will reflect the speaker's assessment of three contextual variables: the power relationship that exists between speaker and hearer (P), the social distance between them (D), and the gravity of the imposition (R). For example, if the act involves a severe imposition and thus a very grave risk to face, speakers may simply choose to sacrifice their communicative goal and not do the act (e.g., deciding not to ask a friend to borrow a very large sum of money). If the benefit of doing the act outweighs the potential risk to face, speakers may choose to go ahead and do the act, and may do so either on record or off-record. Speakers go on record by making their communicative intention clear. They can be maximally clear by performing the act baldly, without redressive action, known as bald-on-record usage. Bald-on-record acts are characteristic during emergencies (e.g. *Watch out!*), or when speakers know each other very well and are in a symmetrical power relationship. They are also typical in situations such as invitations where the benefit to the hearer results in a diminished imposition (e.g. *Come in! Have a seat!*). In situations where the gravity of the imposition is higher, or where interlocutors may not know each other very well, speakers may choose to do the act with redressive action. Redressive action with negative politeness involves attention to the hearer's want to remain unimpeded. For example, a request for a lift might be phrased as *You couldn't give me a lift, could you?* As Brown and Levinson (1978/1987: 172–3) explain, the modal verb, the negative structure, and the tag question encode pessimism, showing that the speaker is being careful not to assume that the hearer will agree to the request. Negative politeness strategies are often chosen when speakers are in a lower social position than hearers. Redressive action with positive politeness involves attention to the hearer's want to be included and valued. A request for a lift made with attention to positive face needs, for example, might be phrased *Give us a lift, love.* As Brown and Levinson (1978/1987: 108, 126) note, the imperative, the inclusive pronoun and the endearment all encode the optimistic assumption that the hearer will not mind complying. This positions the hearer as an intimate, a member of the speaker's inner circle.

Speakers can also choose to go off-record. According to Brown and Levinson (1978/1987: 211), an act 'is done off-record if it is done in such a way that it is not possible to attribute only one clear communicative intention to the act'. This allows the speaker to leave him or herself an 'out', as the act even in context will have several reasonable interpretations. For example, if a speaker says *Is anyone else here cold? I'm a bit cold*, he or she does not have to acknowledge this as a hint to close the window, since the utterance is also plausibly understood as a comment on the weather. Off-record strategies tend to be used, as Brown and Levinson (1978/1987: 211) go on to explain, when speakers want to do a face-threatening act, but do not want to take responsibility for doing so.

Brown and Levinson (1978/1987: 211–27) draw on Grice (1975) in their account of how off-record strategies are understood despite their highly ambiguous nature. They work by failing to observe one or more of the four maxims in various ways. For example, off-record hints operate by failing to observe the relevance maxim. Understatements, overstatements and tautologies, other off-record strategies that Brown and Levinson (1978/1987) list, fail to observe the maxim of quantity. Contradictions, metaphors, rhetorical questions and ironic statements do not observe quality, and strategies such as being ambiguous, vague, too general or incomplete do not observe manner.

Brown and Levinson (1978/1987) have had no small impact on the field, and their account is employed in the analysis of most of the plays in this book. Their work on positive politeness is particularly instrumental in the interpretation of Wesker's *Roots* (see Chapter 4), and their framework of off-record communication is of especial importance in the reading of Rattigan's *In Praise of Love* (see Chapter 5). Their outline of both positive and negative politeness strategies is used in the analysis of Vera's character in Ayckbourn's *Just Between Ourselves* (see Chapter 6).

While speech act theory, the cooperative principle and linguistic politeness have been (and continue to be) of undeniable value in our understanding of the nature of talk, these frameworks pay only passing attention to replies (see Tsui 1994: 160), what hearers say back to speakers (thus becoming speakers in their turn). This is even true of Austin (1962/1975), who noted in the concept of uptake that a bet, for example, was partially defined by an interlocutor who accepted it as such, but did not outline a taxonomy of such accepting acts, and of Grice (1975), who worked on how hearers understood messages but was not especially interested in what they said in response. It is to the conversation and discourse analysts that we must turn for an account of replying acts in talk.

In one of the pioneering papers in conversation analysis, *A Simplest Systematics for the Organization of Turn-Taking for Conversation*, Sacks, Schegloff and Jefferson (1974) set out to develop a model of turn-taking that accounted for 14 'grossly apparently facts' that they noted could be observed in any conversation (1974: 700). While Sacks et al. (1974) list these facts in detail for the purposes of close analysis, the essence of what they want to explain is that speakers in conversation take turns with remarkable precision in an activity that is largely unplanned. The size, order, distribution and specific topic of turns at talk are not organized or known in advance, and the number of participants can vary. And yet, this unplanned activity unfolds in a largely orderly way. Overlapping talk between turns is common but tends to be brief, and turn transitions without gap or overlap are also common.

In order to produce conversations with these observed properties, Sacks and his colleagues reasoned that a system of turn-taking rules known to all participants must exist and operate during talk exchanges. While their use of the term 'rule' at first glance implies a rigid framework to which participants consciously adhere, this is not what Sacks et al. proposed. Rather, their observations of participant behaviour during conversations led them to conclude that interlocutors shared as part of their cultural knowledge a system for allocating turns during conversations that was only brought to conscious awareness when participants went against the norm. The 'rules' of turn-taking can be, and certainly are, broken but this is noticed by participants, who may, for example, apologize for interrupting each other, or comment negatively on people who do interrupt frequently but do not apologize.

So what are these rules that Sacks et al. (1974) suggested must exist? In brief, they can be stated as follows: If the current speaker (C) selects the next speaker (N) in the current turn, then C must stop speaking and allow N to take that allocated turn. Next speakers can be selected in a variety of ways that include asking them questions, identifying them by name, or simply looking at them. If C does not select a next speaker, any one else in the conversation can self-select, and the first person to do so generally wins the turn (of course, brief speaker overlap at this point is common while the turn is negotiated). If C does not select a next speaker, and no one self-selects, C can but does not have to continue.[2]

As Sacks et al. (1974) point out, the turn-taking system also accounts for various silences that can occur in talk. A *gap*, a short and often unproblematic pause, may ensue before a speaker self-selects, or before the current speaker continues. A *lapse*, a longer pause that can be experienced as awkward, may ensue if C does not select N, no one self-selects, and C opts not to continue. As common experience reveals, the longer a lapse like this goes on, the harder it is to re-start the talk. Most problematic of all is the *attributable silence*, the silence that occurs when the current speaker selects a next speaker who chooses not, for whatever reason, to take that turn. This is often a sign that something in the talk has gone wrong and participants in the conversation, in particular the recipient of the attributable silence, will typically attend to this point in an attempt to repair the perceived damage.

The study of talk by conversation analysts has also revealed that turns tend to be organized into what are called *adjacency pairs* (Schegloff and Sacks 1973: 295–7). The first turns in these pairs, or first pair parts as they are called, are named (albeit on a somewhat common-sense basis) in a way that recalls speech act types (e.g. invitations, greetings, requests, etc.). What conversation analysts have contributed is the observation that these first pair parts tend to evoke a rather specific range of second pair parts in natural talk situations. For example, invitations tend to be accepted or rejected, greetings expect return greetings, questions want answers, or reasons for why answers cannot be given, etc. (Schegloff and Sacks 1973: 295–7). Within this range of expected reactions, it has further been observed that acceptances, agreements and indications of compliance seem in general to be *preferred* over disagreements, rejections and denials, which are *dispreferred* (Pomerantz 1984; Sacks 1973/1987; Schegloff and Sacks 1973: 296). This is called preference organization and it has been found that preferred responses differ structurally from those that are dispreferred. Put simply, it is apparently easier and more straightforward to say 'yes' than to say 'no'. Dispreferred responses often include mitigating prefaces (*I'd love to but ...*), apologies, and various hesitation devices (filled pauses such as *er*, *mm*, in-drawn breaths, and items such as *well*). Preferred responses, in contrast, are generally made without delay, and without mitigators or apologies. Preference organization, while normative rather than strictly rule-governed (Taylor and Cameron 1987: 109), nevertheless sets up powerful expectations. The utterance of a first pair part is one way of selecting a next speaker (Sacks et al. 1974: 728), and if neither the preferred nor the dispreferred response occurs, whatever action does occur (e.g. an attributable silence or a request for clarification) will be heard by the recipient as an actual or potential dispreferred response (Davidson 1984).

Conversation analysts have also observed that adjacency pairs are instrumental in building larger sequential patterns of talk that participants mutually recognize, such as opening and closing sequences. These sequences, along with patterns in response types and speaking turn selections, are of especial relevance to the analysis of Pinter's *The Homecoming* and are further discussed in Chapter 3. Work in conversation analysis is also applied in the interpretation of Ayckbourn's *Just Between Ourselves* in Chapter 6.

Conversation analysis is typically contrasted with discourse analysis in textbooks of pragmatics. As Levinson (1983: 295) points out, conversation analysis was initially developed by a group of sociologists who were interested in looking at how members of a society conceptualized their own behaviour within that society, and who turned to everyday conversation for data. In contrast, as Levinson (1983: 286) goes on to note, discourse analysts follow more traditional linguistic methods and principles in applying concepts such as well-formedness. As Levinson (1983: 286) explains, the general procedure in discourse analysis is to isolate units of discourse for study (just as other units, such as clauses and sentences, have been isolated), and then formulate a set of rules that differentiates well-formed, coherent combinations of these units from ill-formed, incoherent combinations. While discourse analysis covers a potentially wide range of activities, the focus here will be on the Birmingham school of discourse analysis, pioneered by Sinclair and Coulthard (1975) and applied widely in the study of talk.

As Sinclair and Coulthard (1975: 6) explain, they turned to the relatively controlled discourse of the classroom in order to devise a framework for the linguistic structure of spoken interactions. Using function in the interaction as a primary criterion, they classify utterances as one of 22 discourse acts (e.g. elicit, nominate, command). As Sinclair (1992: 80) has noted, these acts have a root in speech act theory, but depart significantly from illocutionary acts in being defined not only by function, but also by their place in the discourse (e.g. whether they start, continue or end interactions). The discourse acts combine to form various different kinds of moves (e.g. initiations, responses, follow-ups, etc.). These moves in turn combine to form exchanges, which exhibit a typical structure of initiating, responding and follow-up moves.[3] This kind of structure, called a *rank scale*, is based on Halliday's (1961) scale-and-category grammar. As Sinclair and Coulthard (1975: 20) explain, the basic assumption of a rank scale is that a unit at a given rank, for example, word, is made up of one or more units of the rank below, morphemes, and combines with other units at the same rank to make one unit at the rank above, group.

In devising their framework, Sinclair and Coulthard extended the rank scale to account for not only units larger than the sentence, but also units formed by more than one participant.

As Levinson (1983: 287) has observed, there are various points of contention between conversation analysis and discourse analysis. Discourse analysts, for example, often find that conversation analysts employ analytic categories that are insufficiently defined (Levinson 1983: 287). In theory, conversation analysts want to use categories that participants themselves use in making sense of conversation (Levinson 1983: 295). In practice, however, this often amounts to applying common sense labels with poorly defined technical specifications. According to conversation analysts, however, discourse analysts spend so much time on the theoretical modelling of their pre-established categories that they lose touch with the actual data (Levinson 1983: 287).

While Levinson (1983: 287–8) tentatively floats the possibility of a synthesis between the two approaches, he is more interested in how they contrast rather than compare, and eventually comes down on the side of conversation analysis. The two approaches, however, share in common a fundamental principle of talk, the intimate and dependent relationship between an utterance by one speaker and the one that follows it by the next speaker. Conversation analysts capture this insight in their articulation of adjacency pairs and preference organization (discussed above), and Sacks et al. express it like this:

> … a turn's talk will be heard as directed to a prior turn's talk unless special techniques are used to locate some other talk to which it is directed (1974: 728).

Discourse analysts call this relationship prospection, and articulate it in these terms:

> Each initiation prospects that the utterance following it will be interpreted under the same set of presuppositions as the initiation itself. If the putative response is not compatible with the prospections it will be interpreted as a challenge, and therefore the beginning of a new exchange (Sinclair 1992: 83).

And despite their contrasting methods, conversation analysis and the Birmingham school of discourse analysis have the same goal, the understanding of how conversation works. It should come as no surprise, then, that a synthesis of the two approaches has in fact been successfully developed, as evidenced by the work of A.B.M. Tsui (1994), who characterizes her framework as a '*linguistic description of conversation*' (1994: 3). It is this framework that is used in the present study when a functional analysis of represented discourse moves in drama dialogue is presented, as in the analysis of

Pinter's *The Homecoming* (see Chapter 3), and Ayckbourn's *Just Between Ourselves* (see Chapter 6).

Tsui's framework, set out in full in her book *English Conversation* (1994), uses as data spontaneous, naturally occurring conversational interactions collected over a three-year period. By combining the rigorous standards of act definition and classification characteristic of discourse analytic approaches (which are, as Levinson 1983: 286 has noted, ultimately rooted in speech act theory) with the empirical observations of the conversation analysts regarding turn-taking and preference organization, Tsui (1994) designs a comprehensive framework of English conversation that satisfactorily accounts for her data (Aijmer 1996: 108). One of her most significant contributions is her account of how moves in talk are sequenced throughout an interaction. While conversation analysis accounts for how turns follow one another in the turn-taking mechanism, no correspondingly comprehensive framework is offered for what is accomplished in those turns. In conversation analysis, this tends to be limited to adjacency pairs, local sequences (such as pre-requesting pairs that can precede requests), and highly ritualistic parts of conversations such as openings and closings. Sinclair and Coulthard (1975) sketched out some broad tendencies concerning which acts tended to follow others, but did not fully develop this aspect of their model. Tsui's (1994) framework, however, offers a comprehensive account of how interlocutors sequence their moves throughout an interaction.

Her starting point for this account of sequencing is Halliday's (1963) concept of system, which she characterizes as 'a set of choices that are available in a given environment' (1994: 19). In Tsui's model, systems of choices govern what kinds of moves can be made at any particular point in an interaction. For example, she suggests that speakers at the beginning of an interaction have the choice of realizing one of four different kinds of primary Initiating moves: a Requestive, a Directive, an Elicitation, or an Informative (Tsui 1994: 219).[4] These moves are defined and differentiated from each other by the types of response they prospect. Requestives are moves which expect a non-verbal response, and which allow the addressee to choose between compliance and non-compliance. While Directives also expect a non-verbal response, they, unlike Requestives, are made with the assumption that addressees will comply. Elicitations and Informatives both prospect verbal responses rather than non-verbal ones. However, Elicitations call for answers, usually information of some kind, while Informatives expect only minimal acknowledgements or supportive comments (see Tsui 1994: 54–5 for a detailed account).

Before going on to explain the remaining systems of choices that govern sequences of moves in Tsui's framework, it will be useful to highlight two points. While Tsui (1994) systematically identifies both acts and moves, notice that it is the move which takes precedence in her framework as the primary unit of analysis. A discourse move can be thought of as what people do in their speaking turns (Stenström 1984, especially ch. 4). As Tsui (1994) notes, a move can consist of multiple acts, but only one of those acts will define the move. In an earlier paper (Tsui 1993: 92–3), she notes that she identifies this definitive act (called the *head-act*) by extending Sinclair and Coulthard's (1975: 34) 'push-down' mechanism (where one act in a multi-act move 'pushes down' another) to include the concept of *elicitative force*. This is defined by Arndt and Ryan (1986: 149) as 'the strength of an utterance to call for a response' (see also Stenström 1994: 92).[5] In terms of elicitative force, Directives and Requestives are strongest because they call primarily for actions, whereas Elicitations and Informatives expect only verbal responses. Elicitations, however, are stronger than Informatives, because they call for more substantial verbal responses (e.g. full answers rather than simple acknowledgements). As Tsui (1993: 92) goes on to explain, elicitative force becomes apparent in the data when Directives or Requestives combine with Elicitations or Informatives in a single move. In such cases, addressees typically respond to the Directive or Requestive. Similarly, addressees were observed to respond to the Elicitations when these combined in a single move with Informatives.

The second point to highlight is that the form of an utterance is not the defining criterion of what move it realizes. In Tsui's (1994) framework, moves are classified not by their syntactic or lexical form, but by: 1) the type of response they prospect (as already explained above); and 2) where they occur in the discourse (following Sinclair and Coulthard 1975). As Tsui (1994: 15) explains, formally identical utterances can realize distinct kinds of moves based on whether they serve as initiating moves or responses. Consideration of two of Tsui's own examples will make this clearer.

A: What's the time?
B: It's nearly three.

X: It's nearly three.
Y: Oh my God! (Tsui 1994: 15)

As Tsui (1994: 15) notes, the utterances of B and X above are identical in form, but serve two entirely different functions, and thus are classified as two different kinds of moves. B's *It's nearly three* is the prospected response to A's Elicitation, while X's is an Initiation, an Informative that prospects a response of its own.

Once a speaker chooses one of the primary initiating moves for realization (i.e. a Directive, a Requestive, an Elicitation or an Informative), further choices come into play (Tsui 1994: 219). For example, if the Initiation is a Requestive, it can occur as one of the following subclasses: a Request for Action, a Request for Permission, an Offer, an Invitation, or a Proposal (Tsui 1994: 220). While all Requestives share the feature of allowing addressees not to comply, the subclass types are differentiated from each other according to which participant is expected to act, and which participant will benefit from the action. For example, both Requests for Permission and Offers predicate an action of the speaker. With Requests for Permission, however, it is the speaker who benefits; with Offers, it is the hearer who benefits. Requests for Action and Invitations both predicate an action of the hearer. With Requests for Action, it is the speaker who benefits; with Invitations, it is the hearer who benefits. Proposals predicate an action of both participants, and both participants benefit (Tsui 1994: 101).[6] As will now be evident, Tsui's differentiation of move types according to which addressee benefits and which one is expected to act recalls Searle's (1969) conditions defining speech act types.

After the initiating move has been made, a point in the discourse represented by Tsui (1994: 221) as *Ti*, another set of choices becomes operable. The Initiation can be prospectively or retrospectively classified. Prospective analysis refers to the special relationship between Initiations and Responses noted earlier, and accounts for speaker expectations regarding the responses they have in effect solicited with their Initiations. As Tsui (1994) notes, however, prospective analysis does not account satisfactorily for situations where participants produce something unexpected.[7] In these cases, where the addressee's response indicates that speaker and hearer are interpreting the illocutionary intent of the initiation in different ways (1994: 17–18, 49), Tsui allows retrospective classification. In the following now famous example from Labov and Fanshell (1977: 75, cited by Tsui 1994: 18), for instance, it is clear that B has wilfully interpreted A's Request for Action as an Elicit:Inform (a request for information).

A: Would you mind taking the dust rag and dust around?
B: No. (*does not move*).

Both prospective and retrospective analysis result in the same set of choices at Ti. The new speaker can maintain the discourse framework and respond, or break it by issuing a challenge or another initiation (Tsui 1994: 221). Discourse framework is a concept that Tsui (1994) borrows from Burton (1980). It is based on the concept of prospection, and consists of the initiating move together with the restrictions it places on the moves immediately following. Tsui (1994) also borrows the concept of the challenging move from Burton (1980). Challenging moves are those which do not fulfil the expectations established in the preceding initiation (Burton 1980: 103). Consider the following advice-giving exchange as an example, from part of a longer interaction given in Jefferson and Lee (1981: 406). J has been complaining about going to the dentist, and V offers advice.

1 V: Tell him gas.
2 J: uh-No I don't want no gas, no I wi- I will take it.
(cited in Jefferson and Lee 1981: 406, transcription conventions of the original simplified here).

V's move can be classified as an initiating move consisting of the head-act Advice, which belongs to the class of acts called Advisives, which are themselves from within the class of Directives. According to Tsui (1994), who again is drawing on Searle (1969), Directive:Advisive:Advice presupposes that:

the speaker believes that there is a need for the advocated action;
the speaker believes that the advocated action is in the interest of the addressee;
the addressee is able and willing to carry out the action;
it is not obvious that the addressee will carry out the action of his/her own accord (Tsui 1994: 178).

As can be seen from the example, J's move in line 2 indicates that he is not willing to carry out the action predicated in V's advice. Thus, the third presupposition above is not upheld, and J's move can be classified as a Challenge. As Tsui (1994: 163) explains, Challenges are by definition Initiations, and will occur as a type of Elicitation, Directive, Informative, or Requestive. In the example above, the utterance in line 2 (*uh-No I don't want no gas, no I wi- I will take it*) is a Challenge that occurs as an Informative:Assessment:Assessing (see Tsui 1994: 142–5). Challenging moves are of particular importance in the analysis of Pinter's *The Homecoming* and are further discussed in Chapter 3.

If an Initiation is made at Ti, as happens in the example above, the system starts again from Ti. If a Response is made at Ti, however, a different set of choices opens up (Tsui 1994: 223). Speakers can make one of three different kinds of Responses: Positive Responses, Negative Responses, or Temporizations (Tsui 1994: ch. 8). Tsui's classification of responding moves is based on the preference organization argument put forward by the conversation analysts mentioned earlier (e.g. Pomerantz 1978; 1984; Levinson 1983; Sacks 1973/1987). Tsui (1994: 164) characterises Positive Responses, responses that fulfil the expectations of the Initiation, as preferred. Negative Responses and Temporizations, moves that do not fulfil the expectations set up by the Initiation, are dispreferred.

As Tsui (1994: 223) explains, Elicitations, Informatives and Directives all prospect Positive Responses. The exception is Elicitations of the subclass Commit (utterances such as *Can I talk to you?* which ask the addressee for a commitment to future talk). These prospect all three classes of response. Requestives also prospect all three types of response (Tsui 1994: 222–3). Notice that insights from politeness theory and preference organization are built into these systems of choices. For example, nearly all of the Initiations prospect Positive Responses. This is entirely in keeping with the empirical observation that there is a general preference for agreement over disagreement in English conversation (Heritage 1984; Brown and Yule 1983a: 11; Sacks 1973/1987). The two subclasses that do prospect Negative Responses and Temporizations can be considered to do so for reasons of face. Requestives and Elicit: Commits have in common a prospected action of the hearer without the assumption of speaker authority. As such, they may be treated as threats to the hearer's negative face (Tsui 1994: 102). The greater range of prospected responses for these Initiations is consistent with politeness theory in allowing the hearer a greater range of response options (Leech 1983; Brown and Levinson 1978/1987).

Once a response is made, the current speaker can continue, or there can be a change of speakers (Tsui 1994: 223–4). If the current speaker keeps the floor, the discourse framework is not maintained, and the only move that can be made is an Initiation. This system is demonstrated in the example below.

```
  1 F02:I:Inf:assmt:assng:   He's quite nice really.
  2 F01:R:+veR:              Yeah. He was quite helpful over your settee
  3                          and everything.
→ 4 F01:I:Inf:Rprt          There's a tiger skin settee in there by the
  5                          way this morning.
    (Cobuild S0000000473)[8]
```

F02's utterance, the initiating move, has been classified as an Informative:Assessment: Assessing, a move in which the speaker expresses an opinion about an event, a state of affairs, or a third party (Tsui 1994: 142). After this move is made, the discourse is at Ti. The floor shifts at this point to F01, who can either maintain the discourse framework and respond, or break the discourse framework and issue a Challenge or an Initiation. In the example above, F01 maintains the discourse framework and responds (lines 2–3). The Response is a positive one, as F01 makes a second evaluation that agrees with F02's initial judgement (Tsui 1994: 184). After this Response, the discourse is at Tr, and F01 breaks the discourse framework, keeps the floor, and initiates (lines 4–5). The Initiation is an Informative:Report, a move whose purpose is to provide factual information (Tsui 1994: 137).

If there is a change of speaker at Tr, the new speaker can either maintain the discourse framework and perform a Follow-up move, or break the discourse framework and perform a Challenge or an Initiation (in which case the system would start again from Ti) (Tsui 1994: 224). The latter choice is demonstrated below. F1 breaks the discourse framework and makes an initiating move (line 12–13) after F2's Positive Response in line 11.

6 F1:C:Inf:rprt:	mm I don't know.
7 F2:Back Channel:	No.
8 F1:	I just cannot see myself writing anymore.
9 F2:Back Channel:	No.
10 F1:	I cannot bear it.
11 F2:R+veR:	No.
12 F1:I:Inf:rprt:	I'd rather do something practical like.
13	palaeography.

(author's privately taped data)[9]

If the new speaker at Tr chooses to perform a Follow-up move, that move can occur as one of the four types of Follow-up moves identified in Tsui's framework: an Endorsement, a Concession, an Acknowledgement or a Turn-pass (Tsui 1994: 225, see also ch. 9). Endorsements ratify the positive outcome of an interaction; Concessions accept a negative outcome, often with a view to minimizing damage to face; Acknowledgements display recognition that the exchange has been satisfactory (often with minimal agreement tokens such as 'yeah'); and Turn-passes signal the current speaker's wish to relinquish the floor (for more detail, see Tsui 1994: 200–11).

Tsui (1994: 194, 225) allows Responses to prospect Follow-ups. Positive Responses are typically followed by either Endorsements or Acknowledgements. Negative Responses, on the other hand, are typically followed by Concessions or Acknowledgements. Temporizations prospect only Acknowledgements. A Follow-up: Acknowledgement is demonstrated in the example below, taken from Tsui's (1994) data.

1 D:I:Eli:com:	Alright, well em what what what em what what time
2	d'you what time would you like to do it.

```
      3 H:R:Temp:                  I'll I'll let you know, let me see, let me see h - if I can
                                   get the thing done by the end of the week.
  →   4 D:F:Acknl:                 Okay =
      (Tsui 1994: 208–9)
```

As Tsui (1994: 209) explains, the Response in line 3, a Temporization, allows H to avoid committing himself to a definite time. The prospected Follow-up:Acknowledgement from D occurs in line 4.

If a Follow-up move is made, as in the example above, the system is then at Tf, and a further set of choices is activated (Tsui 1994: 226). The current speaker can again choose whether or not to keep the floor. If they keep the floor, the discourse framework is not maintained, and the only move possible is an Initiation, in which case the system is once again at Ti. If the floor is relinquished, the new speaker can maintain the discourse framework and perform a second Follow-up (re-setting the system to Tf). Because Follow-ups prospect further Follow-up moves, they can be infinitely recursive, but a sequence of more than three Follow-up moves is rare (Tsui 1994: 226). The Turn-pass, available as an option after any number of Follow-ups, is typically realised after the first or second one. An example from Tsui's data is given below.

```
      1 I:S:                       = I'd like to read the story.
      2 R:M:                       Yeah, I'll try to get you a copy of the um of the story
      3                            after this week is over.
      4 F1:S:                      Okay.
  →   5 F_2:M:                     Okay.
      (Tsui 1994: 211)
```

As Tsui (1994: 211) notes, the first Follow-up move (F_1) concludes the business of the exchange, while the second one, the Turn-pass (F_2), indicates that M has nothing further to contribute.

The survey provided in this chapter outlines the explicit linguistic knowledge of conversation that has been brought to bear on the analysis of the plays investigated in the succeeding chapters. What these approaches also do is bring to conscious awareness some of the implicit knowledge that native speakers of English are thought to access, largely subconsciously, when they interact (Herman 1995: 5). In the same way that one can operate a computer without knowing the names of its parts and how they fit together, one can have a perfectly successful conversation without explicit knowledge of speaking turns, speech acts, or the cooperative principle and its maxims. Hymes (1967/1972) called this kind of knowledge communicative competence when he argued that Chomsky's notion of syntactic competence (automatic knowledge that native speakers have concerning the construction of syntactically well-formed sentences in their own language) did not sufficiently account for all that speakers appeared to know (without knowing they knew) about their own language. Hymes (1967/1972: 65) suggested that in deciding what may or may not be appropriately said, native speakers regularly and consistently take into account a range of variables, including the setting of the conversation (both physical and cultural), the participants, the purpose of the utterance, and the topic of the talk (see also Levinson 1979). The concept of communicative competence has been reworked a number of times (e.g. see Cohen 1996; Faerch and Kasper 1984; Canale and Swain 1980: 29) and now includes knowledge of discourse structure; that is, knowledge of how acts are typically structured and distributed in talk, and what sociocultural factors motivate these structures and distributions.

When playwrights represent talk in dialogue, it is these structures and distributions that are presented and exploited (Herman 1995: 6). It should be noted, however, that there is no suggestion here that playwrights typically sit down and say, for example, 'Ah, here I need a dispreferred response', or 'Yes, an instance of reclassified illocutionary intent will do nicely at this juncture'. While more research is certainly necessary on this point, it is reasonable to suggest that playwrights proceed more organically than this, drawing subconsciously on their communicative competence when they write dialogue. A recent guide to writing plays for would-be playwrights (Spencer 2002), for example, presents explicit discussions of dramatic structures (e.g. action, conflict, scene, event) and the representation of emotional states, but rather less clearly articulated discussions of linguistic structures. 'There is not much to say, in my opinion', says Spencer (2002: 196), 'about how dramatic language works except for the following, which is crucial: the words you choose, and the order in which they are delivered, will determine what people think of your play'. But when it comes down to thinking explicitly about these crucial elements — the order of the linguist units, the choices available, and how language actually does operate — it is clear that Spencer (2002) is drawing less on conscious knowledge and more on instinct. Writing good dialogue is writing 'words that sound good together, words that flow easily, words that are, perhaps, poetic' (Spencer 2002: 195), and characters should be allowed to 'speak what they will and how they will' so that the dialogue will 'ring true' (Spencer 2002: 198). For Spencer (2002: 196), the process of manipulating language in the dialogue is essential, but largely subconscious, and he takes care to advise his readers of this.

> You may very well not be consciously aware of your word choice as you write, but you are making choices nevertheless. The degree to which you or your subconscious makes them cohesively or clearly, while still admitting the complexity of the human psyche, will be the degree to which they are perceived by the audience as lifelike (Spencer 2002: 196).

Comments by the playwrights studied here on their own writing indicate that Spencer's experience is not atypical. Rattigan (1953a: xxi) has said that he does not know why understatement and implication work in his plays, only that they do. Wesker (in Leeming 1985: 52) acknowledges a more conscious approach, but notes that what he is conscious of are 'speech rhythms', a largely impressionistic expression. Nelson (1967: 53), drawing on the playwright's own remarks, notes that Pinter employs 'a controlled but essentially intuitive approach' to writing plays.

I merely write and characters create themselves. I don't arbitrarily impose a characterization upon someone, and say you're going to be like this to prove a point that I'm going to make. The stage opens, the curtain goes up and characters move along with it (Pinter with Hallam Tennyson, Interview, BBC General Overseas Service 7 August 1960, cited in Nelson 1967: 153–4).

Clearly, playwrights do not need explicit linguistic knowledge of conversation to write effective dialogue, nor do audiences need such knowledge to be affected by this dialogue. Analysts and critics who would comment on the language of dialogue in plays, however, do not sit in such a privileged position. Their work is best done with conscious knowledge of how the language of talk is thought to work, and the demonstration of this imperative is the subject of the remaining chapters of this book, starting with Pinter's *The Homecoming*.

Chapter 3

Lifting the Smokescreen
The Language of Conversation in Harold Pinter's *The Homecoming*

While Pinter is a favourite playwright among linguists interested in discourse stylistics and drama, his third full-length play *The Homecoming*, considered by many to be his masterpiece (Armstrong 1999: 39–40), has not received much stylistic attention. First performed at London's Aldwych Theatre in 1965, this play affords us several often disturbing glimpses into the lives of a north London family. Teddy, a philosophy professor, and his wife, Ruth, return to London to visit Teddy's family, his father (Max), his uncle (Sam), and his two brothers (Lenny and Joey). During the course of the play, Ruth decides to leave Teddy and stay with his family, accepting their proposal that she support both them and herself through prostitution.

While linguists have not shown any special interest in *The Homecoming*, critics have offered numerous treatments. Despite warnings from both Wellwarth (1996/2001) and Batty (2001) not to seek out any single message in the play, the 'meaning hunt' (Goldstone 1969: 20) seems set to continue. One of Pinter's most controversial works (Cahn 1994: 55), it has been read as a pagan fertility rite drama (Burkman 1971); compared with biblical stories such as the prodigal son and the account of Ruth (Nelson 1967; Armstrong 1999: 54); interpreted with reference to iconic images such as the holy family (Brown 1972: 111–12); considered in relation to Shakespeare's *Troilus and Cressida* and Jonson's *Volpone* (Strunk 1989); and set beside the work of Kafka (Armstrong 1999). It has been viewed as a parody of the working class conflict plays popular in the 1960s (Peacock 1997; Hope-Wallace 1965/1986); read as a study of desperation to fulfil, however inappropriately, the basic need for love (Gale 1987; Knowles 1984); viewed as a portrait of humanity reduced to its basest nature (Batty 2001; Peacock 1997: 87); seen as a gross subversion of family life (Elsom 1978/1986: 99; Cohn 1969: 81); and understood via Freud as an actualization of the subconscious mind (Brown 1972). Criticism of the 1970s revival saw the play as a battle between the sexes (Styan 1981/1998: 135–6; Elsom 1978/1986), and Esslin (1970) has noted that *The Homecoming* works on at least two levels: symbolically as Oedipal wish fulfilment, and realistically as a piece of theatre exploring the harsh realities of the London gangster lifestyle. Critics have also looked to Pinter's own views (as expressed in an interview with Tennyson 1960) in the search for meaning, and have interpreted the play as a variation on the 'invaded room' explored in *The Room* and *The Dumb Waiter* (Batty 2001: 30; Esslin 1968: 265–6).

That so many different interpretations have been put forward is unsurprising. Critics (e.g. Wellwarth 1996/2001: 104; Batty 2001; and Scott 1986: 19) have noted that *The Homecoming* has sparked more critical debates than many of the other plays, and have observed that it provokes a number of emotional reactions in its audiences, ranging from boredom and puzzlement through to shock and outright disgust (e.g. Peacock 1997: 87; Hudgins 1986: 102; Scott 1986; Hope-Wallace 1965/1986; Trussler 1973/1986; Esslin 1970: 157). For all that *The Homecoming* has engendered such debate and controversy, however, critical treatments have stalled when it comes to dealing with the language of the play. This, of course, is not a new thing to say of either Pinter or *The Homecoming*. Writing thirty years ago in his book *The Pinter Problem* (1975), Austin Quigley noted that it was Pinter's 'peculiar use of language' that presented such 'a major stumbling block for criticism of his work' (5). In comparison to many of Pinter's critics, Quigley (1975) was by far the most linguistic in orientation, citing an interest in both literary and linguistic approaches to drama in his preface and acknowledging the direct influence of John Sinclair. He calls for 'demonstrably accurate analytic statements' (1975: 29) and laments what he sees as the forfeit of evidence-based analysis in the criticism of Pinter's plays. He takes issue with many of Pinter's pioneering critics, such as Esslin (1970), Taylor (1962, 1971), Nelson (1967) and Brown (1967), on the grounds that they recognize the need to account for Pinter's use of language, but fail to do so. Instead, they appeal unhelpfully to metaphor and analogy (music, poetry, sculpture, the zoo, etc.); invoke the vague concept of subtext; and manufacture symbols in a vain attempt to account for the supposedly commonplace and mundane in Pinter's language (Quigley 1975). Sometimes, there is even a barely concealed throwing up of hands. Rather than attempting to come to grips with Pinter's exploitation of everyday language, critics retreat behind the assertion that his work simply defies analysis (Quigley 1975: 29). For Quigley (1975), all of these tendencies are symptoms of a deeper problem in attempts to cope with Pinter's work. Metaphoric comparisons, speculation about what lies 'behind' or 'above' or 'beneath' the text (29) and 'symbol-hunting' (7) struck him as ultimately unworkable, since none of these methods succeeded in engaging the 'recalcitrant details of the text' (1975: 19). For Quigley (1975), the subtext that so many critics were fond of citing had to be related to the text in some way, or it would not be detectable (1975: 29), and for Pinter's work to be understood, there could be no 'loss of contact between observable detail [in the text] and reported response [to it]' (1975: 23).

Deeply dissatisfied with existing critical work, Quigley (1975) gave himself the task of accounting for Pinter's 'peculiar use of language' (5). Drawing on Halliday (1970), who was interested in relating language structure to language function, he proposed the 'interrelational function' of language to cope analytically with his primary observation regarding Pinter's dialogue: it is not, essentially, about the transfer of information, but about what the verbal interactions of the characters indicate about the relationship between them (Quigley 1975: 49–53). In addition to drawing on other critics and interviews with Pinter himself, he turned to then-contemporary work in linguistics for a new direction in his analysis. In his chapter 'The Language Problem', he cites some of the key papers and collections of essays in stylistics available when he was writing (e.g. Halliday 1971; Chatman, ed. 1971; Freeman, ed. 1970), and also looks at the text-based work in practical criticism associated with I.A. Richards (1967, 1969).

While Quigley reads linguists and critics interested in language in pursuit of his goal, he also notices that he is limited by what is available to him. Syntactic and phonetic treatments of texts are not helpful in what he wants to do with Pinter's dialogue, and practical criticism, he argues, remains too closely bound to the idea that language is principally about the 'transfer of verifiable facts' (Quigley 1975: 50). This assumption involves isolating linguistic forms from their speakers, and Quigley (1975) thus found it to be of limited use when it came to making sense of what Pinter's characters did with language.

For Quigley (1975: 66) language, and language in Pinter, was not about referring to things and concepts, but about constructing (or destroying) relationships between people. In essence, what he needed in order to fulfil his thesis on language in Pinter was pragmatics, a discipline within linguistics that seeks to account not for what language means but for what speakers mean in the many situations in which they find themselves (see Chapter 2 for further discussion). Interestingly, Quigley's account, informed by Firth (1964/1966), anticipates this concern.

> But if ... the significance of the language is pursued in terms of *its appropriateness to the situation in which it is used*, a whole new set of questions emerges (Quigley 1975: 31, italics mine).

In 1975, however, there were not many sources Quigley could consult to expand his theory, as pragmatics had not then defined itself as a discipline. As Thomas (1995) points out in her preface, it is still a young field, and its major textbooks only began to appear in the early 1980s.

Quigley turns instead to what might be called the 'proto-pragmaticists' (Levinson 1983: xii), scholars such as Wittgenstein (1969), Austin (1962/1975), and Firth (1964/1966) who are more interested in what speakers do with language rather than the structure of the language itself. These authors contribute key ideas to Quigley's work (e.g. people do much more with than language than simply refer; language in use is contextualized, situated language), and from Firth (1964/1966) in particular comes the essential notion that

> you are not free to say just what you like ... The moment a conversation is started, whatever is said is a determining condition for what in any reasonable expectation may follow (Firth 1964/1966: 94).

This relationship between an utterance and what follows it, including silence, as Quigley (1975: 55) also realized, is a key concept in the study of talk, both actual and represented. Discourse analysts after Firth will call this relationship prospection, and conversation analysts will call it preference organization (see Chapter 2). While Quigley may not have had access to these developments in 1975, he is quick to grasp the significance of Firth's statement in relation to understanding Pinter's dialogue.

'There is a strong social pressure available in language to promote the responses one wishes to receive', notes Quigley (1975: 51), but such expectations are, of course, not always met. Rather, 'the tension in much of Pinter's dialogue derives from just that refusal [to produce the expected response]' (1975: 51).

Quigley (1975) recognizes that the relationship between successive utterances in talk is closely bound up with how speakers negotiate relationships with each other. Drawing once again on Firth, he observes that

> no matter how one is addressed there is an implicit demand for a particular range of response. To respond within that range is to accept the relationship on the terms of the first speaker; to reply outside of that range is to qualify or reject the common ground of the relationship as envisaged by the first speaker (Quigley 1975: 55).

Thus, realizes Quigley, what will be of key importance in analyzing Pinter's dialogue, is not so much what is said, but when it is said.

> An understanding of the significance of what any character says in any play requires that we ask not only 'what words did he utter?' but also 'why did he say that *now*?' (1975: 72).

For Quigley, an analysis of how Pinter's dialogue is sequenced will reveal how these sequences communicate changes in the relationships of the characters. It is this 'sequence-oriented interpretation' that separates analysis from re-telling the plot (1975: 74–5).

While Quigley (1975) sketches out quite a reasonable theory, his sources fail him when it comes to applying that theory to the text. Wittgenstein (1969), Austin (1962/1975) and Firth (1964/1966) offer little in the way of comprehensive frameworks with defined units of analysis that can be applied to the data (see Taylor and Cameron's 1987 discussion of rules and units in the study of talk), and so have relatively little to say about how units of conversation are sequenced between participants on a moment-to-moment basis in talk. While Halliday (1971) does work with defined units, Quigley's (1975: 43–4) complaint with his paper is entirely justified. The bulk of it is concerned with identifying and exemplifying ideational clauses, clauses used to express concepts, facts and ideas. Halliday (1971) is less concerned in this paper with Quigley's interest, the interpersonal function of language, and so Quigley finds that it is not helpful to his purpose of analyzing dialogic exchanges.

Undeterred, he set out to build the tool he realized he needed but could not find when he was writing – a framework of analysis for talk exchanges that could be applied to drama dialogue. While Quigley (1975) treats the issue of language in Pinter's dialogue in far more detail than many others, his account nevertheless leaves certain key ideas concerning the sequence of units in talk unclarified. As a result, his own analysis of language in *The Homecoming* does not shed much light on the questions that concerned him. Quigley's (1975) main thesis is that the play explores what happens when different social groups, each with a legitimate claim to the family 'home', come into conflict over that space and what it represents. Following the lead of Cohn (1969: 80), he uses as a unit the duologue, dramatic dialogue between two characters, and explains that

> the sequential juxtaposition of a series of duologues is Pinter's way of organising our perception of change in a relationship so that we may perceive the fact of change, the location of change, and ultimately, the significance of change (Quigley 1975: 74–5).

With specific reference to *The Homecoming*, he suggests that it

> consists of a series of the usual Pinter duologues and also a series of adapted duologues in which the structure is that of one individual versus the rest of the characters present (Quigley 1975: 174).

It makes sense for Quigley to use a dramatic unit such as the duologue, since there was no fully developed discourse unit to use when he was developing his thesis. However, this unit is character-driven rather than language-driven, and this introduces problems. While the play is split into 15 sections (a list of which appears in the argument on page 178 without any explanatory preamble), these sections are delineated by page numbers and characters (e.g., 'pp. 7–11 1. Max and Lenny'), not boundaries in the dialogue itself. In addition, more local developments in the structure of the represented talk (which is presumably what is meant by 'adapted' duologues) will be difficult to determine with such a framework.

Quigley is also vague on the details of sequencing in the dialogue, even when his conceptual understanding of this issue is ahead of its time. While he notes that each 'juxtaposed duologue' is 'heavily dependent for interpretation on its place in the sequence' (1975: 74), he talks about this in terms of 'the 'when' factor' (1975: 74–5). In so doing, he leaves sequencing, the most important issue, in scare quotes, and does so repeatedly throughout the chapter (e.g., see pages 68 and 73). Interestingly, he is here proceeding in much the same way as Kennedy (1975) did with the term 'shaping' (see Chapter 1). As Quigley's account continues, in fact, it becomes clear that the 'when' factor comes to refer not so much to lines of dialogue as sequenced in relation to each other, or even larger exchanges of dialogue as sequenced in relation to each other, but to the order of events in the play. Of the scene when Teddy and Lenny are reunited, for example, Quigley suggests that while it does not make explicit the reason for why the brothers are so tense with each other, 'its location in the *sequence of events* underlines the importance of Lenny's part in the development of future issues' (1975: 193, italics mine).

This confusion with respect to the unit of analysis and how it is sequenced means that many of Quigley's (1975) insights regarding *The Homecoming* are not derived from an analysis of the duologue structure to which he commits himself. For example, he observes that many of the interactions between Sam, Lenny and Max in the first act of the play demonstrate the family is not a sharing, caring cooperative, but an arena for 'mutual exploitation' (Quigley 1975: 184–5). Lenny exploits both Max and Sam for his own ends and Max, the supposed patriarch, is generally powerless, stripped psychologically bare by Lenny's abuse (Quigley 1975: 179–82; see also Esslin 1968:

288, who makes a similar argument). While these are insightful statements on the struggle for territory and power in the play, they do not arise out of an analysis of the interrelational function of language in the duologue structure that Quigley went to such effort to develop. Of the play's beginning, for example, he notes that the 'opening duologue is full of threats, insults and mockery' (1975: 178). While Lenny and Max certainly do threaten, insult and mock each other, what are the linguistic boundaries of the opening duologue? And where are the other duologues with which it can be juxtaposed in order to reveal the conflicts over the physical and conceptual space of the 'home'? Instead of clarifying this, Quigley (1975: 179) moves straight from the opening duologue to differences in dress between the two men, noting that Lenny appears 'dressed to leave the house, Max to stay'. Elsewhere, a similar method is employed with the physical position of the characters on stage being used to forward the thesis that relationships between characters are in transition (see 201). While modes of dress and choreography are clearly relevant in establishing the roles characters play or will play in the family, this kind of analysis does not advance knowledge of how language is used in the struggle for territory in the home.

When language is given explicit focus in the analysis, there is also a tendency to gloss what characters say to each other. For example, Quigley (1975) notes that Lenny

> cleverly guides the conversation towards an extended emphasis on Sam's function in the world outside – an emphasis that can only feed Max's sense of inadequacy in this sphere. This strategy quickly works, as Max is stung into retaliation by suggesting that Sam's popularity as a chauffeur has less to do with his driving ability than with other ways in which an unmarried adult male chauffeur might be 'had' (Quigley 1975: 183).

Such glossing does not identify patterns in the conversational behaviour of the characters that can be related to the conflicts that develop among them concerning who it is that is coming home, and to what.

In addition, weaknesses in the framework sometimes lead Quigley to do that which so frustrated him in the work of the others – retell the plot. For example, he notes that Lenny's response to Max's seemingly innocent request for a pair of scissors (Lenny: 'Why don't you shut up you daft prat?': 4)[1] is understood not so much by its referential meaning, but by what it tells us with respect to the conflict between the two men over who is who in the family (1975: 179). The promised analysis of the duologue structure is difficult to discern, however, and what is given instead seems to be an account of what happens, as in the following example:

> Max's inconsistent estimates of his major role in life are evident in these early remarks to Lenny. First he tries to compete with the image he feels Lenny has in the world outside: 'You think I wasn't a tearaway? I could have taken care of you twice over. I'm still strong' (5). And when Lenny's attention remains on the horse-races in the newspaper, Max tries to claim expertise in this area, too: 'I had a … I had an instinctive understanding of animals. I should have been a trainer. Many times I was offered the job – you know, a proper post, by the Duke of … I forget his name … one of the Dukes' (7). But when Lenny remains

unimpressed by these claims, Max switches to claims of a rather different kind, and these claims are in the nature of both an excuse for failure in the world outside and an avowal of a different kind of success (Quigley 1975: 180).

While Quigley (1975) notes much that is of interest here, interrelational classifications for utterances that occur are not offered, and their place in the sequence of the interaction is primarily chronological (first, next, then, etc.) rather than functionally contrastive.

Quigley's attempt to deal with Pinter's language is laudable and in places impressive, but it does not clearly elucidate a series of juxtaposed duologues. Consequently, the work does not manage to show how these supposedly contrasting duologues reflect character relationships in transition. It is only fair to point out, however, that Quigley (1975) may simply have taken on too much. Many of the most influential frameworks for discourse and conversation are developed as linguistic contributions first in book- or thesis-length treatments, and only later applied to other kinds of data. In contrast, *The Pinter Problem* set out to develop a framework and apply it to several of Pinter's plays all in one work.

Quigley's analysis may have raised more questions than it answered, but it is unfortunate that his critique of Pinter criticism did not have a greater effect on the field than it did. While he is often a starting point for linguists writing on Pinter (e.g. Gautam 1987; Burton 1980), critics have on the whole been less impressed. He crops up reasonably often in bibliographies of secondary works, but few critics engage his argument in detail. He is, for example, cited in Hinchliff (1986: 153), but only in relation to his statement on Pinter's continued popularity with both critics and audiences. Stevenson (1984: 34) briefly praises him for being 'sensitive to Pinter's linguistic complexity', but goes on to suggest that the playwright's work is best dealt with by going outside the text to compare him with his influences among modernist writers such as Joyce and Hemingway. Quigley (1975) gets several mentions in Dukore (1982), but none of them go into any great detail. He cites Quigley briefly to agree with his interpretation of Stanley's interrogation in *The Birthday Party* (1982: 32), and his reading of Aston's electric-shock therapy speech in *The Caretaker* (1982: 49). While he also quotes one of Quigley's paraphrases of Firth on the power of initiating utterances to constrain replies, taking Quigley's linguistic thesis forward is not one of Dukore's (1982) primary concerns.

Such superficial mentions remain the norm even after extracts from Quigley's (1975) work are reprinted in Scott's (1986) casebook. For example, *The Pinter Problem* appears in the bibliography of Esslin (2000) (the sixth edition of *The Peopled Wound*, published as *Pinter: The Playwright*), but is not listed in the index. Cahn (1994: 34), cites Quigley (1975) (once, briefly) in connection with the importance of language and character relationships in *The Collection*, but does not pursue Quigley's linguistic approach to the dialogue. He is given a bit more space in Malkin (1992), but she does not do justice to his account. While she agrees with him that Stanley is beaten into submission through a series of verbal accusations in *The Birthday Party*, she criticizes him for not looking at the content of these accusations in sufficient depth. In not entirely taking on board Quigley's argument, however, Malkin (1992) perhaps fails to fully appreciate the value of his contribution. He was not simply stressing 'the sheer number and variety' (Quigley 1975: 64) of the accusations levelled at Stanley as Malkin (1992) seems to have supposed. Quigley's point was that the referential meaning of the various accusations was less significant than the way they were used.

The tendency to ignore or gloss over Quigley's (1975) contribution, even after landmark work appears in pragmatics (e.g. Levinson 1983), conversation analysis (e.g. Sacks, Schegloff and Jefferson 1974) and discourse analysis (e.g. Sinclair and Coulthard 1975) that could have been used to progress his concerns, has resulted in continued stagnation in Pinter criticism when it comes to dealing with the language of the plays. Peacock (1997: 80), for example, does not look at how pauses in conversation have been dealt with by linguists in his attempt to deal with the interplay of talk and silence in *The Homecoming*. Instead, he draws on the well-worn but vague music metaphor (Quigley 1975: 24), comparing the dialogue to a musical score. In his account of how the males in the family interact, he follows the lead of earlier critics (e.g. Wardle 1971; Hollis 1970: 97–8) in drawing on metaphors of animal behaviour rather than models of talk, noting that 'each of the males, with the exception of Joey, *snarls* and *paws* at one another in an attempt to establish dominance within *the pack* over Ruth' (Peacock 1997: 80). Cahn (1994) adopts a similar strategy. Following the lead of Cohn (1969: 80), he conceptualizes the family as a jungle (74) and its members as animals that inhabit it. Lenny is the 'younger primate standing over' Max, the 'defeated older male' (57); Sam is the outcast, an adult male who has fathered no offspring (57); and Joey enters wanting food, another 'animalistic element' according to Cahn (1994: 57).

More detailed attempts to look at the language of the play tend to rest on the identification of words and word-like units. Knowles (1984), for example, devotes an entire study to the issue of names and naming in *The Homecoming*. Armstrong (1999: 56) is interested in Lenny's verbal skill, describing him as 'a formidable strategist in his deployment of language', a character who 'evinces a high degree of verbal fluency' (56). He bases this, however, on Lenny's seemingly equal ease with both vulgar expressions (a lexical category), and '*words* and *phrases* that seem quite foreign to someone of his socio-economic background', such as *hypothesis* and *criterion* (56, italics mine). In like fashion, Batty (2001: 40) notes that Pinter is careful to set down 'the language of interaction and the currencies of negotiation' that obtain in the household before Ruth is introduced, but his analysis of this language consists primarily of identifying words, in particular slang expressions such as 'bitch', 'tit', and 'slag'.

Another recurring problem in critical treatments dealing with the language of *The Homecoming* is the tendency to use subjective, non-technical terms rather than the appropriate linguistic terminology (see also discussion of this issue in Chapter 1). A number of examples are provided in Cahn's (1994) study. Lenny's replies are '*brief*' and '*sharp*' (55) unless he is threatened, in which case he betrays himself with '*choppy* prose of retreat' (62); the conversation between Max and Lenny '*softens* as the two reflect about horses' (56) (italics mine), and Teddy's 'rhythms and tone of speech' are indicative of his insecurity (59). Words like *sharp* and *choppy* mean nothing linguistically, and so shed little light on the language of the text. *Brief* has meaning only in relation to the expected length of an utterance, and *soften* in its technical sense is related to the use of mitigating devices, but Cahn (1994) appears to be using the ordinary meaning of these terms. Issues of rhythm will be apparent in a performance and are inferable from the written text (Short 1989), but Cahn (1994) does not discuss here how he arrives at this conclusion. Tone of speech, the layperson's expression for what is in reality a cluster of interacting features including pitch, loudness and stress (Crystal and Davy 1975: 14) will also be apparent in performance and inferable from the text, but Cahn (1994) does not provide detailed discussion on these issues.

Consider as well that while a number of frameworks for the analysis of talk are now available (see Chapter 2), glosses of what characters do and say are apparently still acceptable as language analysis. Batty (2001: 40), for example, proposes to explore the power struggle between Max and Lenny, suggesting that their 'verbal interaction is a process of mockery and defence, of belittling one another in a shifting game of power advantage'. He provides ample evidence of Lenny abusing and belittling his father, for example:

> when, in the play's opening moments, Lenny can't get his father to 'shut up' or 'plug it' by calling him a 'daft prat', a 'stupid sod', or 'demented', he reaches for this tactic, firstly by undermining his father's expert opinion over a racehorse and secondly by ridiculing the old man's cooking. When he successfully riles Max, he cowers in mock terror at his father's rising anger and threatened use of his walking stick (Batty 2001: 40–41).

Such a record of events, however, does not do much to show how the structure of the dialogue can be shown to enact as well as reflect the struggle for power. Cahn (1994: 59) is similarly dependent on description in places. He notes that Ruth 'speaks and acts with confidence', observing that when Teddy asks if she is cold she simply answers, 'No'. What is arguably the key piece in the analysis, however, is not covered. What exactly is it in Ruth's refusal that suggests confidence? This can be more effectively explored with reference to prospected or preferred responses to enquiries regarding an interlocutor's welfare, but Cahn's (1994) discussion shows little interest in this type of analysis.

Wellwarth's (1996/2001: 106–7) commentary presents perhaps the most extreme example of critical difficulty in coming to grips with *The Homecoming*. Faced with Pinter's text, he abandons attempts to deal with it because he has such trouble believing that a character of Teddy's background could ever be a PhD in America, much less in philosophy (1996: 106). Instead, he puts forward what he suggests is a more plausible sequence of events: Teddy's marriage, children and academic career are a cover story for his revenge on his family. Teddy has not, in fact, been in America, but in some English city away from London and has become an underworld king in his own right. He returns, having paid Ruth to destroy his family, and thus be liberated from them. As Wellwarth himself admits, however, this is not what Pinter wrote. Clearly, such unanchored speculation sheds little light on either the play or its language.

Also problematic in recent commentary on *The Homecoming* is that while some of the older, landmark texts are still appearing in revised editions, these revisions do not typically take on board developments in linguistic enquiry. Revisions to Esslin's *The Peopled Wound* between 1970 and 2000 take into account new developments in Pinter's career and new developments in drama criticism, but generally do not pay any attention to developments in linguistics that are relevant to the study of drama. Additions to the bibliography do not include any of the texts in linguistics and pragmatics that could have been consulted (see Chapter 2), with the result that the analysis offered of Pinter's language in 1970 is still the analysis being offered today. This is not inconsequential. While Esslin lists references to 'linguistic techniques' in his index, the corresponding discussions do not cover topics that many linguists would recognize as relevant under this heading. For example, 'linguistic techniques' leads to a discussion of one of Ruth's major speeches, during which she observes that 'perhaps the fact that [her lips] move is more significant ... than the words which come through them' (85, ellipses Pinter's). Where a linguist might expect a discussion on the conversational uses of metalanguage and their representation in the play, Esslin identifies this as a 'key sentence' and goes on to talk about how it reveals Pinter's own philosophical attitudes.

When Quigley's (1975) concerns are taken on board and progressed with frameworks for the linguistic investigation of talk that are now available, the dialogue can be analysed to shed light on three issues that emerge as particularly salient in the research record on *The Homecoming*, the struggles for power, the unsettling mix of the usual and the strange, and the disturbing matter of Ruth and her choice. For the rest of this chapter, each of these issues will be dealt with in turn.

Many accounts of *The Homecoming* foreground how the characters struggle for psychological and territorial dominance within the often oppressive institution of the family (Batty 2001; Peacock 1997; Wellwarth 1996/2001: 105; Quigley 1975: 173; Esslin 1968: 288). In this struggle, the Sam-Lenny-Max dynamic has been of interest, and attempts have been made to link the language of the dialogue to this conflict. Cahn (1994: 55), for example, talks about the 'familiar Pinter technique of unanswered, then repeated questions separated by pauses', and suggests that this shows Max to be 'the weaker figure'. While Cahn (1994) makes a reasonable point, adopting methods from conversation and discourse analysis in the study of the dialogue of these three characters can do more to reveal how the represented conversations serve to construct the skewed power relationships within this severely dysfunctional family. As Herman (1998: 24–5) has noted, the order and content of turns at talk are, in a play, 'controlled by the dramatist for a purpose', and looking carefully at patterns in these features in the dialogue reveals a great deal about how the play achieves its effects. This can be demonstrated by looking at an encounter between Sam, Lenny and Max from early in Act One (10–13), from MAX *sits hunched* to SAM *They get very jealous.*

Lenny and Max are on stage, having just finished a violent argument when Sam makes his first entrance in the play.[2]

Lenny:	Hullo, Uncle Sam.
Sam:	Hullo.
Lenny:	How are you, Uncle?
Sam:	Not bad. A bit tired (10).

At first glance, this represented greeting is unremarkable. As with many exchanges represented in drama, two of the most fundamental rules of turn-taking are displayed: one speaker speaks at a time, and speaker change recurs (Burton 1980: 115, drawing on Sacks 1970). In addition, these first four lines are constructed from two adjacency pairs that are typical of conversational openings (Schegloff 1972; Levinson 1983). Lenny and Sam exchange greetings in the first two lines, and this pair is followed by the 'ritual enquiry' *How are you?* (Schegloff 1972: 354) and one of its preferred responses (SAM *Not bad. A bit tired*).

In fact, so normal does this greeting sequence appear that it is easy to dismiss it. Doing so, however, is a mistake, as greetings are actually very significant pieces of talk that can be manipulated to great effect in drama dialogue (Herman 1995: 162). Greetings are exchanges of mutual goodwill (Tsui 1994), examples of what Goffman (1967: 57) called 'interpersonal rituals', the seemingly mundane interchanges through which we daily confirm our relationships with each other. And as Schegloff (1972) points out, greetings are rarely an end in themselves; rather, they exert a measure of control over the rest of the interaction by occasioning further talk and allowing speakers to accomplish a 'coordinated entry into an encounter' (Schegloff 1972: 370). Had only Sam and Lenny been on stage, this greeting would have been largely mimetic, a representation of two family members re-establishing contact after a short absence. However, it must be remembered that Max is also there sitting 'hunched' as the stage directions make clear. He does not take part in the exchange of goodwill (see Herman 1995: 162 for similar instances of Max behaving this way) and he misses (or is denied) his coordinated entry into the talk. Consequently, Sam and Lenny are free to behave for most of the scene as if Max were simply not there. Max's absence while present is exemplified in this fairly typical exchange between Sam and Lenny.

Lenny:	Tired? I bet you're tired. Where you been?
Sam:	I've been to London Airport.
Lenny:	All the way up to London Airport? What, right up the M4?
Sam:	Yes, all the way up there (10).

The contributions that Lenny and Sam make to the represented talk are patterned to ensure that Max's exclusion continues. Lenny directs the flow of talk away from his father by consistently selecting Sam as the next speaker. Notice as well that his selection choice is unambiguous. He linguistically points to Sam with direct questions (*Where you been?*), tag questions (Oh, a Yankee, *was it?*) and direct terms of address (*Uncle*).

When all of Lenny's turns in this extract are considered, only one exception to this general pattern occurs, as indicated below. Items in Lenny's turns that select

Sam as next speaker are underlined, and the exception (more of which later) appears in italics.

Sam as Selected Next Speaker in Lenny's Turns
Hullo, Uncle Sam.
How are you Uncle?
Tired, I bet you're tired. Where you been?
All the way up to London Airport? What, right up the M4?
Tch. Tch. Tch. Well, I think you're entitled to be tired, Uncle.
I know. That's what I'm talking about. I'm talking about the drivers.
Oh, a Yankee, was it?
Had to catch a plane there, did he?

While it can certainly be argued that Lenny's expressed concern for his uncle is less than sincere (Strunk 1989: 174; Quigley 1975: 183), his turns clearly show that he selects Sam as the next speaker, and never his father Max.

While Sam's role is more passive, he too contributes to Max's disenfranchisement. He does not actively exclude Max, but nor does he work especially hard to include him either, and it is not until the end of the extract that he selects Max as next speaker. In the majority of his turns, Sam behaves appropriately as Lenny's nominated participant. He takes his turn at talk, and provides preferred responses to each of Lenny's questions (*I've been to London Airport; Yes, all the way up there*). Notice as well that in contrast to Lenny, the majority of Sam's turns leave the floor open, especially in the first half of the extract.

Speaker Selection Patterns in Sam's Turns
Hullo.
Not bad. A bit tired.
I've been to London Airport.
Yes, all the way up there.
Well it's the drivers.
Knocks you out.

As is clear from these turns, Sam does not select any other participant to speak. The turn-taking pattern established in the first part of the extract is for Lenny to select Sam or himself, but never Max. When Lenny does self-select, he returns the floor immediately to Sam. Sam follows Lenny's lead by providing preferred responses to Lenny's questions in his turns, but does not actively select the other participants as next speaker.

As indicated earlier, there are exceptions to this pattern, breaks in the established routine that are thus particularly noticeable. These exceptions surround Max's much delayed entry into the talk. The single turn of Lenny's that does not select Sam as next speaker (*I know. That's what I'm talking about. I'm talking about the drivers*) initiates the exchange just prior to Max's first attempt to participate.

Lenny:	I know. That's what I'm talking about. I'm talking about the drivers.
Sam:	Knocks you out.
	Pause.
Max:	I'm here, too, you know (11).

In contrast to his earlier turn-taking behaviour, Lenny does not self-select and return the floor to Sam after *Knocks you out*, and a pause ensues that can be analysed as a gap in the turn-taking framework. Sam has not selected anyone as next speaker, and no one immediately self selects. Significantly, this is the first gap in the talk since Sam's arrival. As indicated in the dialogue cited above, it is Max who fills the silence by self-selecting.

It is also significant that Max's late entry into the talk is realized by a face-threatening act, an Informative:Assessment:Criticism (*I'm here, too, you know*). As Tsui (1994: 147) notes, these moves express negative evaluations of the addressee or addressees (see Chapter 2 for a discussion of Tsui's 1994 framework). Notice as well that the force of Max's Criticism is aggravated with the tag *you know*, an item from a class of forms called strengtheners or aggravators that serve to strengthen the illocutionary force of an utterance.

Disruptions in Sam's usual turn-taking behaviour also cluster around Max's entry to the talk. While Sam's responses to Lenny were preferred, his reply to Max's Criticism is a Challenging move. As Tsui (1994) explains, Initiating moves carry certain presuppositions. Responding moves supply the prospected preferred responses, thereby upholding the presuppositions of the initiation, while Challenging moves question or undermine them. As a type of Assessment, for example, Criticisms carry the presupposition that speakers believe their expressed valuations to be accurate (Tsui 1994: 183). Prospected responses to a Criticism, those that confirm the given presupposition, are typically realized as agreements and/or apologies (e.g. *yes, you're right, I'm sorry*). Sam reacts to Max with what is called an attributable silence, the act of saying nothing even when one is expected to speak (see Chapter 2). As the stage directions make clear, he remains silent and simply looks at Max (11). In so doing, he Challenges Max's Criticism instead of supplying the prospected agreement or apology.

This Criticism/Challenge pair is repeated in the next exchange.

Max:	I said I'm here, too. I'm sitting here.
Sam:	I know you're here.
	Pause.
Sam:	I took a Yankee out there today ... to the Airport.
Lenny:	Oh, a Yankee, was it? (11).

Max's first attempt to enter the talk has not succeeded. Sam uncharacteristically self-selects and continues after the gap (marked by *Pause* above), and the normal pattern for this extract is then resumed: Lenny self-selects and returns the floor to Sam with his question about the Yankee. Thus, breaks in the turn-taking pattern highlight Max's entry into the talk, and the resumption of those patterns signal his return to silent non-participation.

Max's second attempt to join the talk is also highlighted by breaks in the established turn-taking pattern between Lenny and Sam. Contrary to type, Sam selects Lenny as the next speaker when the talk turns to a box of cigars that a customer has given to Sam.

Lenny:	Had to catch a plane there, did he?
Sam:	Yes. Look what he gave me. He gave me a book of cigars.
	SAM takes a box of cigars from his pocket.
Max:	Come here. Let's have a look at them (12).

This break in the pattern is followed by another face-threatening attempt from Max to enter the talk. While Sam has selected Lenny as the next speaker, Max performs a turn-grab (Herman 1998), stealing the floor (and arguably the cigars) from Lenny ('Come here. Let's have a look at them').

At this point, it is both Max and Sam who act contrary to type. Instead of Criticisms, Max issues an Informative:Assessment:Compliment directed at Sam. Sam, instead of taking the role of respondent, self-selects with an Informative:Assessment: Self-Commendation ('You know what he said to me? He told me I was the best chauffeur he'd ever had. The best one': 12). These moves prospect agreements and upgrades (Tsui 1994: 144) (e.g. *Of course you're the best. Who could think anything else?*). Max, however, suddenly returns to type and performs a Challenging move ('From what point of view?'), a Challenge that is repeated after Sam's Elicit:Clarify ('Eh?': 13).

The organization of turns in this extract makes this relatively unaggressive Challenge very noticeable. In contrast to many of Max's other Challenges (e.g., 'Listen! I'll chop your spine off [...]' 5), *From what point of view?* is fairly mild. It occurs as a question rather than a statement, and it does not include any aggravators. And yet, the line resonates. Why? There are several reasons for this. Because Max has had to work so hard to get into the talk, we are paying careful attention to what he says. In addition, the Challenge follows an unusual Supporting move from Max (his Compliment regarding Sam's cigars), and the contrast between the two move types captures attention. The Challenge is further highlighted because of Sam's response to it, his request for clarification ('Eh?'). Since we have no reason to believe he has not heard, the assumption is that he is surprised by the question, and perhaps threatened.

Why is this particular Challenge from Max given such prominence in the dialogue when other, more violent Challenges are not? As critics have routinely pointed out, the first act of *The Homecoming* is structurally crucial to the second act (e.g. see Nelson 1967: 148). Max's Challenge regarding why Sam is considered the best driver prepares the audience for a significant revelation in act two, Sam's confession that MacGregor, an associate of the family, had Jessie, Max's wife, in the back of Sam's car while he (Sam) was driving (131). This may actually turn out to be Sam's last living act, as he collapses without apparent recovery (131) shortly after this outburst.

Consideration of the turn-taking patterns and discourse structure in this extract also serves to shed light on a second much-discussed issue in the literature on *The Homecoming*, the way in which the play sets the 'bizarre' against the 'mundane' (Strunk 1989: 169; Brown 1972: 11; Worth 1972; Esslin 1970: 149). Peacock (1997: 83) is also struck by this aspect of the play, noting that events often begin in an unremarkable way, but are then 'gradually transformed ... decorum and normal social interaction soon crumble, taking with them conventional morality'. What has not been said in sufficient detail, however, is how this juxtaposition between the normal and the weird is accomplished in the dialogue. Rather, what we have thus far are either largely intuitive accounts that gloss what characters say and do, or discussions that make use of categories and features that are difficult to systematically define or track in the data. How is a 'normal social interaction' to be defined, and how do we know when this has 'crumbled'? What characterizes a 'crumbled' social interaction? How are events 'gradually transformed'? Looking at the dialogue from a linguistic perspective allows us to explore these intuitions regarding normal and unusual interactions in greater depth.

One of the key passages to demonstrate the mix of the bizarre and the mundane in the play is the goodbye scene between Teddy and the rest of his family (133–6). Critics have been much exercized by Ruth's farewell to Teddy ('Don't become a stranger': 136) and its preface, her once and only use (Knowles 1984: 122) of the intimate nickname 'Eddie' (135) for her husband. In concentrating their language study on the formulaic nature of Ruth's goodbye, however, many of these discussions remain somewhat narrow in focus. After classifying 'Don't become a stranger' as a 'weak cliché', Esslin (1970: 224) turns to its literal meaning to expound on its dramatic significance, rather than its function in the represented talk. He suggests that while Teddy takes the cliché at face value as 'an idiom without any emotional force' (223), for Ruth it is meant as 'a last despairing lament of a wife for the husband she has now lost, who has, in fact, at this very moment become a stranger to her' (223–4). This reading seems to stretch things a bit, however, as there is little evidence to support feelings of sorrow on Ruth's part at the loss of her husband. Nelson (1967: 148), for example, has pointed to the essential sterility of their relationship, and Quigley (1975: 190) comments on their lack of rapport. Gale (1987: 282) suggests that Teddy has always been a stranger to Ruth, but also takes the clichéd goodbye literally. For him, this line indicates that Ruth bears Teddy no grudge: 'like her marriage, he has failed in his role, so she simply dismisses him as one would say good-bye to a casual acquaintance'. Cahn (1994: 72) proposes that the intimate nickname and the cliché betray mixed feelings on Ruth's part, affection for her husband on the one hand and resignation at their inevitable parting on the other. Knowles (1984: 122–3) prefers a metaphoric reading, suggesting that the two elements 'conflate the milieux of home and brothel reflecting [Ruth's] compound rôle of mother-lover-whore'.

Consideration of Ruth's farewell as part of a represented conversational closing allows for a discussion that moves beyond the categories of cliché and naming. The first thing to be pointed out is that the leave-taking (from TEDDY *Well, I'll leave your case, Ruth* to *Teddy goes, shuts the front door*: 133–6) is in many ways presented as normal. As Shegloff and Sacks (1973: 295) observe, the turn-taking mechanism in talk seems designed to foster the continuation of interaction, and leave-takings function to suspend that continuation. Farewells can be tricky, however, as not all parties may be ready to leave the talk at the same time. This, suggest Schegloff and Sacks (1973), may be what accounts for the relatively complicated structure of leave-takings in English. As only a moment's thought will reveal, it is usually not possible to simply leave a conversation by saying 'Good-bye'. Speakers generally expect a bit more warning than this, and Levinson (1983: 317, 325), with reference to the argument put forward by Schegloff and Sacks (1973), sketches out a typical leave-taking structure. The current topic is closed down with the introduction of what is called a closing implicative topic, such as making arrangements for a next meeting or offering regards to the interlocutor's family. This topic itself must then be shut down, and this is normally done with several pairs of passing turns, turns that consist of pre-closing items such as *okay*, *all right*, *yeah* or *so*. These passing turns, while devoid of semantic content, are what speakers use to negotiate the end of an encounter. They signal the approaching close of the conversation, and thus also serve as a platform to introduce any unfinished business. If any such business is introduced, its topic is then closed. Speakers may also sum up their talk by making reference to the type of interaction in which they have engaged (e.g., if a favour has been done, a thank-you/your welcome pair may occur). This typing, as it is referred to, is generally followed by more pairs of passing turns, and then the final exchange of good-byes characteristically occurs.

The leave-taking scene just prior to the close of *The Homecoming* is not, of course, an exact replica of an actual conversational closing. The repetitive turn-passing pairs are abbreviated to a few pre-closing items from Teddy, and Joey is somewhat awkward. The scene does, however, contain most of the generally occurring elements in a plausible order. Teddy initiates a closing implicative topic (his intention to go to the Underground station), and Max replies appropriately with the offer of directions (133–4). Teddy accepts the offer in a preferred response, and this agreeing pair is then repeated (134). Max continues with the closing topic (warning Teddy about cab fare), and Teddy initiates its end with the pre-closing items *Yes* and *Well* (134). He issues the first half of a farewell pair ('bye-bye, Dad. Look after yourself' 134), and he and Max then summarize their interaction with a typing pair (MAX '[…] It's been wonderful to see you / TEDDY It's been wonderful to see you' 134). Max takes the opportunity to introduce some unfinished business (offering pictures of himself for Teddy's children), and then the final exchange of goodbyes begins. After accepting Max's gift of the photograph with a preferred response (the children will 'be thrilled'), Teddy initiates terminal goodbye pairs with both Lenny and Joey in turn (134–5).

One of the things that makes this fairly typical leave-taking scene at the same time so bizarre is that it is utterly laughable in the given circumstances of the play. Teddy's visit has been fraught with conflict, his uncle has just collapsed on the floor and may be dead or dying, and his wife has just agreed to abandon him and their children to remain in London as the family whore. And yet, Teddy and his father and brothers are shown to take their leave of each other in a reasonably normal way, following the ordinary steps in the sequence to minimize the risk of offence during leave-takings.

Ruth's famous line is also significant, but not simply because of its clichéd nature or prefacing nickname. As Laver (1981) points out, it is precisely because leave-takings are so potentially dangerous to positive face (see Chapter 2) that speakers tend to rely on formulaic utterances when they close conversational encounters. The use of fixed phrases familiar to all interlocutors makes it less likely that something face-threatening will be said at such a vulnerable juncture. Also compatible with the goal of softening the blow of saying good-bye will be the use of positive face-enhancing nicknames (Brown and Levinson 1978/1987) with friends and family members. Thus, the fact that Ruth uses a clichéd element during a leave-taking sequence is not in itself extraordinary. Indeed, it can be set beside Teddy's equally clichéd 'Look after yourself' (134) and Lenny's triple-barrelled 'Ta-ta, Ted. Good to see you. Have a good trip' (135). Also noticeable here is that Ruth is not the only character to use a nickname in this scene – Lenny abbreviates 'Teddy' to 'Ted'.

Using conversation analysis to further Quigley's notion of sequencing, it can be shown that what is significant about Ruth's farewell move is *where it occurs* in relation to other such moves, and what interactional goal it accomplishes. After initiating goodbye pairs with his father and both of his brothers, Teddy heads for the front door. He does not initiate a goodbye pair with Ruth. Dukore (1981: 81), one of only two critics located for review to consider the interactional function of Ruth's farewell line, also notices that Teddy avoids saying goodbye to Ruth. Like Lahr (1971: 126), however, Dukore (1982) suggests that Ruth is mocking Teddy with the intimate nickname and the cruelly ironic plea that he not become a stranger. While this may be so, what is of potentially greater significance here is that Ruth has to bid for speaking rights at this point, which takes a great deal of the sting out of her barb. She has to perform what is known as a summons, the first pair part of a summons/answer pair (Levinson 1983: 309), in order to issue her farewell. A summons typically consists of an attention-getting device such as the recipient's name, and Ruth certainly gets Teddy's attention (and the audience's) with the nickname 'Eddie'. It is at this point that she issues her famous cliché in order to elicit a goodbye from Teddy, who shuts the door in her face on his way out, the ultimate dispreferred response. Ruth, generally one of the more powerful characters in the play, is here aligned, if only momentarily, with the powerless Max, who was, as noted earlier, similarly forced to bid for speaking rights in the greeting sequence near the play's opening. And Teddy, while a broken man in many ways by the end of the play, may not be as passively acquiescent to Ruth's choice as is often supposed (as, for example, by Peacock 1997: 86; Wellwarth 1996/2001: 106; Gale 1987: 278; Elsom 1978/1986: 99; and Esslin 1970: 149).

A third major area of concern in the literature on *The Homecoming* is the character of Ruth herself. Most of the critical attention has fallen on the two issues briefly mentioned above, the power she generally wields and the choice she makes. While a few of the earlier critics (Quigley 1975: 225, for example) recognized Ruth as a woman in control of her own destiny, many of them viewed her as passive, and struggled to understand her motives. Esslin (1970: 156), for instance, thought that

Ruth had failed at her marriage, failed to conquer her own base nature, and simply surrendered to her fate, resigned and past caring. While Nelson (1967: 147) somewhat grudgingly admitted that the play did not 'seem to be about the victimization of Ruth', he nevertheless concluded that she drifted through the action in a 'state of trance' having undergone 'a kind of hypnosis presumably imposed upon her by the naked wills of the men among whom she moves'(1967: 159).

As later critics were quick to notice, however, Ruth shows herself to be a powerful force, a woman firmly in charge of her choices, her life, and the people around her (Batty 2001: 41; Strunk 1989: 177). The source of Ruth's power is her use of language. This is readily shown with reference to two of her major scenes, her first meeting with Lenny, and the scene in which she negotiates the terms under which she will consent to remain with Teddy's family.

Ruth's first meeting with Lenny, identified by Scott (1986: 20) as one of the most powerful scenes in play, is also one of the most widely discussed. That Ruth dominates Lenny in this scene is commonly observed, especially in later critical work (e.g. Batty 2001: 42; Strunk 1989: 178; Scott 1986: 19; Peacock 1997: 84). What has not been clearly elucidated thus far is how the structure of their talk serves to communicate this domination. Taylor (1971: 65), for example, observes that 'each piece of the conversation falls perfectly into place' as a move in the game of power the two are playing, but does not have the tools to substantiate his intuition. Instead, he provides a partial list of items he sees as 'pieces', (e.g., 'Ruth's cool superiority of tone, Lenny's apparently rambling discursions about the clock', etc.). Kennedy (1975: 188) suggests that Ruth's transformation from mother to whore can be traced through her language but, given the state of what was known about talk at that time, can offer only vague summations, pointing to Ruth's 'seductive innuendos' with Lenny. Nelson (1967: 147) notices the 'loaded subtext' between Lenny and Ruth, but cannot go much further than this. Esslin (1970: 139) is struck by the 'strangely casual' nature of the meeting between Lenny and Ruth, but has to rely on an account of what the characters say, as in:

> Only after polite nothings about the weather and whether he can offer her a drink have been exchanged does Lenny inquire who the mysterious woman who has just come into his house in the middle of the night might be:
>
> > You must be connected with my brother in some way. The one who's been abroad.
>
> When Ruth replies that she is his brother's wife, Lenny does not react at all. He merely asks her advice about his insomnia (Esslin 1970: 139, with a quote from *The Homecoming*).

An interpretation not available at the time Esslin (1970) was writing is that Lenny's request for advice in the given situation *is* a reaction, just not the prospected or preferred one.

More recent work on this scene follows suit. Peacock (1997: 84) discusses Lenny's failed attempt to dominate Ruth in their first meeting, but his evidence consists primarily of a list of actions (e.g. 'First he refuses to recognize her as Teddy's wife. He then asks to hold her hand. Spurned, he turns to descriptions of physical assaults on two women', etc.). Such a list sheds little light on the process of Lenny's failure, or how Ruth achieves it, primarily because it does not account for the *language* of the interaction, the exchange of turns at talk between the two characters. Cahn (1994: 61) observes that Ruth and Lenny 'compete verbally for power in this scene', and notices that one of Ruth's weapons is her resistance to his offers. While this is an insightful reading, the discussion soon moves on to more intuitive territory.

> When Lenny brings Ruth a glass of water from which she takes a sip, the action may be seen as a gesture of intimacy. Yet Ruth's refusal to thank Lenny or to place herself in any way in his debt *blunts the proposal* (Cahn 1994: 61, italics mine).

'Blunting' is not a recognized technical term in conversation or discourse analysis, and accounting for what is going on between the two characters with such a term results in a discussion that skips over much of the scene's verbal complexity.

Batty's (2001) discussion of this scene is similarly unconvincing. He notes that Ruth gets the better of Lenny 'verbally by adopting assertively maternal and sexual postures' (2001: 42). As evidence, he cites an 18-line stretch of dialogue (from Ruth: *I'll relieve you of your glass* to Ruth: *Why don't I just take you*) but leaves the reader to decide what in Ruth's language makes her 'assertively maternal' and 'sexual'.

So how is language used to convey the power play that is Ruth and Lenny's first meeting? This question is usefully approached through a linguistic analysis of the represented conversation that draws primarily on Tsui (1994) (see Chapter 2). For the purposes of analysis, the scene will be split into three sections, the first from LENNY *Good evening* to RUTH *No, thanks* (41–2). In this opening part of the scene, notice that Ruth does not actually assert power over Lenny so much as let him hand it over. Most of Lenny's moves are those that attempt to open the talk by establishing goodwill and comity (see Tsui 1994 and Aston 1988) between interlocutors. For example, Lenny initiates with an Informative:Expressive:Goodwill ('Good evening': 41); he invites Ruth to participate in further talk by issuing an Elicit:Commit asking her name (42); he makes an Informative:Expressive:Empathy that enquires after her welfare ('Cold?': 42); he tries again to get the talk off the ground by issuing an Elicit:Agree ('It's been a wonderful summer, hasn't it?': 42), a clear attempt to establish common ground, and finally tempts Ruth to participate in an interaction by making an Offer ('Would you like something? Refreshment of some kind? An aperitif, anything like that?': 42), a discourse move whose outcome will benefit Ruth at Lenny's expense.

By taking the initiating role in these exchanges, Lenny gives Ruth the power to either reciprocate his gestures of goodwill or establish distance. With great skill, Ruth does the latter through a series of moves that spurn Lenny's attempts to establish common ground. In reply to Lenny's 'Good evening', for example, Ruth asserts that it is morning (41). For Lahr (1971: 135), this is notable primarily because of its 'hard accuracy'. Looking at this reply in terms of its discourse value, however, is more revealing. Instead of the preferred reciprocation to Lenny's expression of goodwill, Ruth performs a Challenging move with her assertion that it is actually morning. More important than pedantry here is her clear refusal to take part in the interpersonal ritual (Goffman 1967) of greeting. Lenny cedes even more power here by positively responding to Ruth's Challenge, noting that she is right to say it is in fact morning. Ruth, however, remains unresponsive. Despite Lenny's best efforts, the talk lapses. Since there are only two participants, the turn passes to Ruth, but she remains silent, forcing Lenny to self-select if the talk is to resume.

Ruth's unresponsiveness continues. She refuses his Offer of refreshment with a dispreferred Negative Response ('No, thanks': 42), and Challenges his Elicit:Agree with one of the most face-threatening options available, an attributable silence (42). In addition, Ruth reclassifies[3] Lenny's Elicit:Commit and his Informative: Expressive: Empathy as Elicit:Informs. That is, when Lenny asks 'Cold?' Ruth simply says 'No', as though she had been asked a purely factual question (42). When Lenny asks her name, she simple gives it, declining the invitation to further talk (42). In reclassifying Lenny's moves here, notice that Ruth is in effect appropriating Lenny's illocutionary force. She does not even allow him control over his intended meanings.

In effect, Lenny is in the position of having to do the conversational 'shit work' of keeping the talk going, a role generally filled, as Fishman (1983) points out, by women, something Pinter parodies to great comic effect with Meg's repeated questions to a mostly taciturn Petey in the opening of *The Birthday Party*. Lenny, so dominant and powerful when compared to Max and Sam, is with Ruth enacting Meg's role in this first part of their meeting.

The second section to be analysed follows on immediately from the first, beginning with LENNY *I'm glad you said that* and ending with LENNY *Don't call me that, please* (43–51). At the close of the first section, Ruth had refused Lenny's offer of refreshments with a Negative Response ('No, thanks'). Lenny, apparently having had enough of Ruth's refusal to cooperate, replies to this with 'I'm glad you said that. We haven't got a drink in the house' (43). Dukore (1982: 77) reads this as an insult, and suggests that what is most significant is Ruth's refusal to be baited into a response, not even surprise. This is an important observation, but there is something else going on in this exchange. In his reply, Lenny makes his first attempt to take back some of the power he initially ceded. As Tsui (1994: 203) explains, Negative Responses to Offers prospect Concessions as Follow-up moves. Concessions are moves that accept the negative outcome of an exchange (e.g. *Okay, I see, We'll save it for later*, etc.). In so doing they also accept the interactional terms set by the participant who made the Negative Response, much as Quigley (1975), via Firth (1964/1966) suggested. Lenny's move is clearly not a Concession. It is instead an Endorsement, a move that 'enthusiastically endorses the positive outcome' of an exchange (Tsui 1994: 200). In treating Ruth's refusal as though it were a positive outcome, the result he sought in the first place, Lenny attempts to tip the scales of power in his favour.

As Dukore (1982: 78) points out, another strategy of Lenny's is to imply that Ruth is something other than a wife to Teddy. He accomplishes this in part through the use of Elicit:Confirms, moves that presuppose agreement in an attempt to force Ruth into confirming what he has already concluded. Examples include 'You must be connected with my brother in some way' (43) and 'What, you sort of live with him over there, do you?' (45). He makes similar use of moves that request given information be clarified (Elicit:Clarify). When Ruth reports that she and Teddy are on a visit to Europe, for example, Lenny asks, 'What, both of you?' (44). The clear implication here is that Lenny would not expect his brother to take a whore, or a mistress as Dukore (1982: 78) suggests, on holiday with him.

It soon becomes apparent, however, that Ruth remains undaunted. She does not let Lenny get away with trying to membership her as a prostitute or a mistress. According to Dukore (1982: 78), she does this by replying not to Lenny's veiled insults, but to the 'words on the surface'. This is essentially what Ruth does, but a closer analysis serves to show in greater detail how Ruth uses Lenny's own language against him. As before, her real weapon is to deny Lenny control over his own illocutionary force. She reclassifies his presumptive Elicit:Confirms and Elicit:Clarifys as straightforward Elicit:Informs, requests for information, and makes Positive Responses to those, as in the example below.

Lenny:	You must be connected with my brother in some way. The one who's abroad.
Ruth:	*I'm his wife* (43).

Further examples of such reclassifications are found on pages 44 and 45. In proceeding this way, Ruth also allows herself to do as little as possible to recognize Lenny as an interlocutor. Her Positive Responses do not actively select him as the next speaker since they are potentially exchange-final (Eggins and Slade 1997). That is, the question has been asked and answered, the business is done, and the floor passes to Lenny simply by default. In addition, her Responses, being positive, can be unmitigated, devoid of any hedging particles or hesitation devices that weaken the force of disagreements for the benefit of the hearer (Pomerantz 1984; Brown and Levinson 1978/1987). By manipulating the force of Lenny's Initiations, Ruth puts herself under less obligation to use such devices.

It is during this second section of their encounter that Ruth begins to go on the offensive. While Lenny is also becoming increasingly aggressive, he still makes use of Requestives, moves in which the speaker attempts to get the hearer to do something, but which carry no expectation of hearer compliance. To each of Lenny's Requestives, Ruth responds with Challenging moves by calling into question one or more of the following presuppositions: 1) that the speaker sincerely wants the action to be carried out; 2) that the speaker believes the action needs to be carried out; and 3) that the addressee is willing to carry out the action, or have it carried out (as stated in Tsui 1994: 173, with slight modifications). When Lenny offers Ruth a glass of water, she asks what it is (44), a reply that questions Lenny's sincerity and indicates that she herself is not willing to carry out the action of drinking the water. Verbally, this is akin to flinging the drink back in his face. When Lenny offers to move the ashtray out of her way, she Challenges the offer with the assertion that it is not, in fact, in her way, indicating that there is no need to have the action carried out.

Ruth also uses this strategy when Lenny issues a Request for Permission to ask if he can hold her hand. With her reply of 'Why?' (46), Ruth again questions Lenny's sincerity and the assumption that she wants the action to be carried out. It is this refusal to let Lenny hold her hand that leads him to tell his stories of violence against women in an attempt to shock and frighten her. Ruth, however, is not intimidated. Her only reaction to his story about beating up a prostitute is to Challenge his assertion that she was 'falling apart with the pox' (47). This assertion can be classified as an Informative: Report, an account of an event or state of affairs (Tsui 1994: 138). It presupposes that the expressed proposition is true (Tsui 1994: 181). By asking how Lenny knew the prostitute was diseased, she Challenges his Informative:Report, defusing his attempt to threaten her. Indeed, Lenny never really recovers from this Challenge. In his answer ('I decided she was': 48), he is forced to admit that his Informative:Report was actually just an Informative:Assessment, an opinion. The talk then lapses until Lenny self-selects with a new topic (48).

Lenny tries again to get the upper hand, demanding in a series of Directive: Mandatives that Ruth return the glass of water she only grudgingly took after Challenging Lenny's initial Offer. Directive:Mandatives, in contrast to Requestives, presuppose that the speaker has the right to make demands of the hearer (Tsui 1994: 177), and Ruth Challenges this presupposition in her replies to Lenny.

> Lenny: And now perhaps I'll relieve you of your glass.
> Ruth: *I haven't quite finished.*
> Lenny: You've consumed quite enough, in my opinion.
> Ruth: *No, I haven't.*
> Lenny: Quite sufficient, in my own opinion.
> Ruth: *Not in mine, Leonard* (51).

In her final Challenging move, Ruth succeeds in wrong-footing Lenny by addressing him with his full first name, framing the discourse (Goffman 1974) as parent-child. Startled from his string of Directive:Mandatives, Lenny makes a less assertive Request for Action, asking Ruth not to call him by that name and mitigating the force of his Requestive with the politeness marker *please* (51).

In the final section of Ruth and Lenny's initial encounter, from RUTH *Why not?* to the silence after Lenny's *What was that supposed to be? Some kind of proposal?* (51–4), it is clear that Lenny has lost the battle as Ruth's offensive tactics are brought out in force. She continues to Challenge Lenny's Requestives, asking 'Why not?' (51) in reply to his request that she not call him 'Leonard', and also issues Directives of her own. When Lenny menaces her with a Directive:Mandatives:Threat ('I'll take it [the glass of water], then': 52), she Challenges him with a counter Threat ('If you take the glass ... I'll take you': 52). After a lapse, Lenny self-selects, backing down with a Proposal ('How about me taking the glass without you taking me?': 52). By way of reply, Ruth simply repeats her earlier Directive:Mandatives:Threat, and all Lenny can do is counter somewhat feebly with the elicitatively weaker Informatives, a series of Assessments ('You're joking': 52 / 'You're in love, anyway, with another man. You've had a secret liaison with another man': 52) and a Criticism ('Then you come here without a word of warning and start to make trouble':s 52). As noted in Chapter 2, Initiations can be ranked by the strength of the responses they prospect. Directives are stronger than Requestives because they prospect compliance, Directives and Requestives are both stronger than Elicitations and Informatives because the former prospect actions while the latter prospect only verbal responses. Informatives are the weakest class since they prospect mostly acknowledgements or agreements instead of answers, actions or compliance (Tsui 1993).

Ruth ignores Lenny's Assessments and initiates a new series of exchanges with an elicitatively more demanding Offer.

Ruth: Have a sip. Go on. Have a sip from my glass (53).

This line is loaded with aggravators. Each of the verb phrases occurs in the imperative mood, and two of them are repeated. In an ordinary Offer, these would count as normal positive politeness devices serving to enhance solidarity between the interlocutors. As Brown and Levinson (1978/1987: 229–30) point out, however, politeness devices can be used strategically in inappropriate situations to mock or insult, and that is clearly what is going on here. Ruth and Lenny have not established a rapport, and the object of her offer, the glass of water, is the selfsame glass that Lenny has claimed as belonging to him.

Ruth upgrades her Offer when Lenny responds only with stillness, encouraging him to sit on her lap and 'take a long cool sip' (53). In her next two moves, the Offers become so inappropriate to the situation that they are in effect Directive:Mandatives: Threats, the imperative mood now signalling the expectation of compliance rather than mock solidarity.

Ruth: Put your head back and open your mouth (53).
Ruth: Lie on the floor. Go on. I'll pour it down your throat (53).

Lenny's replies to these Threats are indicative of his rapidly diminishing control. He tries to downgrade Ruth's Threat by questioning her intended illocutionary force ('What are doing, making me some kind of proposal?' 53), but she is again non-responsive. She laughs, drinks the water (which ensures Lenny will never get it back), and initiates a new exchange with an Informative:Report, arguably talking mostly to herself ('Oh I was thirsty': 53). She then smiles at Lenny, and exits up the stairs. Lenny is left repeating his question ('What was that supposed to be? Some kind of proposal?: 53) to empty space, watching a supremely indifferent Ruth simply walk away from him.

Critics have also shone the spotlight on Ruth's decision to stay on in London as a prostitute. As Esslin (1970: 149) noted, this choice is one of the most shocking elements in the play, and it apparently remains as such. Peacock (1997: 86) and Wellwarth (1996/2001: 106), commenting some 30 years later, both point to the same set of concerns: how 'unbelievable' (Peacock), how 'implausible' (Wellwarth) it is that Ruth would choose the life she does. While Ruth's choice may be difficult to accept, it has been recognized as being the whole point of the play (Elsom 1978/1986). Indeed, the 'homecoming' of the title is repeatedly identified as hers rather than Teddy's (Batty 2001: 40; Peacock 1997: 86; Quigley 1975: 205; Taylor 1971: 62; Wardle 1971: 42; Esslin 1970: 154; Hollis 1970: 106; Nelson 1967: 148), and various reasons have been put forward for why she makes her infamous choice. For some, it is a shocking but 'logical' course of action (Peacock 1997: 86; Elsom 1978/1986: 199; Nelson 1967: 148) once it is remembered that

> the family depicted is one which has always been living on the fringes of the respectable, normal world, [and] that Ruth, although a college professor's wife, might well also have been a prostitute in the past (Esslin 1970: 152).

Others suggest that Ruth considers herself to be trapped in a lifeless marriage (Batty 2001: 44; Elsom 1978/1986: 198; Wellwarth 1996/2001: 106; Esslin 1970: 140), and enacts her choice as revenge (Wellwarth 1996/2001: 106). For Goldstone (1969: 23), it simply represents her understanding that sexual desire is the most potent force in human life. Gale (1987: 281), on the other hand, saw Ruth as a character driven to extremes in her search for acceptance and affection.

Ruth's motivations may in the end by unknowable. The point is that she makes her choice without a loss of power. While this is acknowledged in the critical record, her methods of exercising control while she negotiates her terms near the close of the play (from LENNY *We'd get you a flat* to LENNY *I think so*: 127–31) remain poorly elucidated. Brown (1972: 101) observes that Ruth's speech is 'business-like', Kennedy (1975: 188) was impressed by her 'mercenary jargon', and Peacock (1997: 86) notes that she accepts the proposal to be run as a whore 'on her own terms'. Such characterizations reveal very little about how Ruth uses language to dominate the men who would exploit her. How is it that Ruth seems, as Batty (2001: 45) suggests 'empowered by her ability to play the game better than the men who make the rules'? It mostly comes down to the use of Elicitations and Requestives, weapons that Ruth wields with far greater effectiveness against Lenny than Lenny does against her.

As noted earlier, Elicitations are weaker than Requestives or Directives in terms of elicitative force because they call primarily for verbal responses rather than actions (Tsui 1993). However, it is precisely this quality of demanding a verbal response that makes Elicitations an effective tool in organizing the talk according to the elicitator's agenda, and this is something Ruth is represented as doing with great skill. As the negotiations begin in earnest, Lenny makes an Offer ('We'd get you a flat' 127). Before accepting or rejecting this offer, Ruth checks its terms against her own requirements in a series of Elicitations that steer the talk in exactly the direction she wants it to go.

Elicit:Clarify	Ruth:	A flat? (127)
Elicit:Inform	Ruth:	Where? (127)
Elicit:Inform	Ruth:	How many rooms would this flat have? (128)

When Lenny responds to the last Elicitation with 'Not many', the negotiations hit a snag since Ruth is unsatisfied. She turns up the pressure with a Request for Action, insisting that Lenny provide a flat that has a bathroom and three rooms (128). Lenny Challenges this Requestive on the grounds that she will not need this many rooms, but Ruth holds firm with counter Challenges such as 'No. Two wouldn't be enough' (128). Lenny eventually gives in and agrees in a Positive Response to carry out the action of getting Ruth a three-bedroom flat with a bathroom.[4]

Having won the first round, Ruth repeats her strategy of directing the negotiations with Elicitations, ensuring that the flat will be appointed to her liking.

Elicit:Clarify   Ruth: With what kind of conveniences? (129)
Elicit:Inform: Ruth: A personal maid? (129)

At this point, Lenny tries to gain some ground in a Request for Action, trying to insist that Ruth pay the family back for the expenses she has managed to wring out of them (129). Ruth rejects this out of hand with a Negative Response ('Oh, no, I wouldn't agree to that' 129), and counters with a Request for Action of her own ('You would have to regard your original outlay simply as a capital investment' 130). Lenny again gives in, making a Positive Response ('I see. All right': 130).

Now in a position of considerable power, Ruth moves from Elicitations to Requestives and closes the deal. A number of these Requestives are phrased optimistically in that they assume agreement (Brown and Levinson 1978/1987: 126), which Ruth duly gets, as in the examples below.

Ruth: You'd supply my wardrobe, of course?
Lenny: We'd supply everything. Everything you need (130).

Ruth: I would naturally want to draw up an inventory of everything I would need, which would require your signatures in the presence of witnesses.
Lenny: Naturally (130).

While it has been suggested that *The Homecoming* (see Nelson 1967: 150), like many other Pinter plays, problematizes the use of language as a means of communication, it is clear that language does not fail Ruth in her interactions with Lenny.

As this chapter has argued, Quigley's (1975) analysis of Pinter and his critics deserved far more recognition than it ultimately got. By applying frameworks for the linguistic study of talk developed since 1975 to the dialogue of *The Homecoming*, it has been possible to progress one of Quigley's (1975) major concerns, relating reactions provoked by the text to its language. A number of critical intuitions have arisen in response to the play with respect to: 1) the characters' struggles for territory; 2) the mix of the bizarre and the mundane; and 3) the character of Ruth, and the probable sources of these intuitions in the text are now more fully illuminated. Looking at turn-taking patterns, speaker selection choices, and the role of greeting sequences has revealed how the dialogue of the play constructs Max as a failed patriarch, an old man full of bile but lacking in real power. Consideration of the represented farewell in *The Homecoming* in relation to actual conversational closings has taken the interpretation of this scene beyond the narrow confines of cliché and jargon to show that Ruth is at this critical point put in the rare position of having to bid for speaking rights. By analyzing key interactions between Ruth and Lenny in terms of the discourse moves they exchange, Ruth's skill in using language as a weapon against Lenny, and Lenny's failure to do so against her, are now understood in more detail. With Elicitations,

Requestives, Challenges, dispreferred responses, and reclassifications, she verbally manipulates Lenny and secures for herself the life and lifestyle she wants. Whether others accept her choice or not is quite beside the point. In the next chapter, we move on to consider the importance of language, dialect and positive politeness in the study of drama with particular reference to Wesker's *Roots*.

Chapter 4

Language and Social Class in Arnold Wesker's *Roots*

Arnold Wesker's *Roots*, first presented in 1959, is generally considered to be the most popular play in what has become known as The Wesker Trilogy (Wilcher 1991: 31; Adler 1979: 429; Worth 1972:20; Leeming and Trussler 1971: 55; Latham 1965: 192; Findlater 1960: 236). The action revolves around Beatie Bryant, a young woman who grew up in rural Norfolk but who has been working and living in London for several years. She returns to her family home for a visit ahead of her urban intellectual boyfriend Ronnie, who is scheduled to come and meet the Bryants in two weeks' time. Beatie is all eager anticipation about the visit, and speaks of little else besides Ronnie. Indeed, she has the habit of quoting Ronnie, so accurately that 'we see a picture of him through her' (Wesker 1959/1976: 88).[1] However, neither the family nor the audience of *Roots* ever meet Ronnie in person. Instead of showing up as promised to meet her family, Ronnie sends a letter explaining to Beatie why he has decided to leave her.

While *Roots* opened to some very favourable reviews, the critical record has not always been kind to the play or Wesker (Wilcher 1991; Latham 1965; Taylor 1962/1969). Despite arguments to the contrary by Leeming and Trussler (1971), many critics found him excessively didactic (Adler 1979), and accused him of using his characters as little more than mouthpieces (Wilcher 1996: 425; Hayman 1970/1979; Taylor 1962/1969; Findlater 1960: 236). While a few critics were impressed by Wesker's blend of realistic and symbolic elements in *Roots* (Mutalik-Desai 1987; Adler 1979), others were more muted in their praise (Brown 1972), and what emerges most saliently in the literature is the view that Wesker more often than not exercised poor structural control of his material (Wilcher 1996: 425–6; Bigsby 1981: 21, 36; Hayman 1970/1979; Taylor 1962/1969; Findlater 1960: 236). Taylor (1962/1969) was particularly harsh. Citing 'basic technical faults of construction' (159), 'some carelessness in detail' (155), and 'patches of boredom' (155), he wondered if the play's initial critical acclaim was mostly a function of Joan Plowright's outstanding performance as Beatie.

While it is perhaps fair to say that Wesker may not have the same artistic control as, for example, Pinter, it can be argued that a number of responses to *Roots* arise more from weaknesses in critical discussions of his work than from any textual failure on Wesker's part. One very common response that can be discussed in this light is Wesker's depiction of the Beales and Bryants, Beatie's Norfolk farming family. Over and over again in the literature, Wesker is said to have portrayed Beatie's family as ignorant oafs. They have been described as slow (Hayman 1970/1979:

40), inarticulate (Innes 1992: 115; Latham 1965: 196; Taylor 1962/1969: 155) bores (Taylor 1962/1969: 155) who suffer from 'mental lethargy' (Wilcher 1991: 45) and are incapable of forming complex arguments (Dornan 1994: 33). They are widely considered to be the product of a 'blinkered society' that offers them only a 'tawdry existence' (Chambers and Prior 1987: 140; see also Innes 1992: 115; Leeming 1983: 50), and are seen to perpetuate 'their own misery' (Dornan 1994: 35) by refusing to accept enlightenment (Chambers and Prior 1987: 143; Leeming 1983: 44, 50). While Findlater (1960: 236) praised Wesker for depicting the rural working class 'as human beings with rights of their own', he nevertheless characterises Beatie, a representative of that class, as 'inarticulate'. Like Findlater (1960), Latham (1965) and Wilcher (1991) have some praise for the Bryants (e.g. they are in tune with nature's cycles; they are justified in their scepticism of Ronnie), and acknowledge that Wesker did not set out to condemn or blame the rural community represented in the play. At the same time, however, they still buy into the notion that the Bryants are unsophisticated and lack the means to fully express themselves. Latham (1965: 195) characterises their vocabulary as 'limited and even crude'; and Wilcher (1991: 44) suggests that 'the world of the Bryants is one in which words are an undemanding accompaniment to the routines of work and domestic life' (Wilcher 1991: 44).

Dornan (1994: 35) wonders why a self-professed socialist playwright, as Wesker was when he wrote the Trilogy, would paint such an unflattering portrait of the people he was trying to reach. She speculates that Wesker's depiction of the Norfolk farmers is part of a much wider pattern of ambivalence that emerges in *Roots*, an ambivalence symptomatic of Wesker's simultaneous commitment to, but doubts about, socialism and the working classes in Britain (1994: 37). Particularly telling in this respect is that Ronnie, the voice of socialism in the play, is such a deeply flawed individual (Dornan 1994: 37; Orr 1981/1989; Latham 1965; Findlater 1960: 241). He lacks the courage of his convictions (Adler 1979); he talks a big game but accomplishes very little (Sanger 2001: 42; Adler 1979: 434; Brown 1972:166), and while he fancies himself an artist, he lacks the discipline to come up with anything original. As Ronnie's brother-in-law puts it in *I'm Talking About Jerusalem* (the third play of the Trilogy), 'I know your kind, you go around the world crooning about brotherhood and yet you can't even see a sordid love affair through to the end' (216).

Roots can certainly be read as a play that manifests doubts and core beliefs in transition. Indeed, this argument has been cogently made in several places (e.g. Wilcher 1991; Chambers and Prior 1987: 136–7, 144; Itzin 1980), and Innes' (1992: 116) suggestion that *Roots* may symbolically represent Wesker's experiences with the arts organisation Centre 42 is particularly convincing. As I will argue here, however, Wesker's reputation for damning the Norfolk farmers is largely undeserved, stemming as it does from criticism that has paid insufficient attention to three rather significant aspects of the language of the text, the representation of everyday talk, the representation of dialect, and the use of direct and indirect speech.

Some of Wesker's earliest critics took an interest in how the Beales and Bryants were represented in conversation with one another but, writing in the early 1960s and 1970s, were not in a position to take advantage of what is now, to borrow a phrase from Meyers (1980), 'known to be known' about everyday talk. One such critic is J.R. Taylor (1962/1969), undeniably one of modern drama's most widely known and prominent voices. He suggests that Wesker's main point was to show 'the *almost inconceivable limitation* of the Bryants' minds' (1962/1969: 154, italics mine). In support of his view, he notes (without citing specific textual examples) that 'again and again the same clichés recur, the same substitutes for thought, the same pointless stories endlessly, inanely repeated' (Taylor 1962/1969: 154). As work in linguistics has since demonstrated, however, clichéd and formulaic elements not only occur frequently in ordinary English conversation (Cowie 1988; Nattinger 1988: 76; Pawley and Syder 1983), but also play important communicative functions in helping to establish and maintain interpersonal relationships (Laver 1981; Brown and Levinson 1978/1987; Goffman 1967). It therefore cannot be assumed that these elements equate to 'substitutes for thought' among dramatic characters. Similar points can be made regarding the trading of stories and gossip in conversation, which have been shown to play important functions in demonstrating solidarity (Cameron 1997/1998: 281; Pilkington 1998: 254; Coates 1989/1998; Brown and Levinson 1978/1987).

Hayman's (1970/1979) account of the Bryants is similar and similarly difficult to accept. He suggests that the farm labourers' '*slow rhythm of thinking* is echoed in their *slow and repetitious way of talking*' (Hayman 1970/1979: 40, italics mine). As evidence, he cites a 14-line stretch of dialogue, given below for ease of reference, between Jenny, Jimmy and Beatie. It is early in Act One, and Beatie has just arrived back in Norfolk.

1 Jenny:	Now shut you up Jimmy Beales and get that food down you. Every
2	time you talk, look, you miss a mouthful! That's why you complain
3	of pain in your shoulder blades.
4 Beatie:	You bin hevin' pains then Jimmy?
5 Jimmy:	Blust yes! Right a'tween my shoulder blades.
6 Jenny:	Mother says it's indigestion.
7 Beatie:	What the hell's indigestion doin' a'tween his shoulder blades?
8 Jenny:	Mother reckon some people get indigestion so bad it go right
9	through their stomach to the back.
10 Beatie:	Don't talk daft!
11 Jenny:	That's what I say. Blust Mother, I say, you don't git indigestion in
12	the back. Don't you tell me, she say, I hed it!
13 Beatie:	What hevn't she hed.

Closer inspection of the text, however, reveals that there is very little evidence to support either of Hayman's assertions. Notice first of all that there is no explicit indication in the text to suggest that the characters are speaking slowly, as the stage directions prior to this scene make no mention of speech tempo. In fact, in a stage direction several pages later pertaining to the play as whole, Wesker states categorically that the characters, including those cited above, 'talk quickly' (92). It is possible that Hayman (1970/1979) may have been drawing here on Dexter's production and its reviews in his account of the Bryants' speech. At Wesker's insistence, Dexter employed a slow pace and made use of long silences (Wesker in Findlater, ed. 1981: 81), and this 'ponderous slowness' (Worsley 1959, extracted in Leeming 1985: 17) may have led, at least in part, to perceptions of the Bryants as 'slow-mouthing' (Jackson 1959: 15). Indeed, it may also have resulted in performances where characters did actually speak slowly. It is clear from the text, however, that they are intended to be speaking quickly, and Hayman does not give these issues detailed consideration when he characterises the Bryants' talk and, by dubious implication, thought, as 'slow'.

Secondly, notice that Hayman's claim regarding repetition is also, in light of subsequent research in linguistics, easily refuted. The repetition present in the dialogue he cites is not only entirely normal in casual talk, but also functional. As Halliday and Hasan (1976) have noted, repetition is a cohesive device in connected text that serves to show how previous ideas are linked to subsequent ones. Tannen (1989: 50–51) and Coates (1989/1998) have demonstrated that repetition plays a similarly important role in ordinary talk. They show that it is instrumental in establishing interpersonal involvement between interlocutors by allowing speakers to show enthusiasm, react to each other's utterances, and demonstrate active listenership. Notice as well that this kind of repetition is not extraordinary or limited to specific kinds of speech events; rather, it is 'pervasive, functional, and often automatic in ordinary conversation' (Tannen 1989: 54).

An analysis of the dialogue cited above between Jenny, Jimmy and Beatie (inspired by Tannen 1989) shows that the repetition of key noun phrases may not represent 'their slow rhythm of thinking' as Hayman claimed; rather, its function is more likely to represent an entirely normal degree of topic cohesion as well as solidarity and personal involvement among the interlocutors. Jenny introduces the topic of Jimmy's pain in lines 2–3 with the noun phrase *pain in your shoulder blades*. In the next turn (line 4), Beatie recycles the head noun of the phrase, *pain*, in a question addressed to Jimmy (*You bin hevin' pains then Jimmy?*). This allows her to orient her question not only back towards Jenny and her previous turn, but also forward towards Jimmy. Jimmy provides a Positive Response (Tsui 1994) to Beatie's question in line 5 (*Blust yes! Right a 'tween my shoulder blades*), and his repetition of *shoulder blades* simultaneously allows him to address Beatie and tie his utterance back to Jenny's turn in lines 2–3. Thus, in addition to sustaining topic coherence, repetition of key noun phrases allows Jimmy and Beatie to ratify and include Jenny as a participant while directly addressing each other.

The repetition of *indigestion* in the second half of the dialogue cited works in a similar way. Jenny introduces the topic with the noun phrase *indigestion* in her turn in line 6, and Beatie and Jenny trade the term back and forth in their ensuing turns (lines 7, 8, and 11). In addition, notice that the repetition of this key noun phrase is essential in allowing the sisters to agree on how ridiculous they both think their mother's theory is. As Aston (1988) points out, the trading of matching assessments is a very common way for speakers of English to establish and maintain rapport, and the repetition of each other's language in these assessments serves to enhance that rapport. Thus, repetition in the dialogue above is not a device used to signal a lack of imagination in Jenny and Beatie; rather it is a device used to demonstrate the bonds of sisterhood.

Taylor (1962/1969) and Hayman (1970/1979) cannot, of course, be held accountable for failing to access work that did not exist when they were writing on *Roots*. Their views, however, have cast a long shadow and have become part of the 'received wisdom' that has accrued around the play. Wilcher (1991: 44), for example, follows in their path when he claims of *Roots* that 'well-tried verbal formulas serve their turn and no topic is pursued for more than a few moments'. It is clear, however, that such arguments are in (desperate) need of review. The function of features such as repetition, cliché and story-telling in the play need to be seriously re-thought in light of advances in pragmatics. It can be argued, for example, that these and related features occur not because the Bryants are slow-witted bores, but because they are given more to the expression of positive politeness with each other than negative politeness. That is, they structure their speech acts to emphasise common ground and shared experience rather than social distance and personal autonomy (see discussion of Brown and Levinson 1978/1987: ch. 2).

Interestingly, this characteristic has not gone entirely unnoticed in the literature. It tends to be referenced, however, only in intuitive terms. While critics are careful to point out that Wesker does not romanticise the lives of the Beales and the Bryants, they also speak of things like 'communal living' (Brown 1972), 'family cohesiveness' (Tynan 1960: 25), and the 'warm, lived in quality' of their dialogue (Worth 1972: 21). Less commonly noticed and appreciated, however, is the connection between these intuitive responses and the use of positive politeness devices such as repetition, matching assessments, and gossip in the dialogue. Some very clear examples are found in the conversation between Stan and Mrs Bryant at the beginning of Act Two (106–8), an interaction that is particularly rich in positive politeness devices (as outlined by Brown and Levinson 1978/1987: 103–29). Mrs Bryant notices Stan's wants and needs ('Sit you down bor and rest a bit'); Stan intensifies his interest in the talk for Mrs Bryant's benefit by using exaggeration ('Time drag so slow, I get to thinkin' it's Monday when it's still Sunday'); they use in-group address forms with each other ('gal', 'my manny'); and Stan engages in small talk with Mrs Bryant about years gone by rather than simply asking the question he came to ask (whether Beatie is home yet) and then leaving. Also noticeable are Stan's jokes ('Just gimme young days again Daphne Bryant an' I'd mount you); the non-problematic use of face-threatening acts due to the assumption of shared interests and wants (Mrs Bryant: 'Shouldn't wear such daf' clothes'. / Stan: 'Daf'clothes? Blust woman, I got on half a cow's hide'); the repetition of each other's utterances ('Stan: Still, I had my day gal I say. *Yearp. I had that* all right. / Mrs Bryant: *Yearp. You had that*'), and Mrs Bryant's use of the conclusory marker *then* to imply that conclusions are shared ('Time drag heavy *then*?'). This is not the talk of people who are backward, boorish, and ignorant. This is the talk of two old friends who have in common a lifetime of shared experiences.

Also clear from the text of the play is that the Bryants and their neighbours talk not only like a close-knit group of family and friends, but like a close-knit group of family and friends from rural Norfolk. That they be represented as doing so was an issue of particular importance to Wesker (Sanger 2001: 38), and his instructions on this point in the prefatory material to *Roots* are clear.

> As [the play] is about Norfolk people it is important that some attempt is made to find out how they talk. A very definite accent and intonation exists and personal experience suggests that this is not difficult to know (83).

He continues with detailed explanatory notes (e.g. *been* sounds like *bin*; *have* sounds like *hev*, the preposition *on* is often used instead of *of*, etc.).

Oddly, critics have been largely dismissive of these efforts to ensure that the dialect of the Norfolk farmers be represented faithfully (Dornan 1994: 34), with many accounts limited to only passing comments on authenticity and realism. Orr (1981/1989: 265) speaks of Wesker's 'magnificent ear for the demotic', for example, and such remarks occur repeatedly (e.g. see Innes 1992: 118; Worth 1972: 21; Findlater 1960: 235; Jackson 1959: 15). The problem with these remarks, however, is that they are just that: remarks. They spring mostly from assumption rather than systematic observation of Wesker's use of language in the play. Worth (1972: 21), for example, talks about the excitement of hearing the 'Norfolk sound' on the London stage, a sound she further characterises as 'full-blooded'. This non-technical description summarises five lines of dialogue, lines that are cited, but not analysed in linguistic detail. Just what is the 'Norfolk sound'? This is often taken for granted in the research record on Wesker.

Other examples are not difficult to find. Leeming and Trussler (1971: 69) suggest that Wesker's representation of rural Norfolk speech has 'authority and conviction', but base this on what they identify as a 'basic rhythm in the word and phrase order'. While this appears to mean the repetition of phrases that include one or two well-known characteristics of the dialect area, further details are not forthcoming. Evans (1977) is more respectful of Wesker's language than many others (Leeming 1983: 48–9), but he is reluctant to engage in systematic linguistic enquiry in his account of Wesker and dialect representation (as stated earlier, Evans considered linguistic terminology to be 'incomprehensible', and some of its methods 'fierce'). As a result, he does the very thing he argued against: he underrates Wesker's use of dialect, suggesting that he created an authentic voice for the Beales and Bryants by leaning on a few signature sounds and structures (Evans 1977: 93). As will be shown below, however, Wesker does considerably more than this in representing the Norfolk speakers in *Roots*.

Taylor (1962/1969) also discusses the issue of authenticity and dialect representation in *Roots*, but suggests, in contrast to a number of his colleagues, that the language of the Beales and Bryants bears very little resemblance to that of actual Norfolk speakers. He depends for evidence on the reactions of local audiences who, he claims, objected to the depiction of their language on the grounds that it did not really represent the way they spoke. Such evidence is problematic. People have been shown to be poor judges of the way they themselves speak, tending (especially in the middle-classes) to over-report their use of certain features, particularly prestige variants that they perceive as being 'correct' (Labov 1972). In addition, Taylor provides no references to the audience reactions he summarises here (a point that also bothered Leeming and Trussler 1971: 69, 200n21). Given the status of self-reported evidence, this is a potentially very serious issue, as it makes the claim difficult to evaluate. For example, were the audiences cited reacting to the features indicated in Wesker's printed text, or their performance? In other words, was it the features *per se* that were found objectionable, or simply their rendition by actors during a particular performance or set of performances? Was the audience made up of rural farmers, or people from more urban areas of the region? Or did the audience include people who had grown up in rural farming communities, but were themselves engaged in white-collar professions? Was the mean age of the audience nearer 20 or 50? Were the reactions voiced mostly by men or by women? Taylor does not answer these questions himself, nor provide references through which they can be answered, and this makes it difficult to accept his evidence. The issue becomes even more serious when we consider that empirical studies of writers, directors, reviewers and audiences in the mid-1960s reveal that the theatrical/critical machine was then still largely a middle-class enterprise (Bigsby 1981: 12–15 drawing on Williams 1961 and Halsey et al. 1980). It is possible that Taylor had in mind here Hunt's (1960) account of letters written to the *Eastern Daily Press* in the wake of a radio broadcast of *Roots* in Norfolk. According to Hunt (1960), many of those who wrote in did object to how the Bryants were depicted. Hunt (1960), however, acknowledges what Taylor does not. The reaction was mainly that of a

> small section of the community which still sit up on Monday nights listening to a radio play (instead of going to bed or watching the telly), and of that still smaller section which writes letters to provincial quality papers (Hunt 1960: 30–31).

Audiences, even local audiences, may not be the best judges of whether *Roots* presents a reasonably convincing snapshot of rural Norfolk speech.

What discussions of language, dialect and realism in *Roots* need is a source such as the *Survey of English Dialects*, a systematic study of variation in English directed by Harold Orton and Eugen Dieth. The *Survey* collected data throughout England between 1950 and 1961 and began publishing its work in 1962. Volume III (Orton and Tilling) contained the findings for Norfolk and appeared as three separately bound parts in 1969 (Part I), 1970 (Part II), and 1971 (Part III). The *Survey,* of course, is not without its problems. There were only a handful of informants per locality; most of them were men (except for the questionnaire items that dealt with housekeeping); and the items detailing grammatical features were left to 'the more alert informant' (Dieth and Orton in Orton 1962: 46). For all its weaknesses, however, the *Survey* provides an in-depth and comprehensive look at the speech of rural agricultural communities in Norfolk not too far removed in time from the people Wesker was representing in *Roots*.

When the accent and dialect features Wesker included are cross-checked with the results for Norfolk in the *Survey*, it turns out that Wesker's ear was, in fact, remarkably reliable, and that he went considerably further than just leaning on a few typical features. For example, the Bryants frequently omit the final velar nasal from progressive verb forms (e.g. *comin', hevin', earnin'*, etc.), and the *Survey* shows this same feature in the Norfolk responses (Orton and Tilling 1970: 680, 755). Similarly, Wesker represents *with* as *wi'*; *won't* as *'on't*; and *have* as *hev*, and a number of the responses for the Norfolk informants show equivalent forms (e.g. see Orton and Tilling 1970: 515, 737). Imperatives (*Shut up!*) and invitations phrased as imperatives (*Come in!*) occur with explicit rather than implied *you* in *Roots* (e.g. *shut you up*: 85; *come you in*: 87), and this was also evident in the *Survey* (Orton and Tilling 1971: 1102, 1105).

While only a minority of items in the questionnaire dealt with grammatical features (Orton 1962: 15), their responses showed the use of demonstrative *them* instead of *those* (e.g. *them two*, Orton and Tilling 1971: 1332); relative *what* in place of *that* (*the man what looks after the cows*, Orton and Tilling 1969: 301); *hisself* for *himself* (Orton and Tilling 1971: 1339); and *all on it, the whole on it* (Orton and Tilling 1971: 939) and *out on it* (Orton and Tilling 1971: 1227) for *all of it, the whole of it*, and *out of it*. In addition, the contracted negative of the verb 'to be' (*I'm not, she isn't*, etc.) occurs as *ain't* and is pronounced *ent*. All of these features occur in the speech of the Bryants, as the following examples from the play demonstrate (ellipses mine).

Jimmy:	Good cream *ent* it? (91).
Jenny:	… the brass overflow pipe *what leads* out from the lavatory (97).
Jenny:	… and all *them cattle* (101).
Stan:	You read in *them ole papers* … (107).
Beatie:	And then he'd … read it *his-self*! (89).
Stan:	None *on* 'em like livin' look, none *on* 'em (107).

Other features shown that are not readily identified in the *Survey* match up well with a list of widely occurring non-standard dialect features compiled by Freeborn et al. (1993: 40–48), such as the extension of *were* to all persons in the past tense of *to be* and the double negative:

Frank:	Blust woman, *she were* in love! (140).
Jimmy:	*don't* give me *no* riddles (93).

One of the most commonly occurring features in the play, the use of the base form of the verb in the third person singular present tense (e.g. *he say* rather than *he says*) (Sanger 2001: 41), has been noted as particularly characteristic of East Anglian dialects (Trudgill 1974: 55). Clearly, Wesker goes far beyond what Sternberg (1982: 88) has called 'formal transposition' in representing rural Norfolk speech. That is, he has not simply picked a few obvious features of the dialect and included them to periodically remind the audience that the characters are intended to be Norfolk farmers, as some critics would have us believe. Rather, he writes their lines fairly consistently in their dialect. This is not ridicule, and it is far more than realism. This is respect.

Authenticity, of course, is not the only issue that needs exploration in discussions of dialect representation. As Evans (1977: 91) has suggested, one of Wesker's major contributions was to 'dissociate dialect from inferiority'. Unfortunately, his is a minority view, and, as stated earlier, his argument is difficult to engage in linguistic detail. Far more frequent and, unfortunately, far more influential, in the literature on *Roots* are accounts that accept the highly problematic notion that non-standard dialects of English are inferior dialects of English. Latham (1965), for example, suggests that Wesker's use of language deserves more credit than it usually gets, and points with precision to a few features of the Bryants' dialect (e.g. the use of the base form of the verb in the third person singular present tense). She still goes on to suggest, however, that the Bryants 'express themselves repetitively, with difficulty, and in a syntactically simple form' (1965: 195). Leeming (1983: 48) finds herself generally impressed with Wesker, and suggests that his use of the Norfolk dialect[2] in *Roots* was largely misunderstood by audiences trained (through long-standing tradition in English theatre) to equate non-standard dialects with characters intended to be objects of humour or ridicule. She, like many others, however, still sees the Bryants as characters of 'limited horizons' (1983: 44) who have a 'blinkered view of the world' (1983: 50).

Even the most recent source located for review, Dornan (1994), follows suit. While there is now quite a large body of research into variation in English, much of it accessible to those without specialist training in linguistics (e.g., Chambers and Trudgill 1980/1998; Freeborn et al. 1993; Trudgill 1990), Dornan has apparently not taken this into account. She does not reference any of this or similar material in her discussion of Norfolk dialect features; topics such as *language, linguistics, stylistics* and *dialect* are absent from her index; and there are no sources on linguistics, stylistics or dialectology listed in her bibliography of secondary works. And yet, she covers the topic of dialect representation in *Roots*, asserting that

> the Bryants, a rural family rooted in Norfolk, speak with a distinct East Anglian dialect indicative of their simple education and way of life (Dornan 1994: 31).

She goes on to characterise the dialect as 'rough' (35), and associates its use with negative attributes she sees as evident in the play – an ignorance of medicine, an absence of common sense, and a want of social graces (35).

Dornan's view of linguistic variation leads her to conclude that Wesker, perhaps unwittingly, 'employs embarrassing stereotypes' to depict the Bryants as 'bumpkins' (1994: 35). From a linguistic point of view, however, such assertions betray an alarming naivete of the subject. While the Norfolk dialect Beatie and her family are represented as speaking differs from standard English,[3] it is not, linguistically speaking, 'rough', nor necessarily indicative of a poor education and a limited life. As linguists routinely point out, standard English is just one dialect among many, and there is no sound evidence to suggest that any one dialect is linguistically better or worse than another (Sanger 2001: 37; Chambers and Trudgill 1980/1998: 3; Freeborn et al. 1993: 39; Trudgill 1990: 3). Rather, to the linguist, as Freeborn et al. (1993: 39) point out, 'all dialects of English are equally regular in their own forms and rules'.

Linguistically speaking, Beatie is not making a mistake born of ignorance when she talks about what 'Ronnie say', but following the rules of the dialect that she is represented as speaking (Sanger 2001: 41). As Freeborn et al. (1993) point out, the conjugation of present tense verbs can differ from dialect to dialect. Standard English uses the base form in every person except the third person singular (*he/she/ it*), which takes the *-s* inflection, as in *I drive, you drive, he/she/it drives, we drive, they drive*. The dialect of rural Norfolk that Beatie is represented as using has simply ironed out the exception by extending the use of the base form to all persons in the paradigm (*I drive, you drive, he/she/it drives, we drive, they drive*) (Trudgill 1974: 55). This kind of regularisation is not indicative of deviance. On the contrary, it is an entirely normal process that has been affecting the conjugation of verbs in English for centuries, including the conjugation of verbs in standard English. The verb *drive* in Anglo-Saxon, for example, had four forms in the present indicative, *drīfe* for the first person singular (*I*), *drīfest* for the second person singular (*you*), *drīfeþ* for the third person singular (*he, she, it*), and *drīfaþ* for the first, second and third person plural (*we, you all, they*). Modern standard English has reduced this distinction to two forms, and many other dialects, Beatie's among them, have simply taken the next step in the process of regularisation and dispensed with this last remaining inflection in the present tense.[4]

Beatie's use of *were* when she talks about the things Ronnie would do when 'he were in a black mood' (90) can be explained in a similar way. While standard English uses two distinct forms of *to be* in the past tense (*was* for singular *I, he, she* and *it*, and *were* for *you, we*, and *they*), many non-standard dialects have regularised the paradigm by using *were* throughout. Standard English is not linguistically 'better' because it has two forms rather than one. The process of regularisation has simply not gone as far in standard English as it has in many other dialects (Freeborn et al. 1993).

As a final example, consider Beatie's use of *hisself* rather than *himself*. While standard English would consider this a mistake, its occurrence is, like the two verb forms previously discussed, entirely rule-governed. As Freeborn et al. (1993) point out, standard English uses the possessive pronouns *my, our* and *your* plus *self* or *selves* to form *myself, yourself, ourselves* and *yourselves*, but the object pronouns *him* and *them* to form *himself* and *themselves*. Many non-standard dialects, Beatie's among them, require that the possessive pronoun be used as the basis of the reflexive for all persons. This generates *myself, yourself* etc. as well as *his-self* and *theirselves* (Freeborn et al. 1993: 39).

These same arguments can be applied to the many other Norfolk dialect features evident in the play. To say that such features are deviant, or 'rough', or 'crude' or wrong is simply untenable linguistically. Consider as well that Wesker presents the Bryants to us in their domestic environment. That they speak their own dialect in their own homes among themselves does not make them stereotypic 'bumpkins' as some critics have supposed. It makes them normal.

When the dialogue of the Bryants is considered from a linguistic perspective, it is perhaps easier to see that they are not actually portrayed as stupid in the text. Sanger (2001: 41–2), for example, adopts a linguistic approach and starts from the view that the Bryants speak a different dialect of English, not an inferior one. Perhaps unsurprisingly, he notices immediately that Mrs Bryant is very perceptive and certainly no one's fool, characteristics that the critical record has not generally acknowledged in her. Taylor (1962/1969: 152–3) called her 'irremediably stupid', and Leeming (1983: 46) saw her as little more than a victim of a dehumanizing life. Both Taylor (1962/1969) and Hayman (1970/1979) saw her as a particularly unsympathetic character, in large part because of her reaction to Beatie after Ronnie's betrayal. Mrs Bryant certainly has a lot to answer for (e.g. she slaps Beatie across the face, and indulges in some very insensitive I-told-you-so's). However, when her temper blows itself out, it is Mrs Bryant who provides words of comfort by noting that Ronnie simply did not deserve Beatie: 'I suppose doin' all those things for him weren't enough. I suppose he weren't satisfied wi' goodness only' (145). Furthermore, her suggestion that the family sit down to eat in the wake of Ronnie's treachery (144) is a good one. In the circumstances, in fact, it is really the only thing that can be done, and Mrs Bryant is the only one present to realise this.

In addition, notice that it is Mrs Bryant who voices the most cogent objections to Beatie's account of Ronnie's views on the dangers of popular culture. When Beatie criticises her mother for enjoying a pop song, her mother's objections, regardless of one's stance on the issue, must be acknowledged as relevant and to the point. How, she asks, can one actually tell if something is third-rate? What are the criteria for differentiating 'high' and 'low' art?

> Mrs Bryant: What make that [song] third-rate and them frilly bits of opera and concert first-rate? (115)

The debate on this issue rages on, and interestingly, Mrs Bryant's view is similar to the stance that McGrath (1970) would very famously take in his review of Wesker's play *The Friends*. While Wesker certainly disagreed (Itzin 1980: 107), he thought McGrath's view important enough to engage him in a lengthy and often heated correspondence about it (see Itzin 1980).

Pearle, Beatie's sister-in-law, comes across as particularly sharp, and answers some of Beatie's remarks with arguments of her own. When Beatie accuses Pearle of gossiping about relatives who have bought a television, Pearle notes that she is not gossiping, but making 'an intelligent observation about the state of television' (139). When her comment is fairly considered, it is clear that she does indeed make 'an intelligent observation'. Pearle suggests that buying the television may have been a waste, since the only programs that ever seem to be on are re-runs (138).

It is also clear that the Bryants are capable of discussing complex issues, as is evident when Beatie sets the family a moral dilemma concerning a young girl's choices (139–40). While they are clearly unaccustomed to speaking in hypotheticals, and not all of them care to join in, Pearle and her husband Frank debate the issue. The moral dilemma concerns a young girl who is in love with a man that does not love her. This man lives across the river and when she hears that he will be leaving the area, she decides to try and persuade him to take her along. To do this, however, she needs to cross the river. She asks the ferryman to take her, but he says she must first remove her clothes. Reluctantly, she agrees, and the ferryman keeps to his side of the bargain.

She arrives naked at the home of the man she loves, and begs him to take her with him when he goes. He promises to do just this, so she sleeps with him that night, only to discover the following morning that he has left her. In desperation, she turns to a man she does not love, but who loves her. He, however, now refuses to help. The question to be answered is who is most responsible for the girl's plight.

Pearle puts forward the view that it is the girl herself who is most responsible, because all of the choices she made were hers to make and she made them freely (140). Frank, on the other hand, is more willing to excuse her, pointing out that she did what she did out of love. Pearle is sufficiently interested in the issue to ask what Ronnie's view was, and it turns out that his position, as reported by Beatie, is compatible with Frank's. Ronnie suggests that the girl is only responsible for the decision to take her clothes off, but this she did for love. Her ultimate circumstance is the fault of the two men, the one who takes advantage of her, and the one who professes to love her but is unwilling to help her. While Pearle disagrees, her view is nevertheless a legitimate response. And Mr. Bryant, who at first dismisses the whole story, professing not to understand or see its relevance (141), later hits the nail right on the head when he points out that the dilemma is also a parable for Beatie's own situation, a parable she has failed to learn from: 'And there she were gettin' us to solve the moral problem and now we know that she didn't even do it herself' (144).

Once the idea that non-standard dialects of English are inferior dialects is dismissed for the unsubstantiated prejudice that it is, other aspects of the play come into clearer focus as well. For example, if we look more closely at direct and indirect speech in the play, it becomes apparent that Wesker may actually be challenging class prejudice against non-standard dialects with his representation of these features. As noted earlier, Ronnie never appears in *Roots*. Instead, Beatie quotes what he has said to her back to her family. She does this either by giving what is understood to be a verbatim account (known as direct speech), or paraphrasing (indirect speech). Examples of each are given below.

Direct Speech
Beatie: […] So then he'd say: 'Bridges! bridges! bridges!' (90).

Indirect Speech
Beatie: He say it serves us right (147).

In both cases, Beatie scaffolds Ronnie's utterances with framing clauses (Toolan 1988: 120) (e.g. *he say, Ronnie say*), and then quotes or reports what Ronnie said in inset clauses (Sternberg 1982).

In the literature on *Roots*, Beatie's quoting and paraphrasing of Ronnie is generally taken to mean that she simply repeats him throughout the play (Adler 1979: 438; Hayman 1970/1979: 31; Brown 1972: 166), often without understanding him (Dornan 1994: 34; Innes 1992: 116; Taylor 1962/1967: 152; Worsley 1959).[5] Feminist critics have been particularly unimpressed by this aspect of the play, objecting to the presentation of Beatie as a woman with no opinions until a man bestows them upon her (Dornan 1994: 34). When direct and indirect speech in the play are considered from a stylistic point of view, however, it becomes apparent that these devices may serve an entirely different function.

The first thing to notice is that Beatie does not actually quote or paraphrase Ronnie all that often. This was determined by looking at selected extracts from each act of the play (see Table 1 on the next page), and counting the number of Beatie's sentences that were hers, the number of sentences that contained directly quoted material from Ronnie, and the number of sentences that paraphrased him. A line was considered a sentence if it ended in a full stop, an exclamation mark, or a question mark. The extracts selected are outlined below. Rather than choose randomly, the extracts were selected based on their position in the play (near the beginning, in the middle, and near the end), and on their prominence in the existing critical record.

As Table 2 shows (see next page), the clear majority of Beatie's 272 sentences (80.51 per cent) were hers and hers alone, with direct quotes and paraphrases of Ronnie's utterances accounting for only 19.48 per cent of Beatie's sentences in the selected extracts. Clearly, the extent to which Beatie quotes Ronnie has been overestimated at the expense of her own contributions in her own dialect.

By allowing Beatie and her family to speak as themselves, and limiting Ronnie's contributions to reports made by Beatie, Wesker has, as Sternberg (1982: 75) would put it, effectively taken Ronnie's language from its original context and recontextualised it within the Bryants' environment. As a result, his utterances become 'expose[d] to the pressures of a new network of relations' (Sternberg 1982: 75), and it is the Bryants' perspective that dominates. What might have been very believable in London after making 'love in the afternoon' (90) becomes less and less credible as the very sensible reactions of Beatie's friends and relatives mount up: 'Ent you married yit?' (Jimmy: 87); 'He sound a queer bor to me' (Jenny: 89); 'He *talk* like that?' (Mrs Bryant, 111).

Using the Bryants' dialect to scaffold the standard as Wesker does is actually quite extraordinary. As Sternberg's (1982) work demonstrates, the more usual model in English literature is a standard English frame with a non-standard inset. Wesker has turned this model on its head, which is, even prior to issues of theme and character, a profound statement against the hegemonic order in itself. The 'stylistic norm' (Sternberg 1982: 72) established in the play is the Bryants' dialect, and it is Ronnie's standard English that differs from it.

While Beatie's quoting and paraphrasing of Ronnie has been overestimated, the use of these devices is not unimportant. They allow Beatie to not only report Ronnie's views, but to express her doubts about them as she does so. Early in the play, for example, Beatie notes that she loses patience with Ronnie when he insists that she ask him what words mean if she does not know.

Beatie: I get annoyed when he keep tellin' me – and he want me to ask. [*Imitates him half-heartedly now*] 'Always ask, people love to tell you what they know, always ask and people will respect you' (94).

As the stage directions clearly indicate, Beatie is not quoting Ronnie here to affirm her blind agreement with his view. Quite the opposite – she disagrees with Ronnie,

Table 1 Extracts analysed for direct and indirect speech in *Roots*

Act	Pages	Text boundaries
1	86–91	From *Beatie: Yoo-hoo!* To *Jenny* [rising to get sweet]: *Shut you up gal and get on wi' your ice-cream.*
2	Part 1: 110–12 Part 2: 114–16	From *Beatie: Yearp. Now listen Mother ...* To *Mrs Bryant: I'll get you the soft water from the tank.* From *Mrs Bryant: I tell you what I reckon's a good song ...* To *Mrs Bryant: Is that your father home already?*
3	144–8	From *Mr Bryant: Well, what do we do now?* To [the end of the play].

Table 2 Beatie's use of direct and indirect speech (measured in sentences)

	Beatie as herself	Beatie quoting Ronnie (direct speech)	Beatie paraphrasing Ronnie (indirect speech)	Total
Act 1	71	26	0	**97**
Act 2	55	19	4	**78**
Act 3	93	0	4	**97**
Total	**219**	**45**	**8**	**272**

as well she might. People do not always have respect for those who show they lack knowledge, something Beatie may have learned through personal experience at the hands of Ronnie and his friends. As Beatie has come to realise, Ronnie is not teaching her, as he declares, 'to save someone from the fire' (115). Rather, she knows that what he actually enjoys is humiliating her, baiting her on subjects he knows she does not understand in front of his friends (94).

Beatie's doubts about Ronnie become apparent even when no overt clues are given in the stage directions. This is the case when Beatie reports Ronnie's views using indirect speech. As an example, we can return to the conversation between Beatie and her mother in Act Two concerning what makes a pop song third rate.

> Beatie: [...] I ask him [Ronnie] exactly the same questions – what make a pop song third-rate. And he answer and I don't know what he talk about. Something about registers, something about commercial world blunting our responses (115).

Here, Beatie gives an account of what he said, but does not use his exact words. This has been taken to mean that she is simply absorbing his 'theoretical phrases' without yet understanding them (Leeming and Trussler 1971: 61). There is, however, another interpretation available. Drawing on Toolan (1988: 120), it can be argued that Ronnie's message is cast to make sense from Beatie's point of view, and this is further underlined by the fact that Wesker has 'homogenised' (Sternberg 1982) Ronnie's voice into Beatie's here, not the other way round. With Beatie's point of view presented as dominant, it is possible to view Ronnie as the one who does not know what he is talking about rather than Beatie. While Beatie may not have understood Ronnie's answer, this may have more to do with his lack of conviction than with her supposed inability to understand.

Clearly, there is more to Beatie than Ronnie. She has concerns not only about some of his views, but about their relationship, as well. When Jenny suggests that Ronnie and Beatie may not be particularly suited to each other, Beatie at first protests ('[*loudly*]: It's not true! We're in love!') (95), but then goes on to admit her own doubts about their relationship (95). Beatie also indicates that Ronnie's influence on her, both cultural and linguistic, may be superficial. She 'belongs to Norfolk' (Mutalik-Desai 1987: 7):

> Soon ever I'm home again I'm like I always was – it don' even seem I bin away. I do the same lazy things an' I talk the same (88).

And while she is self-deprecating here, the audience does not necessarily have to believe her. As Wilcher (1991: 46) notes, Beatie is ironically unaware of the strength and value of her own roots.

When Beatie's use of dialect is considered from a linguistic perspective, we see that she is not, as many critics have claimed, 'static until the one moment of acute revelation' at the end of the play (Chambers and Prior 1987: 141; see also Hayman 1970/1979: 31; Latham 1965: 192; Findlater 1960: 241). In contrast to the dominant critical view, Beatie does not find her own words, discover her own voice (Dornan 1994: 34; Brown 1972: 166; Hayman 1970/1979: 31; Taylor 1962/1969: 153; Adler 1979: 429; Innes 1992: 116), or liberate herself through language (Innes 1992: 115; Dornan 1994: 34) at the end of the play. She has always had her own language and spoken in her own voice, something that is only infrequently acknowledged in the critical record (e.g., see Wilcher 1991: 46 and Leeming 1983: 50). While the final stage direction suggests she is 'articulate at last' (148), it can be argued that this refers to her new-found confidence to express herself politically rather than to her language. As is noted from time to time in the critical record, Beatie's final speech does not entail a shift in dialect (Bigsby 1981; Evans 1977: 91; Latham 1965: 197). Less often noticed, however, is that Beatie's final speech shows her directly quoting her oppressors in *her* voice.

> We know where the money lie', they say, 'hell we do! The workers've got it so let's give them what they want. If they want slop songs and film idols we'll give 'em that then. If they want words of one syllable, we'll give 'em that then. If they want third-rate, *blust*! We'll give 'em *that* then. Anything's good enough for them 'cos they don't ask for no more (148).

When Beatie quotes the faceless 'they' of the capitalist power machine, 'they' are actually recorded as speaking in Beatie's voice, even though inverted commas are used to indicate 'verbatim' speech. They are, in essence, divested of an independent existence, and such life as they have is narrated entirely through Beatie's language. She owns them.

Ronnie tells Beatie that words are bridges (90) – bridges to education, to independence, to a better life (Dornan 1994: 33–4; Peter 1989: C9). It is through language that we can ask questions, challenge assumptions, and seek knowledge (Dornan 1994: 33). Peter (1989: C9) suggests that Wesker is telling us in the play to 'only connect', and it is language that connects us, not only to each other, but to our roots, by which Wesker means the wider historical and cultural context that underlies much of Western society and thought (Dornan 1994: 33). What Wesker may be showing us not only in Beatie's last speech but throughout the play is that her home dialect serves just as well as Ronnie's standard English when it comes to asking questions, challenging the status quo, debating, and ultimately connecting. Ronnie has no right to tell Beatie she does not know how to use her own language (90), and can in fact stand to learn a thing or two from the Bryants. If they are to be 'saved', they must first be understood, and above all respected. If Beatie succeeds in rescuing only herself (Dornan 1994), it is because she, like Ronnie, does not see the value in her own roots.

As demonstrated in this chapter, a linguistic analysis of *Roots* has added much to our understanding of the play. It has been shown that Wesker wrote the play in the Bryants' dialect and from their perspective. While their life is certainly harsh and impoverished in many ways, the portrait he offers is not without respect. Views to the contrary betray something of a critical blind spot, a superiority complex, if you will, based on nothing more than an outmoded and insupportable view of linguistic variation in English. Speakers of non-standard dialects are not by definition ignorant 'bumpkins', repetition does not necessarily indicate 'a slow way of thinking', and cliché and formulae are not automatically 'substitutes for thought'. It is unfortunate that such views have thus far been allowed to dominate the debate on *Roots*, a play explicitly identified as dealing directly with 'the need to respect language' as an 'essential tool for living' (Wilcher 1991: 15).

In the next chapter, a stylistic analysis is employed to consider how it is possible to understand what is not said in Rattigan's *In Praise of Love*. While Rattigan has often been compared unfavourably to playwrights such as Pinter and Wesker, this analysis of his dialogue shows that his linguistic achievements are no less deserving of serious critical attention.

Chapter 5

Brave Silences
Understanding What Is Not Said in
Terence Rattigan's *In Praise of Love*

In Praise of Love, one of Rattigan's last plays, presents a painful episode in the lives of Lydia and Sebastian Cruttwell, their son Joey, and their friend Mark Walters, a writer of popular fiction.[1] Lydia is in the final stages of a terminal illness but conceals this fact from her husband and son in order to protect them. She does, however, confide in Mark, who has come to visit the Cruttwells and who was at one time (and perhaps still is) in love with Lydia. Throughout Act One Sebastian, a former novelist turned critic, treats his wife with what appears to be casual disregard. As the audience eventually discovers, however, this is simply a false front. Sebastian knows about Lydia's illness, but believes he is concealing it from her in order to protect her.

Lydia's illness and the deceptions surrounding it create further complications for the family. Joey has written a play that is going to be performed on television, and an evening to celebrate the broadcast has been arranged. Sebastian, however, fails to arrive, forgetting the occasion after having received definitive confirmation of Lydia's terminal condition that afternoon. Because he has concealed his knowledge of Lydia's illness from both Lydia and Joey, he cannot use the bad news to absolve himself. However, he has confessed all to Mark, who arranges for Lydia to discover the truth behind Sebastian's behaviour. Lydia helps Sebastian engineer a reconciliation with their son, who remains blissfully ignorant of her illness, and the play ends with the family united if not in complete honesty at least in peace.

The literature on *In Praise of Love* reveals a number of different strategies for its interpretation. The play has been labelled 'a domestic tragi-comedy', (Young 1978: xv), and read as 'an agonized examination' of Rattigan's own life (Rebellato 2001: xxiii). Parallels have been drawn between Lydia's condition and Rattigan's own struggle with leukaemia, and connections have been made between the events in the play and Rattigan's observation of the situation concerning his friends Rex Harrison and Kay Kendall. Harrison, when informed by Kendall's doctor that she was dying of leukaemia – Kendall apparently having not been told – chose to spare her the pain and keep up the pretence that nothing was wrong (Rusinko 1983: 10).

Critics have also identified significant themes explored in the play, such as the father/son conflict, the role of writers in society, and the repression of emotion (Rusinko 1983). Evidence of such themes is found in key 'load-bearing' lines that are isolated and interpreted, such as 'Do you know what "*le vice Anglais*" – the English vice – really is? [...] It's our refusal to admit to our emotions' (52). Of especial interest in the critical record on *In Praise of Love*, however, is the relationship between honesty and concealment in the play (Rebellato 2001: xxv; Rusinko 1983: 11), with Rattigan's ability to write dialogue that communicates indirectly through hint, suggestion and even deception receiving frequent comment. For Rusinko (1983: 132), *In Praise of Love* is a play of 'subtle unspoken truths'; for Young (1986: 186), it is 'a masterpiece of deceit;' for Rebellato (2001: xx) it is a 'meticulous interweaving of white lies, painful deceptions and compassionate untruth'. These unspoken truths and compassionate falsehoods arise out of love as Lydia and Sebastian attempt to shield each other from the painful reality of Lydia's illness (Foulkes 1979: 380). Young (1978: xviii) was impressed by their 'quiet bravery', and Rusinko (1983: 132) was moved by their sacrifices for each other, noting that their strength was tempered with 'a delicacy and finesse possible only by *implicit* means' (Rusinko 1983: 132, italics mine).

Interestingly, critics have not paid much attention to how it is that readers and viewers manage to fill in the gaps left by the deceptions and silences in the material. Instead, they tend to catalogue actions that underline themes of deception. For example, Rebellato (2001: xxvii) notes that Sebastian pretends not to love Lydia; that Lydia pretends not to be dying; that Mark pretends to be Sebastian; and that Joey calls himself 'Joseph' to seem more like a serious writer. Young (1986: 190) compiles a similar list, articulated in terms of what characters do and do not know. Sebastian knows that Lydia is dying, but cannot tell anyone; Lydia knows that she is dying, but can tell no one but Mark; Mark knows that Lydia is dying, but does not know (at first) that Sebastian knows; Joey remains none the wiser throughout.

Critics have proved equally adept at cataloguing revelations. Lydia reveals her true diagnosis to Mark; Sebastian confesses to Mark that he has known all along about Lydia's illness, and has discovered (too late) that he loves her; Mark 'tells' Lydia that Sebastian knows about her illness by directing her to look at the hat box where Sebastian has been hiding her doctor's reports (Rebellato 2001: xxix-xxx). While critics have been much exercised by Rattigan's talent for 'saying without saying', they appear to have taken for granted their ability, and the ability of readers and viewers, to recover a coherent narrative from a text that is, by most accounts, purposefully unreliable in key places.

One explanation for this curtailed interpretative endeavour may be the critical climate in the wake of John Osborne's *Look Back in Anger*. As Taylor (1962/1969: 12) has observed, Osborne's premiere in 1956 is typically taken as something of a watershed moment in British theatre and drama, an event that put onto page and stage a 'new wave' of overtly political, socially responsible, anti-establishment, and formally innovative drama. While *In Praise of Love* came out in 1973, it can still be refracted through the prism of the 1956 'revolution', as it played to a generation of critics schooled in 'new wave' ethics (Rebellato 2001: xviii).

After Osborne's premiere, Rattigan's genius for 'subtl[y] tracing the emotional lives of the middle classes' (Rebellato 2001: v) suddenly became a liability, at least as far as criticism was concerned (Gross 1990; Worsley 1964: 67). As a result, Rattigan's work was fixed with labels (shallow, complacent, sentimental, old-fashioned) that were largely undeserved. Serious drama after Osborne had to be ideological (Hill

1982: 41; Chambers and Prior 1987: 105-6), and Rattigan was not, at least for the purposes of his plays, interested in any of the 'isms' of the day (Worsley 1964: 63). Considered 'second rate' and 'superseded' (Worsley 1964: 60), he was accused of being 'ideologically empty' (Hill 1982: 41) and of 'fail[ing] to respond dramatically to the needs of the time' (Chambers and Prior 1987: 105–6).

By the mid-1960s however, some critics had begun to point out that 'new wave' reactions to Rattigan amounted to little more than prejudice against a playwright who chose to maintain older traditions (Taylor 1967; Worsley 1964: 60), and this sentiment has been voiced repeatedly in the literature since then (Rebellato 2001: xiii; Gross 1990: 346; Rusinko 1983; Hill 1982). As welcome as these correctives are, they have not undone the worst of the damage wrought by new wave fervour. Three issues important in the understanding of how ambiguities and deceptions nevertheless make sense in Rattigan's dialogue are still overlooked or de-emphasised in the critical literature. One of these issues concerns the careful manipulation of information in what are called 'well-made' plays. Deriving from a tradition in French theatre, the term *well-made* refers to plays with carefully crafted plots and tidy, resolved endings (Lennard and Luckhurst 2002: 371; Rusinko 1983: 26; Taylor 1981: 179; for a full discussion, see Taylor 1967). After 1956, plays structured in this way fall out of fashion. 'Well-made' becomes an insult (Rusinko 1983: 25; Hill 1982: 39; Taylor 1967; Worsley 1964: 65) synonymous with concepts such as 'bourgeois complacency, hypocrisy, moral cowardice, and intellectual laziness' (Dalrymple 2000: 13), and Rattigan found himself severely criticised for writing such plays.

In the rush to condemn well-made plays, however, the significance of a crucial element in their construction was overlooked: the controlled release of information (Rusinko 1983: 25; Taylor 1981: 179).[2] *In Praise of Love* in particular depends on this kind of manipulation, but many critics, in throwing the 'information' baby out with the 'well-made play' bath water, missed opportunities to relate carefully controlled states of knowledge with dialogue so heavily dependent on lies that nevertheless pointed to the truth.

A second casualty of new-wave critical sensitivities was Rattigan's faith in his audience. Perhaps unwisely, Rattigan (1953b: xi–xii) attempted to explain this through the creation of *Aunt Edna*, a conceptual embodiment of a typical theatre-goer he described as 'a nice respectable, middle-class, middle-aged, maiden lady with time on her hands and the money to help her pass it'. While Rattigan (1953b) maintained that Aunt Edna was to be challenged as well as respected, she was widely regarded in the post-1956 critical climate as yet another indication that Rattigan was guilty of 'an insipid pandering' to his audience (quote from Rebellato 2001: xii; see also Worsley 1964: 62).

In their zeal to read Rattigan's work as complacent and unchallenging, however, new wave critics paid perhaps less attention than was due to a very relevant aspect of Rattigan's faith in audiences: his belief that they would take an inherent delight in the challenge of working things out for themselves. Writing on his 'sense of theatre', Rattigan explained that an analysis of those moments in the great plays at which we have all caught our breaths would surely lead to the conclusion that they are nearly always those moments when the least is being said, and the most suggested (Rattigan 1953a: xix–xx).

While Rattigan's comments on the value of audience discovery are well-covered in the literature, Aunt Edna 'dogged' his career, becoming a 'by-word for what theatre should not be' (Rebellato 2001: xii), and questions concerning *why* it was that Rattigan could trust her to do so much of the interpretative work went largely unasked. This is curious, as *In Praise of Love* virtually requires its audience to 'read between the lines'.

The third issue to receive short shrift in the critical literature, Rattigan's use of language, relates directly to Aunt Edna's capacity for discerning clarity in ambiguity and truth in falsehood. This too has unfortunately gone out with the bath water. While Rattigan gets credit for his ability to convincingly represent conversational English (Young 1986: 189; Rusinko 1983: 15; Foulkes 1979: 380), it is noted that what he represents so naturally is the conversational speech of the middle classes rather than the working classes (Evans 1977: 82; Worsley 1964: 71). Worthy drama after 1956 was expected to attack middle-class values, and Rattigan's choice to present middle class characters without criticizing their 'middle-class-ness' was unpopular (Bigsby 1981; Taylor 1967).

On the very few occasions when critics have looked beyond the issue of Rattigan's choice to represent the middle-class vernacular in his dialogue, their attempts to link issues of deception and suggestion to the language of the text are in the main unconvincing. Rusinko (1983), for instance, notes Sebastian's tendency, particularly in Act One, to focus on anything but Lydia's illness (e.g. the state of his library, his political views, Lydia's former life, etc.). At the linguistic level, however, this is explained as the couple playing 'witty games', a tactic of Sebastian's that Lydia has apparently mastered 'as a defensive strategy' (Rusinko 1983: 129). 'Witty games' and Lydia's talent for giving as good as she gets, however, do not do justice to the language of the text, since the games that Sebastian and Lydia play so well are not ends in themselves but signposts towards a deeper truth.

Young (1986: 189–90) notices that the text generates a number of questions (e.g. why has Lydia stayed with Sebastian when he is such a bully? Why does Lydia say Britain is a nice place to *have* lived?) but accounts for this by comparing *In Praise of Love* to an Agatha Christie thriller. For Young (1986), Rattigan prompts readers to ask such questions by leaving psychological clues in the text. Young's comparison of the play to an Agatha Christie mystery, however, has little to say about how the audience is able to interpret such clues.

Rebellato (2001) and Rusinko (1983) deal with similar issues, but appeal unhelpfully to the notion of performance. Both authors grapple (briefly) with the issue of why certain lines in the play appear to have a kind of weightiness, a resonance unexplained by the syntactic structure and semantic content of the clauses themselves (e.g. Sebastian's 'Is there *nothing* I can keep concealed in this house?': 6). For both authors, the suggested answer is that Rattigan's words on their own are insufficient and can only be appreciated in performance. Rebellato (2001: xxix) suggests that 'Rattigan's dialogue may seem flat on the printed page, but in performance the iron structure of the play charges and animates some of the simplest utterances'. In very similar terms, Rusinko (1983: 15) supposes that 'the flat, terse extraordinarily ordinary language succeeds in evoking complex realities and in giving actors the freedom they need to communicate those realities'.

While such appeals to performance may have precedent in the literature (e.g. see Styan 1960/1976: 11), they are ultimately unhelpful when it comes to dealing with the language of the text. It is not that the words on the page are 'flat' and can only be fully appreciated in performance. What the accounts of Rebellato and Rusinko show here is not necessarily a weakness in Rattigan's dialogue as written, but a weakness in the critical idiom employed for dealing with it. Appeals to performance, while certainly legitimate in discussions of dramatic texts, are not the only (or even the most convincing) account of why seemingly 'ordinary' utterances appear to take on added meanings in Rattigan's text.

What is needed in the interpretation of *In Praise of Love* is an analytical tool that can: 1) cope with dialogue that manages to transcend its own surface structure; and 2) account for how audiences cope with such dialogue. Such a tool is available in Brown and Levinson's (1978/1987: 211–27) framework of off-record communication (see also discussion of this topic in Chapter 2). Speakers go off-record when they hint at what they mean instead of stating their case unambiguously. Brown and Levinson (1978/1987), drawing on Grice (1975), outline a number of these strategies in their account of how off-record speech acts are understood. After observing that ambiguous, incomplete utterances do not generally present problems for participants in ordinary talk, Grice (1975) reasoned that for this to be possible interlocutors in talk must proceed under the assumption that both they themselves and everyone else will behave cooperatively. That is, the starting assumption in communication is that people will design their contributions to be informative (the maxim of quantity), relevant (the maxim of relation), truthful (the maxim of quality) and clear (the maxim of manner) (for a more detailed account of Grice's Cooperative Principle and its four maxims, see Chapter 2).

According to Grice (1975), it is precisely because of these expectations regarding informativeness, truthfulness, clarity and relevance that uninformative, vague, irrelevant and false utterances have meaning. It is not uncommon, for example, for speakers to simply leave their utterances unfinished.

A   So how was your meeting yesterday?
B   Well ...

According to Grice's (1975) theory, B's reply above *flouts* the maxims of quantity and manner. That is, B blatantly and obviously remains vague and says too little in the given circumstances. By doing so, he invites A to search for an interpretation of his utterance that makes sense in context. By generating an *implicature*, as Grice (1975) calls it, B can leave A to work out his meaning (the meeting was not successful) without having to 'spell it out' directly.

Grice's (1975) theory has engendered a veritable industry of research in philosophy, pragmatics and psychology, much of it beyond the scope of the current investigation. Leech's (1983) extension of Grice (1975), however, is of particular relevance. Leech (1983) proposed that interlocutors in talk also started with assumptions concerning more affective variables (tact, generosity, modesty, etc.) and suggested a number of additional maxims to account for this. One of these maxims, the sympathy maxim, will be adopted here. This maxim states that speakers will (and expect others to) minimize the expression of antipathy and maximize the expression of sympathy in talk unless they have a good reason not to (Leech 1983: 132).

Had new wave criticism not been so eager to devalue Rattigan's workmanship and respect for his audience, frameworks of off-record communication might have been applied to *In Praise of Love* much earlier. As critics themselves have noticed, the play is built from dialogue that implies more than it says, and frameworks of off-record communication are designed to account for exactly these kinds of utterances. They seem almost tailor-made to evaluate *In Praise of Love* in a way that some critics have themselves called for: on its own terms (Rusinko 1983: 17) as an exploration of love and honesty in intimate relationships (Chambers and Prior 1987). Such a reassessment is long overdue (Chambers and Prior 1987; Rusinko 1983: 17). As Gross (1996) has noted,

> Rattigan scholarship has yet to move out of the controversies of the 1950s and 1960s to a more considered understanding of this meticulous and reserved playwright (349).

By applying a Gricean perspective to the language of *In Praise of Love*, significant steps towards this 'more considered understanding' can be made. In particular, questions of how Rattigan's skilful manipulation of information enables audiences to see through the gaps and lies in the dialogue can be explored in greater depth and to greater effect than appeals to performance (Rebellato 2001; Rusinko 1983), wittiness (Rusinko 1983: 129), and comparisons (Young 1986: 189–90) to other genres allow.

The relationship between truth and deception in *In Praise of Love* becomes remarkably clear once it is realised that a great deal of information in the play is communicated off-record. In fact, what is arguably the most important piece of information in the play is revealed in this manner. Mark allows Lydia to discover Sebastian's secret (that he has known about her illness all along and has been hiding this knowledge from her out of love) without actually revealing it. Having found out from Sebastian that he has been hiding Lydia's genuine medical records in the hat-box in the hall, which has been there 'looking incongruous' (1) from the very start of the play, Mark finds himself in a difficult position towards the end of Act Two. Lydia is furious with Sebastian for forgetting about Joey's play, but Mark knows he has a genuine excuse, and finds that he cannot support Lydia in her anger against Sebastian.

Lydia:	(*amazed*) You take his side?
Mark:	Yes, on this.
Lydia:	Well, what *is* his excuse?
Mark:	Good night, Lydia. (*He goes to the door, leaving Lydia looking bewildered. Turning*) Oh Christ! Has anybody ever been in such a spot? Look. (*He points to the hat-box*) That thing up there. It needs dusting.
Lydia:	The hat-box?
Mark:	Yes. You can see the dust from here.
Lydia:	But I can't reach it (53).

Mark's hints continue. He tells her to dust the box inside and out when Sebastian is not at home, and further demonstrates to her how she can reach the hat-box by extending the library steps. At no point does he say, for example, 'Sebastian has known all along about your illness and has hidden your medical reports in the hat-box'. This would be unambiguous, on record communication in that Mark, after saying something like this, would not be able to maintain plausible deniability (Brown and Levinson 1978/1987: 211). He could not, that is, feasibly maintain that he meant something else.

As evident from the text, however, Mark does leave himself room for plausible deniability. He goes off-record with a flout of relevance. Instead of answering Lydia's question about what Sebastian's excuse might be with an expected, preferred response, he says 'Good night'. However, he finds that he cannot leave it at that. One of the dangers of going off-record is that the hint will not be understood, and this is clearly what happens. Mark's farewell serves only to bewilder Lydia.

In his second attempt, he is clearer, but still off-record. He suggests that Lydia dust the hat-box. This is another flout of relevance, so much so that Lydia queries the suggestion, protesting that it is out of her reach. After several more hints on how to dust the hat-box, Lydia completes the implicature. Notice, however, that Mark still retains plausible deniability. If questioned, he can say 'I merely suggested she dust the hat-box, which was plainly in need of dusting'. He moves towards clarity by confirming Lydia's guesses (Lydia: 'Love letters? / Sebastian: 'Kind of': 53), but can still claim that he did not actually tell her Sebastian's secret. Thus is the key revelation of the play communicated. Mark says something that seems irrelevant at first (*dust the hat-box*) and Lydia, working under the assumption that Mark's utterance must be relevant, no matter how odd it seems, arrives at the conclusion that Mark is suggesting she look in the hat-box. When she does, she understands the truth of Sebastian's behaviour.

While Sebastian's love and concern for Lydia may come as a surprise to her, reading and viewing audiences are prepared for this from the very start of the play. For most of Act One, audiences are given just enough information to suspect things, but not enough to put the full picture together (yet). In Gricean terms, the dialogue provides enough information to set in motion the process of reasoning that will enable audiences to work out what is implied from what is said, but stops just short of allowing the full implicature to be generated. In proceeding this way, Rattigan has taken full advantage of what Short (1989) calls the embedded nature of discourse in drama.[3]

This embeddedness is how Short (1989) accounts for dramatic irony. As he explains, ordinary communicative events involve an addresser who sends a message to an addressee. While drama shares this structure, 'it is arranged to be overheard on purpose' (149), and thus includes another level of discourse. As characters speak to each other, the playwright is speaking to the audience, and implicatures generated at one level (e.g. between the playwright and the audience) may not be generated at the other level (between the characters) (Short 1989: 149).

Much of the dialogue in Act One is effective in its purpose of raising audience suspicion because flouts, deliberate failures to observe the various maxims, occur at the level of discourse obtaining between the playwright and the audience. What we come to discover in Act Two is that these flouts are for Sebastian and Lydia violations, quiet and unostentatious failures to observe the maxims as they attempt to mislead each other on the painful subject of Lydia's illness.

The process begins with the opening stage directions. As Herman (1995) has pointed out, audiences are likely to interpret interactions between characters in light of the information supplied in the stage directions (whether they read them or see them realised on stage). The first glimpses of Lydia reveal that she is utterly exhausted, barely having made it up two flights of stairs even when she has nothing to carry (1). As for Sebastian, the stage directions make clear that as he comes out of his study with 'a cigarette between his lips, an empty glass in his hand, and spectacles over his nose' (1), he encounters Lydia in her exhausted state, sitting down and staring 'blankly in front of her while she regains her breath' (1). Thus, it is established in the opening stage directions that Lydia is unwell, perhaps even very ill, and that Sebastian is in a position to notice this. Audiences, armed with this information and widely held norms of communication many of them will have brought to the text, can reasonably expect an expression of concern from Sebastian here. Lydia's behaviour can be interpreted as the non-verbal equivalent of what Tsui (1994) calls an Informative:Report (see Chapter 2), a move in discourse in which speakers report on a condition or state of affairs. Reports that express or are taken to express bad news typically prospect sympathetic responses (e.g. *Feeling better?* or *Darling, you look tired. Can I get you anything?*) (Tsui 1994: 140). What Sebastian actually says flies in the face of this expectation.

| Sebastian: | Oh good, darling, you're back. The heating has gone wrong (1). |
| Sebastian: | It's icy in my room (1). |

Coming upon his wife in an obvious state of physical exhaustion, he makes two Requestives (Tsui 1994), both of which are requests for Lydia to engage in an action that will benefit him. While the requests are mitigated (he makes no overt demands), that they occur at all at this particular point in the discourse is odd, and therefore noticeable. Sebastian has clearly failed to observe the sympathy maxim.

For Rebellato (2001: xxix), Lydia's clear physical distress and Sebastian's equally clear lack of concern indicate 'two people locked together in mysterious mutual isolation'. While an overt explanation of Sebastian's behaviour is indeed withheld from the audience at this point, what Rebellato (2001) has not considered is that the dialogue is written in such a way that the audience will go looking for an explanation that fits the information that is given. Sebastian's flouts of the sympathy maxim trigger the first steps in a reasoning process outlined by Grice (1975: 50, see also Thomas 1995: 65) and adapted to the present purposes as follows. Sebastian does not behave as expected → He has not upheld the sympathy maxim → There must be a reason for this. However, the reasoning process has to (for the moment) stop here, as not enough information is given at this point to home in on a plausible interpretation. Is Sebastian the type not to notice what is plainly before his eyes? Perhaps. Is he momentarily, or even typically, preoccupied with his work? Maybe. Does he drink too much? It is possible. Is he just selfish? This could be. Is he wilfully ignoring Lydia's distress? Perhaps. None of these possibilities, or others that can be put forward, can be ruled out at this point. What is important is that these possibilities are generated, and that they come about by Sebastian's flouts of the sympathy maxim.

Also noticeable here is the fact that Lydia seems to take Sebastian's aberrant behaviour in her stride. She sorts out the heat, gently chiding him for not turning it on in the first place, and later refills his empty glass without Sebastian having to ask, an action she can do 'in her sleep' (2). Thus, for Lydia, Sebastian's remarks concerning the heat may not generate any implicatures. As his wife, she is long-accustomed to his ways. While Lydia may not notice anything unusual, Sebastian's contributions to the discourse at this point still run contrary to the more generally held expectations of support in English conversational interactions. As Short (1989) notes,

> the assumptions which the characters share in [a play] are presumably not thought of as odd by the characters. But the fact that they clash with our own assumptions in a play world which at first sight appears to be isomorphous with our own itself constitutes one of a number of accumulated messages which [the playwright] is giving us about the world in which [his/her] characters live (153).

Sebastian's failure to observe the sympathy maxim will prompt the audience to question his reactions here, even if Lydia does not.[4] From the very first lines of the dialogue, the audience is beginning to suspect that something is clearly not right between these two people.

Audiences do not have to wait long for more extreme flouts of sympathy. Soon after the opening of the play, Sebastian and Lydia talk about why she has been out so long.

Sebastian:	[...] And you got held up by the bus-strike?
Lydia:	Not really. I found a new way on the tube.
Sebastian	(*worried*) Should you have?
Lydia:	Oh, it was quite easy ...
Sebastian:	I meant isn't it a bit like strike-breaking?
Lydia:	Your social conscience would have preferred I walked?
Sebastian:	It's not all that far, is it? (2)

Here, audiences and Lydia suspect at first that Sebastian is finally showing some concern, as he appears to be worried that Lydia over-exerted herself by finding a new way home on the tube. However, he goes to the trouble of interrupting her to clarify that his concern is not for her welfare, but his (supposed) political sensitivities. In other words, he goes out of his way to not observe the sympathy maxim. This is the conversational equivalent of running someone down in a car and then reversing back over them to be sure the job is done. Once again, Sebastian's conversational behaviour raises more questions than it answers. Why is Sebastian going to such trouble to show he does not care? Is he simply insensitive? Can someone actually be this insensitive? Does he have some deep-seated problem that causes him to behave this way? At this point in the dialogue, no firm conclusion can be reached and the audience is left to wonder whether Sebastian really is just an ass, or whether his repeated and very obvious attempts to show he does not care signify something else.

Flouts of manner and quantity prompt further questions. In the following interaction between Sebastian and Lydia, issues of clarity that arise between them are dealt with through local requests for repair such as 'That doesn't answer my question' (see Chapter 3 for a technical account of repair). For the audience, however, this interaction exhibits what are flouts of manner, places where the dialogue is obviously and purposely obscure (ellipses within brackets indicate where lines not essential to the analysis have been omitted).

Sebastian:	[…] (*He reaches up and grabs another book*) *Plain Talk about Sex* – next to *Peter Pan*.
Lydia:	(*taking it*) That's mine.
Sebastian:	For God's sake, why?
Lydia:	I bought it for a train, sometime.
Sebastian:	(*taking off his spectacles*) That doesn't answer my question. Darling, I mean, with your early life …
Lydia:	Perhaps it needed a bit of brushing up.
	Pause
Sebastian:	(*blowing on his glasses, carefully*) A criticism?
Lydia:	No. A comment.
[…]	
Sebastian:	You're in a stinking mood this evening, aren't you?
Lydia:	Am I?
Sebastian:	Was it what I said about your earlier misadventures?
Lydia:	(*smiling*) No, stupid. You of all people have the right to talk about that. I mean thirty years after – nearly thirty – St George must have occasionally reminded his damsel of the dragon he rescued her from.
Sebastian	(*embarrassed*) St George! Really! Anyway St George didn't have several ding-dongs with his damsel before he rescued her …
[…]	
Sebastian:	You meant something a bit harsh by 'comment'! Oh yes. I know. Now, darling, you must realize …
Lydia:	You can't be expected to poke an old skeleton. I know.
Sebastian:	Darling, really! That wasn't very – tasteful, was it?
Lydia:	It was your taste. You said it (3).

Brushing up on sexual techniques? Early life? Being rescued? Lydia as damsel in distress to Sebastian's St. George? Several ding-dongs before being rescued? Old skeleton? These references are at this point unclear for the audience, and deliberately so by virtue of the way the play has been structured. The effect of these deliberately obscured references is to prompt the audience to put the clues together and begin wondering what happened to Lydia. That is, flouts of manner send interlocutors (in this case, readers and audiences) in search of clarity, and a reasonable interpretation is that Sebastian rescued Lydia from some dire circumstance, and that that rescue involved a sexual relationship to which Lydia was clearly no stranger. But what, exactly, happened, and what does it have to do with Lydia and Sebastian now? The audience is left wondering.

Flouts of quantity are also clues that Lydia may be up to something as well as Sebastian. Lydia produces test results for Sebastian to inspect, and notes that these results are from her latest tests (4), which clearly indicates that she has had more than one round. Sebastian reads out the results, which are (apparently) all normal (4), and then makes a joke about how dull that sounds (4). Lydia encourages Sebastian to read further, and joins him in his levity, noting how wonderful it will be to eat and drink what she likes (4). Readers and audiences, however, who know Lydia is clearly unwell and who now know she has been to the doctor for at least two batteries of tests, are likely to hear these utterances as flouts of quantity. All of this emphasis on how normal and wonderful everything is serves only to reinforce the interpretation that something is most definitely not normal and wonderful.

Lydia and Sebastian also collude to shift the topic from her test results to a joking discussion about the national health service (4). This can be interpreted with respect to the maxim of relation. Is a satirical discussion of the NHS relevant to Lydia's potentially serious situation and its impact on her family? Not really. It appears that both Sebastian and Lydia are hiding behind banter at this point (Herman 1995). The flouts of manner in their talk reinforce this view. Lydia refers to the results of her 'wee-wee' (4) test, a term that is not appropriate to the situation. Sebastian seizes on this euphemism to retreat even further behind the banter. For the overhearing audience, he flouts the maxim of relation when he chooses to correct Lydia by telling her the proper term instead of focusing on the actual results.

A further hint to the audience occurs in the exchange between Sebastian and Lydia concerning the people at the laboratory (4). When Sebastian asks if 'the lab. people' wrote the results, Lydia responds with a Positive Response ('Of course'), and this is followed in turn by a Follow-up Move from Sebastian, a repetition of *Of course* that ratifies the positive outcome of their exchange (Tsui 1994). The problem, however, is that in context, Sebastian's question is entirely redundant, a flout of the maxim of quantity. Who else would write a lab report but lab people? Their shared insistence that the lab people wrote the lab report is yet another very noticeable instance of Sebastian and Lydia saying too much. This plants a seed of doubt in readers' minds concerning the provenance of the report.

Particular lines in Act One that have left critics perplexed can also be interpreted with reference to off-record communication and Grice (1975). One of these is Sebastian's first mention of Lydia's doctor.

Sebastian: Oh, of course, old Doctor Scheister (2).

For Rusinko (1983: 15), this is one of the lines that is 'extraordinarily ordinary'. Why? Why is this apparently off-hand remark so noticeable? Sebastian is not observing the maxim of quantity and while Lydia may not notice, the audience does. It has been established that Lydia is suffering from severe fatigue, and it is now apparent that she has been to the doctor. And yet Sebastian's first reference to this doctor is loaded with indicators of de-emphasis. With the discourse markers *oh* and *of course*, Sebastian marks Lydia's visit to the doctor as previously given information that had momentarily slipped his mind, old news that is not of any special importance. He reinforces this by referring to the doctor, whose actual name is Schuster, as Scheister, a play on words that suggests the doctor need not be taken seriously. The adjective *old* in this context serves, at least from Sebastian's perspective, to further undermine the doctor's status. Sebastian's too obvious declaration that the doctor is NOT IMPORTANT leads the audience to suspect that he actually *is* important. What is not known at this point is why.

As noted earlier, another line that has been of interest in the critical record but not satisfactorily explained is Sebastian's response to Lydia when she mentions that she just happened to find some of his notes for a new novel. 'Is there *nothing* I can keep concealed in this house?' is Sebastian's roared reply (6). This line resonates, but why? Why do we feel that Sebastian is talking about something other than novel notes in a conversation about his next novel? In the given circumstances, Sebastian's reply flouts manner and quantity. He not only roars his response, we are purposely told, but he does so in a construction that Greenbaum and Quirk (1990: 427) have identified as an existential sentence ('Is there *nothing*') with a relative clause ('[that] I can keep concealed in this house?'). Such structures are similar to cleft sentences, where what might have been expressed in one finite clause is split into two instead. Cleft sentences and existential + relative clause constructions serve emphatic purposes, and in the example that Sebastian uses it is the already italicised *nothing* that is given further focus (Greenbaum and Quirk 1990: 427). Sebastian's reply, roared out and overly emphatic on the issue of how nothing can be kept hidden in his home, leads the audience to suspect that it is not really the novel notes he is worried about hiding.

Approaching the close of Act One, the audience has been able to use the clues given via the flouted maxims to reach a hypothesis that runs along the following lines. Lydia is ill, seriously enough to require regular visits to the doctor and multiple rounds of laboratory tests. Oddly, both Sebastian and Lydia down-play her visits to the doctor and insist (despite clear evidence to the contrary) that she is healthy. Relevant in some way to the present circumstances is Lydia's past, which involved some sort of trauma from which Sebastian apparently saved her. The problems in their current relationship may stem from this event. Sebastian, who cannot fail to notice his wife's condition, acts as though he does not care. This behaviour is so overdone, however, that the audience begins to suspect some other motive for it. Reinforcing this suspicion is his worry about keeping things concealed in his own home.

Questions regarding Sebastian's behaviour are kept active until the very end of Act One. It is at this point that Lydia collapses. For all Sebastian's supposed callousness, he drops everything and almost runs across the stage to assist her. While her collapse is explained away by too much drink, audiences at this point know better. Lydia is very ill, as we have suspected, and Sebastian not only knows but, we are now sure, also cares. His earlier failures to observe the maxims of quantity, relation, manner and sympathy have done their job, which is why this moment does not, as Rebellato (2001: xxvii) claims, 'jar with our understanding of Sebastian at this point'. According to Rebellato (2001: xxvii), we do not realise that Sebastian is putting on a cold front until 'towards the end of the play' when he confesses all to Mark. As a result, says Rebellato (2001), we lose sympathy for Sebastian when Lydia reveals the truth of her diagnosis, since what might have at first been considered 'amusing foibles' are now exposed as thoughtless, even callous behaviour (Rebellato 2001: xxix). This dependence on the overt revelations in the play leads Rebellato to view Sebastian's behaviour as 'the curious moment that ends Act I' (2001: xxvi). As the analysis has shown, however, the language of the play raises our suspicions about Sebastian from his very first lines. When he rushes to help Lydia, we integrate this information with what we have previously uncovered about him and discover that his behaviour at the end of Act One makes perfect sense. Sebastian does know about Lydia's illness, and is not the callous and hard-hearted creature he has been pretending to be.

When the interactions between Lydia and Sebastian are viewed through a Gricean framework, their confessions to Mark, widely understood as the 'all-purpose family confidante' (Young 1986: 187), slot into place not so much as revelations but as on-record confirmations of what had previously been conveyed off-record. In Act One, Lydia's candid discussion with Mark (10–17) reveals that she is not only ill, but in the terminal stages of the disease polyarteritis. While she is brutally truthful with Mark, she has been hiding her illness from Sebastian. It is also revealed that Lydia was a refugee, took part in the Estonian resistance, and spent time in a Russian labour camp where she was forced into sexual slavery. It was this latter situation from which Sebastian rescued her, but we further find out that Lydia thinks it was out of honour rather than love. While Lydia loves Sebastian, their marriage has been, Lydia believes, one of convenience on his part.

Lydia's confession to Mark can be read as a kind of 'reward' to the audience. Utterances that were noticeable because they flouted one of the maxims of conversation can now be fully understood. For example, what were flouts of manner for the audience when Lydia spoke to Sebastian about her 'wee-wee' tests are now revealed as violations at the character-character level of discourse. Lydia permits the inappropriate banter to quietly mislead Sebastian, allowing him to believe (she thinks) that her condition is no cause for real concern. Similarly, their shared insistence that the lab people wrote the lab report, a flout of quantity for the audience, is now revealed as a violation of quality at the character-character level. Lydia knows that her doctor has been giving her overly optimistic reports. What she does not know at this point is that he is doing so at Sebastian's request.

Sebastian's confession to Mark in Act Two (45–6) is also more confirmation than revelation for the audience. What were flouts of manner, sympathy, quantity and relation for the audience turn out to be violations of quality at the character-character level. Sebastian has been lying to Lydia with the intent of quietly misleading her in order to protect her (he thinks) from the truth of her illness. Sebastian reveals to Mark that he is acutely aware of Lydia's illness, and has been acting as though he does not care to shield her, having discovered that he loves her. While maintaining his false front, he has been ensuring that she sees the best doctors and gets the best care, all without her knowing. While this is clearly news to Mark, it may for the audience be more of an *Ah-ha! I-knew-it!* moment.

A similar strategy involving violations and flouts is used in Act Two. Sebastian and Lydia violate maxims in order to quietly mislead their son Joey, but audiences hear these as flouts, deliberate lies designed to protect the young man from some painful truths regarding his parents. As Rebellato (2001: xxv) has noted, *In Praise of Love* can be read as a debate concerning a commitment to the truth at all costs on one hand (embodied in the character of Joey), and the need for compassionate untruths on the other (represented by Sebastian and Lydia). An analysis of key interactions between each of the Cruttwells and their son in Act Two along Gricean lines brings this conflict between uncompromising truth and sheltering fiction into sharper focus.

As Act Two opens, Lydia and Joey are at home preparing to watch Joey's play, which debuts on television that evening. They expect to be joined by Mark, who arrives dressed specially for the occasion and bearing gifts; and by Sebastian, who arrives only after the play has finished, clearly having forgotten his son's big night. Lydia is put in the position of not only having to protect Joey from the truth of her illness, but also having to protect him from what she supposes at the time is his father's crass thoughtlessness.

This is apparent in the dialogue that occurs as Lydia and Joey wait for their guests. The stage directions very clearly indicate that Lydia comes from the kitchen with champagne and only three glasses, and Joey, noticing immediately that something is not right, asks why (33). Lydia responds like this:

> Lydia: Darling, if you forgive me, I think I'll stick to Vichy water (*She sits down, exhausted*) (33).

At the character-character level, Lydia has violated the maxim of manner here by being ambiguous. She lets Joey believe that she is not drinking because of her previous night's excess. As Lydia and the audience know, however, Lydia is affected more by her illness than her alcohol consumption of the night before. For the audience, then, Lydia's line here is a flout. She blatantly fails to disambiguate her statement, which prompts the audience to wonder why. The most likely conclusion given the context is that Lydia is letting Joey believe she is hung-over to prevent him from guessing that she is seriously ill. To ensure the implicature, Rattigan adds a stage direction that recalls the truth of her condition. Lydia 'sits down, exhausted', (33) much as she did when we first encountered her.

Violations from one character to another that get heard as flouts by the audience occur regularly while Lydia and Joey wait for Sebastian, as evidenced in the following extract that occurs later in Act Two.

Joey:	(*looking at his watch*) You don't suppose Dad's forgotten, do you?
Lydia:	Of course not. He's been talking of nothing else all day. Go on.
Joey:	Where is he?
Lydia:	They wanted him at the office. An obituary or something. He'll be well on his way back by now.
Joey:	Did you call him?
Lydia:	Yes. He said he'd be back in plenty of time.
Joey:	Good. (*He runs up the stairs*) (34).

In each of her turns above, Lydia violates the maxim of quality by lying to Joey, and Joey appears to innocently accept Lydia's explanations, concentrating most of his attention on preparing for the evening. For the audience, however, these are flouts, blatant lies. Given Sebastian's almost continual arguments with Joey in Act One, and his dismissive attitude towards Joey's play (27), we are quite certain that he has forgotten and will not make any special effort. Lydia's flouts, then, cue the audience that she is up to something for the sake of her son.

Once again, the audience's interpretative work is rewarded. While Joey is in the kitchen, Lydia gets straight on the phone to Prunella Larkin (a 'friend' of Sebastian's), desperately trying to find him (34). Her conversation dovetails with our suspicions that Sebastian has not remembered his son's debut. These suspicions are confirmed when Mark arrives. Lydia enlists him as a co-conspirator, arranging for him to leave again in order to call the flat so that she can pretend it is Sebastian phoning to report that he is watching the play with his editor. These violations of quality, the lies Lydia tells her son to protect him, are made all the more poignant by their occurrence alongside Joey's strident declarations that people should always be honest.

Joey:	but hell, Mum, that's *dishonest* (41).
Joey:	(*outraged*) We should *pretend*, you mean? (41).

Sebastian, too, does his part to protect Joey. In an uncharacteristically on-record conversation for him, Sebastian apologises to his son for being so deplorable a father as to miss the debut of his television play. In the middle of this conversation, Sebastian violates quality even as he declares to his son that he is telling the truth: 'The plain, sordid fact is that I forgot' (56). Readers and audiences, who have been privy to Sebastian's confession to Mark, hear this violation as a flout. We know that Sebastian is deliberately being less than truthful with his son, and our search for an interpretation that makes sense in context leads us back to Sebastian's heart-to-heart with Mark. On the day of Joey's premiere, Sebastian received official word that Lydia's illness was terminal. He did forget Joey's television debut, but had a good reason for doing so. Revealing this reason, however, would mean telling Joey about his mother, so Sebastian takes all the blame on himself, and pretends that he just forgot.

Consideration of off-record communication in *In Praise of Love* also provides a way to interpret the chess games that occur. For readers familiar with chess, this will be immediately apparent. For readers who do not play chess, the fact that two games are played, and that one of them goes on for some length (nine pages), are clues that the games are not simply background detail. Interestingly, the communicative possibilities of the chess games have not received much comment in the literature on the play. Most of the sources, in fact, either do not mention the chess games, or make only passing comments to them. It is surprising that more attention has not been paid to this aspect of the play, given that chess so readily lends itself to metaphor. Chess pieces (king, queen, bishop, knight, rook) and pawns are symbolic in themselves (e.g. success requires checkmating the opponent's king, but the queen is the most powerful piece on the board; pawns, overtly the least powerful, covertly control the mobility of the higher-ranking pieces) (Harwood 1975: 12; Eade 1999), and the game, dialectical in nature with 'attacking gambits' and 'dashing sacrifices' (Harwood 1975: 34, 50), can be used to represent conflicts not only of war (the historic origin of the game), but also of love, sex, politics, morality, religion, and race (Harwood 1975: 9). Careful attention to the chess games represented during *In Praise of Love* shows that they are not played for their own sake, but serve as metaphors, tools of off-record communication. As Brown and Levinson (1978/1987: 222) note, metaphors, which are 'literally false', invite implicatures by failing to observe the maxim of quality.

The first chess game is between Sebastian and Mark in Act One and occurs after Lydia's confession to Mark. Thus, the audience knows that Lydia is dying, and also knows that Mark knows this. Mark and Lydia think Sebastian ignorant of the situation, but there is, as established earlier, enough evidence to suggest that Sebastian is not as oblivious or uncaring as he seems. What might the chess game metaphorically communicate about the situation between Sebastian, Lydia, and Mark? While for Young (1986: 187) the typical love-triangle situation in Rattigan's plays is in *In Praise of Love* more or less settled, with Lydia, Sebastian and Mark living 'in an atmosphere of friendly compatibility', closer study of the chess game in Act One reveals that the conflict between the two men over Lydia is either ongoing, or has resurfaced in response to her illness.

While the game between Sebastian and Mark is not presented in sufficient detail to follow move by move (player turns occur out of sequence, and moves are left unspecified), the details that have been given, in combination with the surrounding discourse, can be read as off-record tips to the audience concerning Sebastian's behaviour. Just prior to the chess game, for example, Sebastian sees Lydia and Mark embracing twice. Lydia and Mark show no embarrassment, and Sebastian is apparently not bothered either. He ignores the first embrace, and responds with banter to the second ('Have you two nothing better to do?': 20). Close attention to the text, however, reveals that the audience is invited, via the metaphor of the chess game, to believe that Sebastian might actually be very bothered by their intimacy.

The game opens with Mark, playing white, moving the pawn in front of his queen two spaces forward (four spaces from his back rank, so 'Pawn to queen four').[5] Sebastian comments on this immediately ('Pawn to *Queen* four? What's the matter? You've got bored with pawn to King four?': 21). Pawn to King four, moving the pawn in front of the king two spaces forward, is the more usual opening. It allows for more 'open' games with greater mobility and greater potential control of the centre of the board (often the key to winning the game). Pawn to Queen four, by contrast, often leads to more closed games. Movements of pieces are more restricted, and much of the play occurs outside the centre of the board. In effect, the play is more furtive and less direct. In addition, this opening, while it restricts the mobility of the queen, also makes her less vulnerable.

This state of play, opening with Pawn to Queen four, mirrors the situation Mark and Sebastian find themselves in. They are in a contest for Lydia (the queen), but they cannot engage in open battle because of the secret of her illness. With his first move of the game, Mark signals his intention to protect Lydia, and his recognition that he must nevertheless avoid open combat with Sebastian while he does so.

We are next told that Sebastian answers appropriately, and this is very likely to be the mirroring move, moving his queen's pawn four spaces to directly face Mark's pawn. It is now Mark's move again. While we are not told precisely what it is, we are told that as Sebastian studies the board, he says 'Ah. The Queen's gambit' (21). This means that Mark has moved the pawn in front of his queen's bishop two spaces to be in a position to capture Sebastian's pawn. However, since Sebastian has the next move, he can capture Mark's pawn before Mark can attack. In effect, Mark offers a sacrifice (a 'gambit' is an opening move that involves a sacrifice, usually a pawn), which Sebastian can either accept or decline. If Sebastian accepts, he will have weakened Mark's position in terms of material (number of pieces and pawns), but will have lost some vital control over the centre of the board. For this reason, the queen's gambit is usually declined, i.e. players forgo the gain in material to keep their position of strength in the centre. Notice, however, that Sebastian accepts the gambit, and thus the loss of control. Here again, the chess game suggests a metaphor for the conflict between the two men over Lydia. With his move, Sebastian signals not only that he is going to enter into combat, but also that he is going to accept the established terms of covert warfare.

Just as Sebastian has accepted the Queen's gambit, Lydia appears, flaunting the new mink wrap that Mark has given her (22). As Lydia herself notes, it is not entirely appropriate for Mark to give such a gift to the wife of another man. Nevertheless, she accepts the gift, vowing to never take it off, and enters the room (22). However, the same stage direction also reveals that she is 'unobserved'. Sebastian does eventually notice her, but says nothing about the wrap ('Darling, can you leave the ashtrays till later? It's a bit distracting, all that moving about': 22). Apparently, he has not noticed the (inappropriate) gift, which prompts Lydia to point it out. Still, Sebastian is apparently unmoved, replying first with only minimal responses, and then suggesting that she may be too old for such a garment. These flouts of quantity and sympathy raise questions. Can Sebastian really not care about Mark's gift? Has he really not noticed? Is he really not upset? Is his insult a way of showing his displeasure, or simply part of his callous attitude towards Lydia? What is going on with these three people? While the on-record answers to these questions are not provided until Sebastian's confession in Act Two, more evidence of what the audience is beginning to suspect (that Sebastian has seen and is bothered) is provided off-record via metaphor in the chess game.

After Sebastian's hurtful comment about the mink, Lydia loses her temper and swats Sebastian with the wrap, disturbing several game pieces as she does so. Sebastian takes advantage of this moment to change his previous move. Instead of reconfirming his acceptance of the queen's gambit, he announces that he had just moved his pawn to King three (22), the classic move in the Queen's gambit *declined* game. On the face of it, this is cheating, something that can certainly be expected of Sebastian at this point. But metaphorically, it can also be read as an off-record indication that Sebastian has changed the rules of engagement between himself and Mark. He is not happy about their intimate embraces, he is not pleased by Mark's gift to his wife, and he signals this by making a chess move, albeit an illegal one, indicative of a more open conflict.

The next major move in the chess game is from Mark, who castles. This involves moving the king two spaces towards either corner of the board, and then placing the rook on the square just vacated by the king. This is a protective move, as the corners are generally safer, and the king is now protected by the rook and, very probably, several pawns. It is a prudent move, and not unusual in the Queen's gambit declined game, which Sebastian and Mark may indeed be playing (Mark does not challenge Sebastian's cheating move). In the Queen's gambit declined game, both players can be expected to make this move. And yet, Sebastian rather savagely characterises Mark's castling as cowardly (24). Why? Mark would typically castle at a point when Sebastian has gained reasonable control of the centre, but when he, Mark, has more freedom of movement. Once again, the state of play metaphorically reflects the conflict between the two men. While Sebastian may be married to Lydia (he thus 'controls the centre'), it is Mark who can openly show concern (he has 'greater freedom of movement'). Reference to the context surrounding the game at this moment makes the point even clearer. Lydia, who has remained on stage since swinging her wrap at Sebastian, takes two pills. Mark, who knows of her condition, can show concern without revealing this knowledge, and says ('sharply', we are told) 'You've already had two of those' (23). As we later discover in Sebastian's confession to Mark, Sebastian is just as aware as Mark is of the pills, but cannot at this point show his concern without revealing his secret: that he knows and cares about Lydia's illness. The metaphor of the chess game invites the implicature that it is jealousy at Mark's show of concern that provokes Sebastian's comment regarding Mark's cowardice.

The game continues, and the talk turns to when Mark first met Lydia and Sebastian. With the same mix of apparent disinterest and distancing humour that he has shown throughout Act One, Sebastian recounts how Mark had told him on the night they met that he (Mark) was in love with Lydia, and planning to steal her away. Not long into the story, Mark reveals that he might still be in love with Lydia. At the end of this interaction, talk about chess once again serves as an off-record metaphor for talk about Sebastian, Lydia and Mark. Sebastian asks 'Are you making that move?' (26), but can be understood to be asking 'Are you still planning to steal my wife?' Mark's answer is equally revealing. With supposed reference to the chess game, he indicates that he does not yet know what he has decided. While Mark reports a next move, we are not told exactly what it is, only that Sebastian thinks it is silly. Sebastian's answering move, while equally unspecified, makes his emotional position, if not his position on the board, very clear: 'This move will lead to your ultimate annihilation'(26) (i.e., stay away from my wife). Mark, however, turns out to be equal to the battle. He belittles Sebastian's move (26), and then puts Sebastian in check. Sebastian replies by passing off his blunder (being put in check) as a superior move that actually has Mark in a trap. Joey, who has just arrived, notices immediately that in reality, it is the other way around. It is Mark who has Sebastian in a trap. While Joey is referring only to the chess game, the metaphoric meaning available is that Sebastian is trapped by the circumstances of his life. The nature of the trap becomes clear after his confession to Mark. As long as Sebastian is hemmed in by his own pretence of not caring for Lydia, he cannot fight openly for her.

Sebastian signals his realisation of this bind in his final move which, he says while helping Lydia after her collapse, 'would have been pawn to Queen's rook three' (32). This is a flanking move, a move away from the centre that postpones immediate gratification. Direct attack of one's opponent is put off in favour of attempting to weaken their game by stealthier means. While Sebastian may want to tell Mark to leave his wife alone, he can see that this will hurt her and so does not do so. For Lydia's sake, he will not provoke an open conflict with Mark, but the implication is clear – Mark had best watch his step. In the end, conflict between the two men does not develop, since Mark never actually 'makes his move'. True friend that he is, he graciously bows out of the contest after hearing the truth from Sebastian.

The chess game in Act One also suggests that Sebastian may actually know of Lydia's condition and how serious it is. Once again, this is communicated off-record and the audience is invited to do the interpretative work. During the game, Sebastian quotes Shakespeare on death ('Ay, but to die and go we know not where; To lie in cold obstruction and to rot': 26), something Young (1986: 189–90) notices but does not explain with reference to Grice (1975). Mark is so alarmed by Sebastian's quote that it arrests him in his play. As the stage directions indicate, he had been about to make a move, but 'stops with his hand on the piece, staring at Sebastian' (26). For Mark, Sebastian has flouted the maxim of relation. Why quote Shakespeare, on death of all topics, in the middle of a chess game? As he stares at Sebastian, both he and the audience are searching for an implicature, an answer to that question. Given what is known at this point in the play about Lydia's physical state, her visits to the doctor, and her tests, audiences, like Mark, may well suspect at this point that Sebastian is aware Lydia is dying. On-record, Mark asks why Sebastian quoted that particular verse, and accepts his explanation that it is part of an article he is working on. Off-record, however, the audience has one more piece of evidence.

A second chess game occurs towards the end of Act Two, this one between father and son. As with the game in Act One, it is not played for its own sake. Sebastian mixes up the placement of the King and Queen as he and Joey sit down to play, the error of a rank amateur (Whyld 1993: 19). How is this to be understood? This flout of quality (Sebastian is clearly not a novice player) invites the implicature that Sebastian has purposely made this error in order to foster a resolution with this son. It allows Joey to win, and Sebastian to be (for once) a gracious loser. This error also allows the play to end 'with the right pieces in the right places' (57), a metaphor for the restoration of harmony in the family. Symbolically, they are clearing the board and starting over while they still have time. Sebastian continues to keep up the pretence ('Oh sorry, darling. Didn't see you were still there': 58), but it no longer matters. The truth is out.

As shown in this chapter, a Gricean analysis of the dialogue has revealed how readers and viewers are able to piece together the truth of the Crutwells' relationship for themselves. Key pieces of information are conveyed off-record first, and only made fully explicit later. Flouts of maxims at the playwright-audience level of discourse in Act One are in Act Two revealed to have been violations at the character-character level as Lydia and Sebastian secretly attempt to protect each other. The investigation has also shown how the chess games, so infrequently analysed in previous work, potentially operate as important vehicles of off-record communication. In the next and final analysis chapter, we will consider the play *Just Between Ourselves* by Alan Ayckbourn, another playwright whose linguistic achievements have been largely overlooked in the critical record.

Chapter 6

Talking at the Edge
Alan Ayckbourn's
Just Between Ourselves

As unlikely as it may seem today given his current standing in the world of the theatre, Alan Ayckbourn's work did not meet with instant critical acclaim. While his professional debut as a playwright was made in 1959 not long after the advent of the 'angry young men' in 1956, he chose to write comedies that dealt with the private concerns of the middle class (Tucker 2003: 71; Holt 1999: 11; Distler 1991; Ruskino 1991: 41; Page 1983: 44) set, as Taylor (1981: 183) remarked, 'wherever in the scampi-belt the garden gnomes grow thickest'. He was not overtly political in his drama (Fisher 1996: 23; Page 1983: 44), nor was he especially interested (at least early in his career) in challenging the nature or existence of reality (Taylor 1981: 182–3; Fisher 1996: 24). To top it all off, he also achieved commercial success. As Holt (1999: 11) has put it, he focused on the 'wrong' class, wrote in the 'wrong' genre, and presented a 'wrong basic attitude'. Identified as an inheritor of Rattigan (Tucker 2003: 71; Holt 1999: 1–2; Taylor 1981: 183), he was initially dismissed as a writer of lightweight comedies that were suited to the tastes of holiday audiences in Scarborough (Holt 1999: 1; Distler 1991; Rusinko 1991: 41).

While a number of turning points in Ayckbourn's critical reception have been identified (e.g. see Tucker 2003; Fisher 1996: 22; Distler 1991; Hornby 1991: 109; Rusinko 1991: 42), a fair summation of this material is that the tide began to turn in the mid-1970s with the *The Norman Conquests* and the National Theatre production of *Bedroom Farce*, picked up speed with the publication of Billington's 1983 study, the first significant book-length treatment of Ayckbourn's work, and was secured with the critically acclaimed production of *Woman in Mind* (London, 1986). Much of the material located for review written after 1980 is united in the stance that Ayckbourn's early dismissal as a popular but insignificant writer of comedies was unfair, and concerned to show that his work, while certainly comic, nevertheless presented probing studies of ordinary people in extraordinary pain, more often than not brought on by the casual thoughtlessness of their intimates (Tucker 2003: 71; Holt 1999; Distler 1991; Hornby 1991; Rusinko 1991: 41; Blistein 1983: 34; Page 1983).

Just Between Ourselves (Scarborough, 1976; London, 1977) was one of the plays in the mid-1970s that helped to bring about a change in the way critics responded to Ayckbourn's work. The play revolves around Dennis and Vera, a married couple in their 40s, Dennis's mother Marjorie, who lives with them, and Neil and Pam, a younger couple in their 30s. They meet several times to celebrate various birthdays, and it becomes increasingly clear that Vera may be seriously depressed. Dennis only adds to the problem, ignoring the situation when he can and turning it into a joke when he cannot.

Like Vera, Pam feels trapped in her marriage. After giving up a promising career and financial independence to be a wife and mother, she regrets her choice and grows increasingly resentful of her husband Neil. At the close of the play, Pam's escape is left ambiguous. She is temporarily back with Neil after a separation, but only while 'working on her qualifications' (69). Vera's fate, however, is clearer and clearly more bleak. She has lost the battle with Dennis's mother, who serves the coffee (obviously enjoying keeping house for her son) while Vera sits swaddled in a blanket in a near catatonic state, barely speaking or eating. The pain of her loss is made all the greater by the final cruelty: on this Saturday, the birthday being celebrated is hers.

As Ayckbourn himself has said, the play was written during the winter storms of December for a January opening, and this perhaps resulted in 'a rather sad (some say a rather savage) play with themes concerned with total lack of understanding, with growing old and with spiritual and mental collapse' (1979: 7–8). Some considered it to be one of the plays that demonstrated an expansion in Ayckbourn's range (Distler 1991: 157), a shift from writing farce to writing about 'real people in real trouble' (Page 1983: 43). Page (1983: 38) also thought it very effectively demonstrated Ayckbourn's talent for writing 'the scene that is both amusing and disturbing'. A number of readings have been offered, most of them compatible with Allen's (2001: 158) succinctly articulated view that the play is about 'unhappiness so desperate that it drives people mad'. Billington (1983: 111) described it as 'an uncompromising study of uncomprehending destructiveness', a 'bleak, mordant, biting tragic-comedy about what Terence Rattigan once called the real *vice anglais*: fear of expressing emotion'. In sympathy with this view, Hornby (1991: 104) points to the essential irony of the title, noting that *Just Between Ourselves* is actually a play about 'emotional isolation'. Vera and Dennis, as well as Pam and Neil, are trapped in lonely, soul-destroying marriages, a recurring theme in Ayckbourn's work (Londré 1991: 89; Billington 1983: 1; Page 1983: 44). Postlewait (1991: 67) points to another recurring theme evident in *Just Between Ourselves*, particularly in the character of Vera – the struggle against confining systems that are powerful, but mostly arbitrary and unnecessary (see also Holt 1999: 25, who makes a similar point about husbands in Ayckbourn's work).

As noted earlier, Ayckbourn is not especially noted for dealing with overtly political subjects, but a number of critics have expressed surprise that feminists have paid him so little attention (e.g. Page 1983: 37). According to Billington (1983: 115), there is an implicitly feminist theme running through much of Ayckbourn's work, and it is especially apparent in *Just Between Ourselves* with the wasted lives of both Pam and Vera. Londré (1991) suggests a reason for the feminist dismissal of Ayckbourn's apparently feminist work. While she acknowledges that many male characters are also unsympathetically drawn in Ayckbourn's drama, she suggests that the female characters were, almost without exception, not worthy of feminist attention until the appearance of Suzy in *Mr A's Amazing Maze Plays* (1991: 99). Prior to this, argues

Londré, Ayckbourn's female characters were either confined to largely stereotypic roles (wife, mother, etc.) or defined entirely by their relationships with men.

Interestingly, very few of these readings have considered the role of language in the dialogue. In fact, Ayckbourn's use of language does not emerge as a particularly salient topic in the literature on his work at all, unless it is with reference to what Ayckbourn does not do with language. It has been noted several times, for instance, that witty turns of phrase – the clever one-liners (Blistein 1983), the 'verbal jokes' (Hornby 1991: 104), the 'careful barbed verbal responses' (Holt 1999: 30) – are not how Ayckbourn achieves his effects, and what critics seem most impressed by are his technical theatrical skills, in particular his innovative manipulations of time and space (Holt 1999: 30; Postlewait 1991: 67; Blistein 1983: 34), and his feel for theatre-in-the-round (Holt 1999: 5). Critics typically cite as the primary influence on Ayckbourn's writing not his ear for dialogue or his gift for rendering the vernacular, but his experience as an actor, director and theatre manager (Holt 1999; Blistein 1983: 34; Page 1983: 37).

Critics have also been impressed by the visual aspects of Ayckbourn's plays, and Ayckbourn himself has stressed the visual over the verbal in discussions of his work (in an interview with Dukore 1991: 19). Dukore (1991: 75) connects space and environment with character, suggesting that 'Ayckbourn's settings, his plays' visual environment, reveal the characters who inhabit them', and Hornby (1991: 109) makes a similar point, noting that the characters' interactions with various props (e.g. kettles, doors, tools, etc.) represent their interactions with each other.

Holt (1999) has shown more interest than many other Ayckbourn critics in the playwright's language, describing him as 'a wordsmith of great precision' (31). With the following example from Tristram, the young solicitor in *Taking Steps* (1979), he attempts to demonstrate 'his sensitivity to speech patterns and the care with which words are placed' (31–2). Tristram is delivering some papers to a client for his employer.

> Yes … Sorry, my name's … No, I'm from Speake, Tacket and … er … Whatsname … Sorry. Hot. I'm – my name's … er … well, I'm here on behalf of Mr Winthrop who's been … er … taken ill, you see. Not seriously. So, I'm here instead (Ayckbourn 1979 *Taking Steps*, cited in Holt 1999: 32).

Holt (1999) concludes that this speech presents 'a wonderful character sketch of a very anxious young man labouring under his first responsibility' (32). While this is a perfectly reasonable conclusion, Holt's (1999) account could have gone further to illustrate how this conclusion is related to the language of the text, the 'speech patterns' and the 'care with which words are placed'. Only two specific examples are identified, the single word 'hot' and the phrase 'not seriously'. What Holt (1999) means by 'speech patterns' is not specified. Instead, he concentrates on the word and the phrase, suggesting that

> 'Hot' seems at first either misplaced or a non sequitur, until one realizes that it is an excuse to cover embarrassment. Then it seems perfectly positioned to give the actor maximum

opportunity, especially when, almost immediately, it is followed by the confusing double meaning of 'Not seriously' (Holt 1999: 32).

The portrait of an anxious young man, however, is drawn by much more than the word 'Hot' and the phrase 'Not seriously'. It is not the words and phrases and their placement that are best suited to support Holt's (1999) argument, but the construction of turns. This can be demonstrated by looking at Tan's (1998) stylistic analysis of another bumbling Ayckbourn character, Henry in *The Revengers' Comedies* (1989).[1] When Holt's (1999) work is compared to Tan's (1998), we find that there is a great deal more to say about Ayckbourn's language and the characters he creates.

Tan (1998: 166) looks at the opening scene where Henry first encounters Karen, noting that they meet on the bridge where both of them have gone to commit suicide, and it is Karen's failed attempt that distracts Henry from his own as he goes to help her instead of killing himself. Tan (1998: 166) begins his analysis with a study of Henry's turn-taking behaviour, noticing that when Henry interacts with Karen he appears to have trouble completing his turns. They occur with a number of hesitations and filled pauses, often in incomplete grammatical units (e.g. 'Look, I think I'd better …'). Tan (1998) further notes that this degree of tentativeness is not only unusual, but also comic, since it occurs in a speech act that offers help to Karen in a moment of urgent need. This very urgency normally licenses direct and unmitigated speech acts (Brown and Levinson 1978/1987), yet Henry hesitates and shows concern for Karen's negative face, her desire to remain free from imposition, even as she hangs precariously from a bridge ('Would you mind if I – tried to lift you …?') (Tan 1998: 169) (see also discussion of politeness theory in Chapter 2).

When this type of analysis is applied to Tristram's turn in the excerpt from *Taking Steps* cited in Holt (1999), it becomes clear that the perception of Tristram as an anxious young man arises in large part from his severe difficulty in completing, or even starting, a turn. In just five sentences, there are three pauses (marked by '…'), three filled pauses (marked by 'er'), and three false starts, instances where the speaker begins a turn, but stops suddenly to begin it again in a different way (Yes …; Sorry, my name's …; I'm – my name's …). While hesitations and false starts occur normally in talk (see Chapter 1), the appearance of so many in such a short space of time, especially surrounding attempts to give one's own name, represents an unusual degree of difficulty in bringing a turn to completion. While Holt (1999) attempts to account for his impression of Tristram by looking at a word and a phrase, it is clear that the investigation of turn construction features is the more productive avenue for analysis.

Witty one-liners may not be a signature Ayckbourn feature, and what Tan (1998: 166) suggests of *The Revengers' Comedies* is also true of *Just Between Ourselves* – the dialogue is not especially 'poetic' or 'lyrical'. Such characteristics do not mean, however, that language in Ayckbourn's dialogue is not worth studying. When the dialogue is subject to a linguistic analysis, we find that language is just as important as visual metaphor in revealing Ayckbourn's characters, 'the very heart and soul of his plays' (Fisher 1996: 23). Vera, for example, is typically seen as the product of what was for her generation a conventional upbringing. This has left her inarticulate, unassertive, and inhibited (Cornish and Ketels 1986: 6), as well as vulnerable to Dennis's constant put-down humour (Holt 1999: 26; Hornby 1991: 108; Billington 1983: 111). There is certainly much in her language that drives this interpretation. Her usual tendency is towards the expression of negative politeness, which stresses the wish not to impose on others more than is absolutely necessary (see discussion of Brown and Levinson 1978/1987 in Chapter 2). This is evident in some of her requests, such as 'Dennis dear, can you open the door for me, please? It's stuck again' (15). With the exception of the endearment *dear*, this request is negatively polite. Phrased as a question concerning Dennis's ability, it is conventionally indirect rather than direct, and followed by a stated reason for making the request (*It's stuck again*). This, as Brown and Levinson (1978/1987) note, allows her to imply that she ordinarily 'wouldn't dream of infringing H's negative face' (189). When making a request of Neil, an acquaintance rather than an intimate, her expression of negative politeness is even stronger, as in

> Neil, I wonder if you'd be very kind and ask Dennis if he would look out the chairs for us. They're probably tucked away at the back there somewhere. Only he's the only one who'll know where he put them (36).[2]

With the conditional hedging clause *I wonder if you'd be very kind*, Vera signals that she is not presuming Neil will agree to the request. She further minimizes the imposition by giving what information she can to help (*They're probably tucked away at the back there somewhere*) and, as she did before, gives a reason for making the request (*Only he's the only one who'll know where he put them*). Even in a very frank talk with Pam about the state of their lives (37–9), Vera tends towards negative politeness, taking care to minimize the force of her statements with hedging devices such as 'I think' (37), 'probably' (37), and 'I suppose' (38).

There are also times when Vera expresses not just negative politeness, but what is arguably true tentativeness, actual doubt. When Pam asks if it was Vera's idea to sell the car, Vera is too emphatic in her reply.

> Vera: Er – yes. I think it was, yes. I mean, after all it's my car. Dennis bought it for me but it is mine (37).

She responds to Pam's question with two affirmatives, and follows these with two assertions that the car is hers. The first of these assertions is aggravated, strengthened in force, with the discourse marker *I mean* and the adverbial *after all*. In being too informative for the purposes of the given exchange, these are flouts of the maxim of quantity (Grice 1975) at the audience/playwright level of discourse (Short 1989), and they cause us to doubt if even Vera really believes what she is saying (see discussion of Grice 1975 and Short 1989 in Chapter 2 and Chapter 5).

All of this adds up to a character who tries to do what is expected of her and simply seeks to stay out of the way, an interpretation that is much in keeping with the consensus view on Vera in the literature. There is, however, much more to Vera than this. A spirited and articulate woman is visible just beneath the frayed surface if we look more closely at the interactional potential of joking in the dialogue. This is the Vera that once was or might have been before the 'last vestiges of self-confidence are drained from her' (Ayckbourn 1979: 8).

As Brown and Levinson (1978/1987: 124) have observed, joking is not only a means of ridicule, but can also serve as a positive politeness device, a way of enhancing intimacy. Since jokes assume shared values and common ground between interlocutors, they can also be used to assert these things (Brown and Levinson 1978/1987: 229). Of course, this strategy only works if values are actually shared and common ground does actually exist (Tannen 1984: 129). Jokes are a poor means of establishing rapport if the recipient is offended, and evidence of this kind of interaction between Vera and Dennis is easy to find in the play. A particularly clear example is provided in the much-cited interchange (e.g., Allen 2001: 157; Cornish and Ketels 1986: 6; Page 1983: 40; Billington 1983: 112–13) where Dennis teases Vera for 'catching' things with her elbow.

1 Dennis:	[…] If I told you, Mr Andrews, the things my wife had caught
2	with her elbow …
3 Vera:	[*shy and embarrassed*] All right.
4 Dennis:	You would not believe it, Mr Andrews, cups, saucers, dinner plates,
5	radio sets …
6 Neil:	Really.
7 Dennis:	Whole tray of glasses.
8 Vera:	Dennis …
9 Dennis:	And that's just for this month. You ever want a demolition job
10	doing, Mr Andrews, she's your woman. [*he laughs*]
11	[NEIL *joins in halfheartedly*]
12	[VERA *less so still*]
13	Elbows going away like pistons …
14 Neil:	Well, I suppose we all tend to … occasionally (16–17).

Here, Dennis's attempts at positive politeness joking do not succeed in reflecting or asserting intimacy. Quite the opposite. Vera is, as the stage directions specify, 'shy and embarrassed'. She begins what is most likely a Request for Action in line 8 in an attempt to put an end to the teasing, and her laughter is forced. Neil can see her discomfort and is clearly embarrassed. He attempts to steer a path between Dennis and Vera, making a prospected Positive Response to Dennis that manages to agree with his Assessments while diverting attention away from Vera (line 14).

There are times, however, when an analysis of the joking behaviour in the dialogue shows us a very different Vera. This is evident in a rarely cited interaction between Dennis and Vera in Act One, Scene Two (39–40). It is Dennis's birthday, and he and Neil join Vera and Pam on the patio. Dennis enters announcing his star sign, Taurus the Bull. Vera asks Dennis to get some chairs from the garage, but does so with a joke that works as a positive politeness strategy.

What about some chairs then, Mr Taurus? We're both standing around here like sore thumbs (39).

Requests such as Vera's above that are realized as jokes work by attempting to minimize the imposition of the request through 'positive politeness optimism', the assumption that the hearer wants for the speaker what the speaker wants: impositions are less likely to cause offence if the hearer, the recipient of the request, wants what the speaker wants anyway (Brown and Levinson 1978/1987: 228).

Vera's request leads to an exchange of banter with Dennis, a series of playful jokes and insults. As Brown and Levinson (1978/1987) note, intimate relationships tend to be characterized by a low risk of threat to face, and jokes and light-hearted insults between intimates can reflect and reinforce this low face-threat environment. Dennis resists complying with Vera's request with a joke of his own, a pseudo off-record[3] suggestion that Vera is too weak to get the chairs himself ('Oh dear me, they're not that heavy': 39), and Vera counters with an equally insulting suggestion concerning his poor behaviour ('Get on with you. I'm glad it's not your birthday everyday': 39). They then become fully explicit. Dennis warns Vera not to go too far, since the football scores have him feeling anxious, but Vera remains undaunted. She makes two bald-on-record insults ('Oh, sport, sport, sport': 40 / 'Every Saturday afternoon, running, kicking, shooting, jumping. All afternoon': 40), and when Dennis asserts that she likes the wrestling in an Informative:Report, her Challenge, as indicated below, is not only bald-on-record, but aggravated (with *at all* and *great flabby things*)

Vera: I don't like it all. Great flabby things.

While it might be tempting to argue that such moves are not good natured teasing but just more examples of discord in the marriage, the text does not support this interpretation of the given interaction. The jokes and insults are reciprocal rather than unidirectional (in response to Vera's Challenge above, Dennis leaps at her 'ape-like': 40), and there are no stage-directions indicating annoyance or tension. In addition, Pam and Neil show no signs of awkwardness or embarrassment. Perhaps most tellingly, Vera is not dropping anything or stumbling. Here we see a spirited Vera holding her own with Dennis as the two of them enjoy teasing each other. Here also we see what might have been between the two of them, the wasted potential of a couple that might just have been in love once upon a time.

We see more and more of this other Vera the closer she gets to breaking point. She is quite capable, for example, of using humour that wounds Dennis. He is not amused when Vera mocks his mother by pretending to be her, directly performing (Toolan 1988) what are purported to be Marjorie's own words.

Vera: Sixty-seven today. I don't look sixty-seven do I Dennis? Everyone was amazed when they heard I was sixty-seven (55).

Rather than reciprocate Vera's humour here, Dennis tries to put a stop to the mockery with two Requests for Action, suggesting that Vera 'calm down' and just wish his mother a happy birthday (55).

Vera also shows us that she is capable of expressing herself without any hesitation or tentativeness. In the following Request for Action to Dennis, for example, she is direct and bald-on-record.

> Vera: Dennis, will you please come down at once. Come into the house, go into the sitting room and ask your mother, ever so nicely, if she would mind turning down the television (55).

Please in combination with the modal *will* is peremptory rather than negatively polite in a declarative sentence (after Brown and Levinson 1978/1987: 135), and the request is further aggravated by *at once*. In addition, three of the clauses in the second sentence are in the imperative mood (*come, go, ask*), the most direct way of phrasing a request.

Just before she snaps, Vera tells Marjorie what the interfering old woman so richly deserves to hear in a number of aggravated, bald-on-record Informative: Assessment: Criticisms.

> Vera: You poisonous old woman (63).

> Vera: You nasty old toad (63).

> Vera: Bitch, bitch, bitch (63).

While perhaps darkly comic for the audience, this is clearly not an instance of playful banter between the two women. Nowhere in the play is there evidence of a rapport between the two women, and neither Marjorie nor Dennis treat these Criticisms as playful banter. Any lingering doubt regarding Vera's intention is quickly dispelled with her Directive: Mandative:Threat, in which she advances on Marjorie with the electric drill, wanting to 'sandpaper [her] rotten face' (63).

Vera's bald-on-record behaviour here is also interesting in light of the relationship between this strategy and power. As Brown and Levinson (1978/1987: 228) note, powerful, high-status speakers have little need to worry about the consequences of face-threats to their less powerful, lower-status interlocutors, which is what licenses the relatively direct, unmitigated requests made, for example, by employers to their employees (e.g., *Have the papers ready for tomorrow*). It is because of this association between bald-on-record speech acts and powerful speakers that bald-on-record acts can be used to claim or assert power (Brown and Levinson 1978/1987: 228), and this is what Vera seems to do in her last substantive speech acts of the play. Just before breaking point, she asserts the last of her power, speaking as though she no longer fears the consequences of openly and publicly threatening Marjorie's face (and body, as it happens). When we next see Vera, utterly defeated, this is all the more heart-rending because we are aware of the spirited, energetic woman she might or could have been at one point, no matter how warped that spirit and energy became in the end.

Dennis's character has also been closely investigated in the critical literature. It is frequently pointed out that he is not intentionally unkind to Vera, just incapable and unaware (Holt 1999: 26; Hornby 1991: 108; Page 1983; 42). Instead of dealing with his problems he prefers to hide, particularly in his garage (Holt 1999; 26; Cornish and Ketels 1986: 2; Billington 1983). For Dukore (1991: 75), this location is a symbol of Dennis's retreat from both his home and his wife. It has also been observed that 'Dennis treats people like objects and objects like people' (Hornby 1991: 109), and attempts to fix appliances when what really needs attention is his marriage (Holt 1999: 26). This commitment to avoidance results in behaviour that is callous and thoughtless, although not deliberately so. Dennis is simply a 'know-it-all' with no real expertise (Hornby 1991: 108), blithely sending Neil down the path of financial destruction with his investment advice, and slowly driving his wife mad, secure in the knowledge that he understands her (Page 1983: 44). For Hornby (1991: 103), Dennis, like many other Ayckbourn males, is a kind of twisted tragic hero: he unknowingly commits foul deeds, but never realizes what he has done.

Dennis's behaviour has been explained a number of times, usually with reference to popular psychology. Billington (1983: 114) and Hornby (1991: 109), for example, both point to Dennis's difficult childhood, seeing him as a product of a negligent father and an overbearing mother. Allen (2001: 158) reasons that because Dennis's failure to understand Vera's needs is a wilful failure, a refusal to see what is right under his nose, he 'therefore at some level knows he is withholding himself from her'. While these observations provide valuable insights into what Dennis is like and why he behaves the way he does, Dennis's language is an equally important component in how he is drawn for the audience and also needs to be considered. When we look at how Dennis talks, we see someone who does not listen and who is almost entirely self-absorbed, only minimally engaging with those around him.

The extent to which Dennis uses things to insulate himself from people is reflected in his language, which is at times so heavily deictic that really only he can know what it means. Deixis can be explained as the relationship that exists between the speaker, his or her context of utterance, and the utterance itself (Herman 1995: 26). When linguistic items are used deictically, they can only be understood with reference to the speaker's perspective and environment. The classic examples of deictic usage are the first and second person personal pronouns (*I*, *you*, etc.), adverbs such as *here* and *there*, demonstrative pronouns (*this*, *that*, *these*, *those*), and temporal expressions such as *now* and *then* (Levinson 1983: 54). The deictic context originates from the speaker, and includes his or her interlocutor(s) and immediate environment (Herman 1995: 26). What is so unusual about Dennis is the focus on things in his deictic circle at the expense of other people. This is evident from the very first time we see Dennis. As the play opens, Dennis is alone in his garage frowning at the kettle.

Dennis: That goes in there … and then that one goes … through there to that one … which should join up with the other one (15).

Dennis's first clause of the play begins with a demonstrative pronoun *that*, referring to something only he can see clearly. This thing goes to a location that only Dennis knows, identified for the audience simply by the adverb *there*. The second and third clauses work in a similar way with a second item known only to Dennis (*that one*) going to another location only he knows (*through there*) to join another item (*that one*), which in turn will join with either one of the already mentioned items, or some new item (*the other one*). Only Dennis could say for sure. While Dennis works on the kettle, Vera has to fight for his attention. She makes two summoning turns, calling Dennis by name twice, but he continues talking to himself, with the deictic use of *that one* ('that one ... should be joined to that one ...': 15), before answering.

Dennis's attention is only temporarily wrested from the kettle. After perfunctorily answering Vera's summons, he immediately returns to his task, the placement of the items denoted by *that* and *that one*. This continues with another summons-answer pair which immediately follows. Vera again summons Dennis by name, and he completes the adjacency pair with an answer ('Come in': 15), but then immediately returns to working on the kettle and talking to himself. The speech act performed in his answering turn, an invitation, is in any case infelicitous, since one of its constituting conditions is not met (Searle 1969) – Vera cannot possibly enter the garage because its door is, as always, stuck. Only on her third attempt to get Dennis's attention, a Request for Action asking him to open the door, does Vera succeed in tearing Dennis away from his deictic circle of himself, the kettle and the garage. Even then, however, he is extremely reluctant to leave, continuing his conversation with himself regarding the kettle ('if that's the earth it goes in there': 16) even as he tells Vera to stand away from the door so that he can open it.

Later in Act One, when Dennis can finally get back to the garage and the kettle, he resumes his conversation, this time explicitly including the kettle as a person in his deictic circle with his use of the first person plural pronoun *we* ('Now then. Where were we?: 30). As before, the deictic references to things and locations in his immediate environment continue (noted in italics).

Dennis: [...] *This little one* come up *there* and joins up with *this one* (30).

Dennis's retreat to the garage and his projects is not only physical and visual, but linguistic.

Dennis's reluctance to be torn from his rather warped deictic centre becomes even more apparent when other characters look to him for emotional support. At the beginning of Act Two, for example, Neil confesses to Dennis that his relationship with Pam is becoming increasingly troubled, and that she has started drinking. He does this in a series of Informative: Assessment:Assessings, moves that express evaluations of states of affairs (Tsui 1994: 143).

1 Neil: ... you see, my trouble – Pam's trouble is this. I think we –
2 [DENNIS *starts drilling, the next is inaudible*]
3 – both expect things from each other. Things that the other one is not
4 prepared to give –

5 [DENNIS *stops drilling*]
6 – to the other one. Do you get me?
7 Dennis: Uh-huh (49).

As Tsui (1994: 144–5) notes, such Assessings prospect as positive responses agreeing second evaluations. Such agreements support the speaker's point of view. As evident from Dennis's replies, however, he does not offer this kind of support. His first reaction is to interrupt Neil's turn by drilling, literally drowning out Neil's talk. When Neil resorts to pursuing the expected response (Davidson 1984) with his Elicit: Commit (Tsui 1994: 87) in line 6, Dennis replies with only a minimal acknowledgement (line 7), a weak agreement that is rejection implicative (Davidson 1984: 109; Heritage and Sefi 1992: 391). While some might argue that Dennis's *Uh-huh* can be considered a back-channel device, an affirmative noize that shows the addressee is actively listening (Tsui 1994: 139), this is unlikely. Neil continues pursuing a response in his next move as the interaction continues ('I suppose its nature really, isn't it?': 49), an indication that he was not satisfied with Dennis's minimal *Uh-huh*. In response, all he receives from Dennis is yet another minimal response ('Ah': 49). Further indication that Dennis is not actually listening comes when he starts drilling again in the middle of one of Neil's turns – a clear signal that he is trying hard *not* to listen.

A few turns later in the same interaction (50), Neil suggests in an Informative: Assessment: Self-denigration that he is the reason Pam has started drinking. Self-denigrations are Assessments in which speakers express negative evaluations of themselves and as such are one of the few moves that prospect disagreements as a Positive Response (Tsui 1994: 188). This Dennis readily supplies ('Oh, I shouldn't think so': 50), but only in a perfunctory fashion. Instead of allowing the turn to pass back to Neil, thus allowing Neil's topic to develop, he continues holding the floor himself, changing the topic with an Elicit:Inform to the birthday present he is making for his mother ('Does this look level to you?': 50).

Also very telling is the fact that Dennis responds with advice when Neil initiates the topic of his indigestive pain (21–2). Conversation analysts Jefferson and Lee (1981) have termed such interactions – those in which speakers tell their friends or family members about a problem – as troubles-telling encounters. In their study of these interactions, Jefferson and Lee (1981) found that any advice offered tended to be rejected or resisted. They suggested as a reason for this the sudden disruption in discourse roles caused by the giving of advice. In a troubles-telling encounter, the participants are aligned as troubles-teller and troubles-recipient, and the recipient's primary role is to listen. Advice-giving interactions, on the other hand, are more like service encounters. Participants are aligned as advice-giver and advice-recipient in a problem-solving interaction rather than a problem-sharing one, and this introduces a degree of participant asymmetry. The troubles recipient suddenly takes on the role of expert, the giver of advice, and the troubles teller becomes a novice, the passive advice-recipient. That is, tellers of troubles initiate troubles talk expecting to be listened to, and suddenly find that they must become the listeners when those troubles receive advice. Resisting or rejecting that advice is their way of trying to re-establish their role as teller in a troubles-telling (Jefferson and Lee 1981).

The interaction between Neil and Dennis following Neil's admission of stomach pains can be said to reflect a troubles telling encounter that has to cope with the sudden introduction of advice. Dennis does not listen to Neil's trouble; instead, he gives advice ('I'd get it looked at, if I were you': 21). Neil replies with a question ('Think so?: 21) that allows him to resist the advice without openly rejecting it.[4] A few turns later, Neil changes the topic, shutting down Dennis' advice altogether. While Neil may indeed resist Dennis's advice during this conversation,[5] notice that Dennis's advice may itself be a way of resisting Neil's troubles-talk. Such an interaction shows us that Dennis is not the type to listen to others and offer support.

When the trouble broached is indigestion, Dennis's behaviour does not seem so problematic. When Neil later confesses to having suicidal thoughts and Dennis still reveals himself as someone who does not want to listen, his distancing behaviour takes a much darker turn. To Neil's admission that he sometimes feels like killing himself (52), Dennis again responds with advice, and very casual advice at that, telling him to 'cheer up' on his birthday (52). Neil continues to confess to suicidal thoughts in his next turn, and Dennis retreats even further. He picks up his hammer and starts hammering, right in the middle of Neil's turn. When Neil finishes his turn, Dennis uses his opportunity as next speaker to shift the talk to his own interests, the birthday present he is making for his mother. He simply will not allow himself to be cast as the recipient of Neil's troubles.

In some cases, Dennis does not need a hammer or a drill to drown out the emotional needs of those around him. When Pam and Neil have a heated argument while he is present (53–4), language alone suffices to shield him from their strife. He and Neil are still in the garage working on Marjorie's birthday surprise when Pam enters demanding that Neil join her in the house. Neil resists complying and the conflict escalates. Dennis, who is up a ladder at this point, could presumably reinforce this distance by maintaining a discrete silence, simply waiting for the argument to finish in order to avoid embarrassing his friends. Instead, however, he actively intrudes, making repeated Requests for Action for Neil to assist him in his task.

Dennis: Could you pass me one of those bulbs, please, from the box? (53).

Dennis: And another one, please (54).

Dennis: Bulb, bulb, bulb (54).

Dennis's conversational behaviour presents us with a character so unable to cope with emotional needs, either his own or those of his friends and family, that he is compelled to try and extinguish these needs whenever they threaten to compromise his insulated world of self, tools, and garage.

Dennis's talent for shielding himself from the needs of others is also evident in the way he tends to use Informative moves. As noted earlier (see Chapter 3), such moves play an important part in rapport building in English conversation. Dennis, however, is adept at using these moves to keep the conversation focussed on his own interests.

Dennis: I'm really glad you came round today, Neil. I appreciate it very much.
Neil: Oh, that's …
Dennis: [*moving to the back of the garage and rummaging*] Now where the hell did I put them last year? No, I really appreciate it. And Pam as well. I don't know what it is about birthdays. Some people, you know, they get to our age they start to forget about them but I've always – ever since I was a kid this is – [the story continues] (40–41).

While Dennis twice uses an Informative:Expressive to thank Neil for coming, notice that he is not interested in allowing Neil to respond. As Tsui (1994: 152) notes, Expressives are highly ritualistic moves integral to the performance of interpersonal rituals (Goffman 1967, see also discussion of this issue in Chapter 3), the everyday acts of greeting, thanking, apologizing and the like that help bind members of a society to one another in a network of reciprocal ties. By effectively ending the ritual once his part his done, Dennis gives the impression that he is not truly sincere. Rather, his use of the move is as someone going through the motions of learned behaviour that is nevertheless still alien to him. His real interest is the Informative:Report, the account of his own birthdays when he was a child that is realized as a long narrative turn overriding Neil's opportunity to respond. While Dennis will not listen to Neil, he has no problems enlisting Neil to listen to him.

The way Dennis and Vera talk tells us not only about them, but about the dysfunctional relationship between them. Dukore (1991: 73) has argued that this is represented primarily visually in the play, giving as an example the climax of Act One. Pam and Neil have joined Dennis, Vera and Marjorie for sandwiches. During the meal Vera manages to spill tea and sugar, and Dennis's only reaction to her distress is poorly suppressed mirth. According to Dukore (1991: 73), this situation reflects the strained relationship between husband and wife.

While Ayckbourn's talent for relating situation and setting to character is not to be underestimated, the fractured relationship between Dennis and Vera is also drawn at the level of the dialogue, and nowhere more clearly than in what is arguably the most commonly cited interaction between them, Vera's final request for help in Act Two, Scene One (56–7). It is here, as Billington (1983: 117) has put it, that Vera's 'desperation confronts, with hideous irony, [Dennis's] emotional deafness'. Visual metaphors do not characterize this stretch of dialogue, and there are no sight gags. Language is the primary dramatic device here, and this language succeeds in encapsulating the tragedy that is Dennis and Vera's marriage.

At first glance Dennis seems helpful in this interaction, doing just enough, perhaps, to allow himself to believe he is doing all he can. He initiates with an Elicit:Inform asking Vera to tell him what is wrong ('Now, Vee. What's the trouble?': 56). While Vera answers with a Positive Response supplying the information requested ('It's just – I think I need help, Dennis': 56), Dennis very neatly side steps the expectation to act on this information by requesting further information in an Elicit:Clarify ('How do you mean, help?': 56). Vera once again responds positively ('From you': 56), and goes on to reveal that she is dangerously near breaking point. Instead of her more usual Requests for Action, she upgrades to a Directive: Mandative :Warn ('I don't think I can manage much longer unless I get your help': 56). Here, she does not ask Dennis to do something and simply hope that he will comply; rather, she declares that negative consequences are likely to ensue if he does not comply (Tsui 1994: 132). While Dennis Challenges this Directive, he does so relatively gently, minimizing the threat to Vera's face (see Tsui 1994: 177) and allowing himself to maintain the fiction that he is being supportive. He does not question the need for the action, or even Vera's right to make such a demand, but simply indicates with his second Elicit: Clarify that he is unable to comply because he still lacks the requisite information to do so ('Help. What way? With mother? Do you mean with mother?': 56).

While Dennis clearly has much to answer for here, Vera is not entirely blameless. As with a number of other Ayckbourn characters, some of her problems are of her own making (Holt 1999: 11), and when a way out presents itself she does not take it. In his Elicit:Clarify, Dennis has actually put his finger directly on the heart of the problem, his mother. And yet, Vera's reaction to this opening is to shy away from it. She responds positively by providing the requested clarification, but this clarification de-emphasizes Marjorie's role in their problems ('Partly. No, not just her': 56). Vera then keeps the turn and issues an Informative:Assessment:Criticism directed at Dennis ('You never seem to be here, Dennis': 56), virtually ensuring that he replies to this rather than the clarification regarding his mother. The real issue is thus successfully avoided while Dennis and Vera argue over Dennis's tendency to hide in the garage, a symptom of their problem, not its cause. The argument loops back to where it began, Vera's Request for Action seeking Dennis's help ('I need help, Dennis': 56), and Dennis's Elicitation of further information to avoid actually doing anything ('You say help, but what sort of help do you mean?': 56). When Vera can provide nothing more explicit than a reiteration of *Just help* and *From you*, Dennis initiates a new exchange with an Offer.

Dennis: Yes. Well, look, tell you what. When you've got a moment, why don't you sit down, get a bit of paper and just make a little list of all the things you'd like me to help you with. Things you'd like me to do, things that need mending or fixing and then we can talk about them and see what I can do to help. All right? (56–7)

In making an Offer, Dennis commits himself to a future action that will benefit Vera. This characteristic of speaker action/hearer benefit makes Offers ideal intimacy-enhancing devices (Brown and Levinson 1978/1987: 125). Dennis, however, manages to deploy the move as a tool of disengagement. The topic of the Offer marks a return to Dennis's world of tools and appliances, and he uses a number of minimizing hedges to further de-emphasize the gravity of Vera's situation – it will only take a *moment* for her to write *just* a *little* list on a *bit* of paper. When Vera's reply is an attributable silence, he pursues a positive response (Davidson 1984) ('How about that, Vee? All right? Does that suit you?': 57 / 'Vee?': 57 / 'Vee. Vee': 57), apparently having convinced himself that since he has done all he can the rest is now up to Vera. He does not get the response he pursues, as Vera's reaction each time is an attributable silence accompanied by progressive moves away from Dennis. This is the beginning of the end for Vera. While Dennis has made repeated requests for clarification (e.g., *What do you mean?*), she knows that an explicit response is pointless since Dennis will not listen. It is hardly a surprise, then, that her answer is to stop talking.

Discussions of language do not fill pages and pages of Ayckbourn criticism, perhaps because his verbal manipulations are more subtle than those of Pinter, Rattigan or Wesker. As this chapter has shown, however, language is just as important a device as visual metaphor and situation in the interpretation of *Just Between Ourselves*. The study of Dennis's talk has shown us a character that will not listen, the study of Vera's talk has revealed the woman of spirit and verve she could or might have been, and the study of how the two talk to each other has demonstrated how they interact, but ultimately fail to connect.

Chapter 7

Conclusion

The aim of this book has been to demonstrate that methods, findings and perspectives from linguistics are relevant to critical discussions of plays that explicitly engage issues of language. This aim has been met. As the preceding analyses have demonstrated, drama criticism can benefit from taking on board what linguists have known for years: bringing explicit linguistic knowledge of talk to bear on the study of dialogue in plays can enrich our understanding of those plays.

Using linguistic methods and categories of analysis, new light has been shed on all of the plays studied in this volume. In Pinter's *The Homecoming*, a number of critical intuitions can now be more fully related to their probable sources in the text. Consideration of turn-taking patterns, speaker selection options, and greeting sequences has demonstrated not only that Max is constructed as a powerless and disenfranchised patriarch, but also *how* he is so constructed through the dialogue. A look at the discourse moves represented in the dialogue has shown not only how Ruth uses language against Lenny, but also how Lenny fails to use language against her. Consideration of farewell sequences and summoning moves has revealed something else about Ruth, a little-noticed chink in her armour. She does not have the upper hand when she has to bid for speaking rights in order to say goodbye to Teddy. Consideration of dialect representation, direct and indirect speech, and positive politeness in *Roots* has shown that Wesker wrote the play not only in the Bryants' dialect, but entirely from their perspective. This starting point has led to a rethinking of how the Bryants are represented in the play: that they use their own dialect rather than standard English is not cause to assume they are ignorant.

The studies in this book have also shown that the representation of middle class language, while perhaps contrary to 'new wave' sentiments, is just as interesting stylistically as the representation of working class language. In Ayckbourn's *Just Between Ourselves*, a linguistic analysis of the dialogue has revealed that the language of the text is just as instrumental in drawing character as setting and situation. Dennis's resistance to being cast as a troubles recipient, his reluctance to provide supportive prospected Responses, his use of deictic forms, and his subversion of Informative moves all paint him as a self-absorbed and emotionally distanced character. In addition, the investigation of positive politeness devices in the dialogue has shown that there is more to Vera than is typically supposed. The strong and confident woman she once was or may have been is there to be seen once we know where to look. With respect to *In Praise of Love*, the use of the cooperative principle (Grice 1975) and Brown and Levinson's (1978/1987) framework of off-record communication has revealed not only how Rattigan is able to leave only partly specified clues for the audience in the dialogue, but also how the audience is able to recover and interpret those clues.

As noted in Chapter 2, playwrights may not need explicit linguistic knowledge of talk to write plays, and audiences, be they readers or viewers, may not need conscious awareness of this knowledge in order to understand and appreciate these plays. Critics and analysts, however, do not have this luxury. As the studies in this book have demonstrated, linguistics is relevant to drama criticism, and those interested in writing about the language of drama have much to gain by adding its tools to their tool-kits.

Notes

Chapter 1: Drama Dialogue and Talk

1   This analysis was suggested by work on noun phrases presented in Wright and Hope (1996: 7–9).
2   It is worth pointing out that linguistic terminology is no more or less difficult than critical terminology or, for that matter, the terminology of any other field.
3   While Malkin could not have accessed Tsui (1994), Tsui's framework is based on Sinclair and Coulthard (1975), which appeared much earlier.

Chapter 2: Approaches to Talk

1   Austin (1962/1975) also proposed the perlocutionary act, an action or effect that came about as a result of the illocutionary act.
2   This is, of course, a necessarily simplified account of the turn-taking system and readers are referred to the original paper for a complete articulation of the model.
3   Sinclair and Coulthard (1975) also suggested that exchanges combined to form transactions, which in turn combined to form lessons. However, structural evidence for transactions and lessons was weak, and it is the act-move-exchange combination that has been most influential in studies of conversation.
4   Here and throughout the rest of the book, names of acts and moves are capitalised to differentiate the technical definitions of these terms from their everyday definitions. There is a difference between the everyday word 'informative,' and the class of acts labelled as Informative within Tsui's framework of conversation.
5   Interestingly, it can be argued that Searle anticipated the concept of elicitative force in his 1976 argument for a speech act taxonomy. In this paper, he suggests 'direction of fit' with the world as one of the ways that speech acts differ from each other, and this criterion seems to implicitly recognise that directives and commissives are in some sense stronger than representatives. Representatives, such as statements and assertions, for example, simply matched themselves to the world in that they described or attempted to describe a state of affairs without effecting a change. Directives and commissives, however, were attempts to make the world fit with them in that they tried to bring about actual changes (Searle 1976: 3).
6   Providing a complete list of the acts and moves defined in Tsui's (1994) framework is not possible in the present work. Rather, acts and moves that are used in the analysis are defined as they occur, and the reader is referred to Tsui's book *English Conversation*, where her framework is fully elucidated.
7   While participants may make unexpected replies in discourse, note that these are still related to the preceding initiations. This is true even of sudden changes in topic which, as conversation analysts have pointed out (see Davidson 1984), tend to be heard as signals that the previous utterance was problematic in some way. Instances of truly bizarre replies,

those that cannot in any way be connected to the preceding utterance, have not been found to be frequent in ordinary conversation.

8   Material from the Bank of English® reproduced with the kind permission of HarperCollins Publishers Ltd.

9   This example is from the author's collection of privately taped conversational data.

Chapter 3: Lifting the Smokescreen: The Language of Conversation in Harold Pinter's *The Homecoming*

1   This and all subsequent page references to the play are from the 1991 Faber and Faber edition.

2   It would also have been possible to begin the analysis with Sam's sigh as he enters the room. This could count as a non-verbal summons (Schegloff 1972: 357–8, 376–7), an attention-getting device designed to occasion further talk. This would not, however, change the overall interpretation. The talk between Lenny and Sam still unfolds from this point in a way that excludes Max. Interesting in connection with this point is Herman's (1995) take on the opening lines of *The Homecoming*. She points out that when Lenny is alone with his father (i.e., when he cannot use anyone else to help him exclude Max), his strategies are attributable silences and lapsed turns (94–5).

3   Reclassification is one of the more controversial aspects of Tsui's (1994) framework in the analysis of actual talk. Since it is essentially an unobservable cognitive process, only its apparent result can be observed in the data, involving the analyst in what is essentially guesswork regarding the hearer's motives. Its use with drama dialogue, however, is less problematic, since these exchanges are, as Short (1989) points out, designed to be overheard. It is therefore reasonable to assume that instances of apparent reclassification have been included to provoke certain effects available to interpretation as to character motive, purpose, etc.

4   Dukore (1984: 174; 1982: 84) suggests that Lenny may well be lying when he agrees to Ruth's demands, and that the end of the play is thus ambiguous with respect to Ruth's supposed victory over this family of men. While certainly food for thought, this is a minority view in the literature, and one that is not easily reconciled with Ruth's clear victory over Lenny during their first meeting.

Chapter 4: Language and Social Class in Arnold Wesker's *Roots*

1   I have used the 1976 Penguin Plays edition of *The Wesker Trilogy*. All subsequent page references to *Roots* and the other plays in the Trilogy are from this edition.

2   Speaking as though there is only one Norfolk dialect is, of course, an analytical convenience. In reality, regional dialects exist in a continuum and it is often difficult to tell exactly where one ends and another begins.

3   Work on English as an international language (e.g., Trudgill and Hannah 1982/1994; Cheshire, ed. 1991/1996) has shown that there are multiple standard Englishes. The use of the singular in this chapter denotes standard British English, the variety that Ronnie is represented as speaking.

4   As Cheshire's (1978) work on present tense verbs in Reading shows, some dialects go the opposite route and use -*s* throughout the paradigm.

5   Other interpretations have, of course, been put forward. Wandor (1987: 23), for example, sees Beatie as a symbolic mother, and suggests that she tries to give birth to Ronnie every time she quotes him.

Chapter 5: Brave Silences: Understanding What Is Not Said in Rattigan's *In Praise of Love*

1   While there are several different versions of what is now entitled *In Praise of Love*, two major versions are typically cited (Rebellato 2001: xxxii). One version began as *After Lydia*, a piece that was to be performed with *Before Dawn*. *Before Dawn* was eventually dropped, and *After Lydia* expanded into a full-length play and retitled *In Praise of Love* (Rusinko 1983: 129; Young 1978:xiii). It is the expanded, full-length play (with Lydia's disease as polyarteritis rather than leukaemia) that is analysed here (published by Samuel French, ISBN number 0 573 11170 7, first presented in 1973).

2   Young (1986: 190) is an exception to the prevailingly negative current in accounts of Rattigan's work in the years after 1956. He credits Rattigan for writing well-made plays, and is impressed by Rattigan's ability to keep such tight control over audiences' states of knowledge. He does not, however, give detailed consideration as to why this strategy is effective.

3   This is not to say that the other playwrights studied here do not take advantage of the dual nature of drama dialogue. As Short (1989: 149) notes, this embeddedness is an ever present given in drama, but becomes explicitly relevant when Grice's (1975) co-operative principle is applied.

4   There is no suggestion here that Rattigan sat down and said, for example, 'Ah, at this moment I will have Sebastian violate the maxim of quality.' As Rattigan (1953a: xxi) himself has said, he does not know *why* understatement and implication work in his plays, only that they do work. Nor is it the case that audiences have to understand Grice (1975) in order to work out what is meant from what is said. Rather, Grice (1975) observed that people appear to be able to infer intended but unstated meanings as a matter of course in ordinary conversation, and formalised these observations in terms of the co-operative principle and its maxims. These formalisations allow analysts with explicit knowledge of his theory to suggest reasons for why audiences, who bring their inferencing abilities with them when they read or hear a play, can recover meaning from purposefully vague and incomplete texts.

5   I myself am not a chess player, and have drawn on the very helpful texts of Eade (1999), Whyld (1993) and Harwood (1975) for my knowledge of the game.

Chapter 6: Talking at the Edge: Alan Ayckbourn's *Just Between Ourselves*

1   Interestingly, Tan's analysis is given as part of a demonstration for students on how to write essays in stylistics. While critics have not had much to say concerning Ayckbourn and language, Tan (1998) finds the effects of the playwright's language sufficiently 'obvious' to be suitable as a teaching device.

2   This and all other references I make to the play are from *Alan Ayckbourn: Joking Apart and Other Plays* (1979 London: Chatto and Windus Ltd, 15–71).

3   As Brown and Levinson (1978/1987: 212) note, speakers can make use of off-record
     strategies even when it is clear in the given context that the utterance has only one plausible
     interpretation (and is thus actually on-record).
4   These are instances of deflecting advice. See Mandala (2002) for further discussion.
5   While Neil later decides to take Dennis's advice, it is significant that he does not openly
     accept it during their face-to-face encounter.

Bibliography

Abercrombie, D. 1963/1965. 'Conversation and Spoken Prose', in Abercrombie, D. 1965. *Studies in Phonetics and Linguistics*. 1–9. London: Oxford University Press.

Adamson, S. 1989. 'With Double Tongue: Diglossia, Stylistics, and the Teaching of English', in Short, M. (ed.). 1989. *Reading, Analysing and Teaching Literature*. 204–240. London and New York: Longman.

Adler, T. 1979. 'The Wesker Trilogy Revisited: Games to Compensate for the Inadequacy of Words'. *Quarterly Journal of Speech*. 65: 429–38.

Aijmer, K. 1996. 'Tsui, Amy B.M., English Conversation'. *Moderna Språk*. XC (1): 108–9.

Allen, P. 2001. *Alan Ayckbourn: Grinning at the Edge*. London: Methuen.

Armstrong, R. 1999. *Kafka and Pinter: Shadow-Boxing: The Struggle Between Father and Son*. Houndmills: Macmillan.

Arndt, H. and Ryan, A. 1986. 'An Ordered Inventory Of Communicative Functions Of General FLT', in Kasper, G. (ed.). 1986. *Learning, Teaching and Communication in the Foreign Language Classroom*. Aarhus: Aarhus University Press.

Aston, G. 1988. *Learning Comity*. Bologna: Editrice CLUEB.

Atkinson, J.M. and Heritage, J. (eds). 1984. *Structures of Social Action: Studies in Conversation Analysis*. Cambridge: Cambridge University Press.

Attridge, D. 1987/1996. 'Closing Statement: Linguistics and Poetics in Retrospect', in Weber, J. (ed.). 1996. *The Stylistics Reader*. 36–53. London: Arnold. Originally published in Fabb, N., Attridge, D., Durant, A. and MacCabe, C. (eds). 1987. *The Linguistics of Writing*. Manchester: Manchester University Press.

Austin, J.L. 1962/1975. *How to Do Things with Words*. Oxford: Clarendon Press.

Ayckbourn, A. 1979. *Alan Ayckbourn: Joking Apart and Other Plays*. London: Chatto and Windus, Ltd.

Ayckbourn, A. 1979. 'Preface', in Ayckbourn, A. *Three Plays: Joking Apart, Just Between Ourselves, Ten Times Table*. London: Chatto and Windus.

Ayckbourn, A. 1979/1981. *Taking Steps*. London: Samuel French.

Ayckbourn, A. 1991. *The Revengers' Comedies*. London: Faber and Faber.

Babb, S. (ed.). 1972. *Essays in Stylistic Analysis*. New York: Harcourt Brace Jovanovich, Inc.

Baker, M., Francis, G. and Tognini-Bonelli, E. (eds). 1993. *Text and Technology*. Amsterdam: John Benjamins.

Batty, M. 2001. *Harold Pinter*. Devon: Northcote House/British Council.

Beard, A. 2001. *Texts and Contexts: Introducing Literature and Language Study*. London and New York: Routledge.

Beckerman, B. 1970. *The Dynamics of Drama*. New York: Alfred A. Knopf.

Bennison, N. 1993. 'Discourse Analysis, Pragmatics and the Dramatic "Character": Tom Stoppard's *Professional Foul'. Language and Literature* 2 (2): 79–99.

Bigsby, C.W.E. (ed.). 1981. *Contemporary English Drama*. London: Edward Arnold.

Bigsby, C.W.E. 1981. 'The Language of Crisis in British Theatre: The Drama of Cultural Pathology', in Bigsby, C.W.E. (ed.). *Contemporary English Drama*. 11–51. London: Edward Arnold.

Billington, M. 1983. *Alan Ayckbourn*. London: Macmillan.

Blistein, E.M. 1983. 'Alan Ayckbourn: Few Jokes Much Comedy'. *Modern Drama* 26: 26–35.

Bold, A. (ed.). 1984. *Harold Pinter: You Never Heard Such Silence*. London: Vision Press.

Brown, J.R. 1967. 'Dialogue in Pinter and Others', in Brown, J.R. (ed.). *Modern British Dramatists: A Collection of Critical Essays*. 122–44. Englewood Cliffs, NJ: Prentice Hall. Originally published in 1965 in *The Critical Quarterly* 7 (3): 225–43.

Brown, J.R. 1972. *Theatre Language*. London: Allen Lane/The Penguin Press.

Brown, P. and Levinson, S. 1978/1987. *Politeness*. Cambridge: Cambridge University Press.

Brown, G. and Yule, G. 1983a. *Teaching the Spoken Language*. Cambridge: Cambridge University Press.

Brown, G. and Yule, G. 1983b. *Discourse Analysis*. Cambridge: Cambridge University Press.

Burgess, G. 1997/2000. *The Mammoth Book of Chess*. London: Constable and Robinson.

Burkman, K.H. 1971. *The Dramatic World of Harold Pinter: Its Basis in Ritual*. Ohio: Ohio State University Press.

Burton, D. 1980. *Dialogue and Discourse*. London: Routledge and Kegan Paul.

Button, G. and Lee, J. (eds). 1987. *Talk and Social Organisation*. Clevedon and Philadelphia: Multilingual Matters.

Cahn, V. 1994. *Gender and Power in the Plays of Harold Pinter*. Basingstoke: Macmillan.

Calderwood, J.L. and Tolliver, H.E. (eds). 1968. *Perspectives on Drama*. New York: Oxford University Press.

Cameron, D. 1997/1998. 'Performing Gender Identity: Young Men's Talk and the Construction of Heterosexual Masculinity', in Coates, J. (ed.). 1998. *Language and Gender: A Reader*. 270–84. Oxford: Blackwell.

Canale, M. and Swain, M. 1980. 'Theoretical Bases of Communicative Approaches to Second Language Teaching'. *Applied Linguistics* 1 (1): 1–47.

Carter, R. 1982. 'Introduction', in Carter, R. (ed.). *Language and Literature*. 1–17. London: Routledge.

Carter, R. and McCarthy, M. 1995. 'Grammar and The Spoken Language'. *Applied Linguistics* 16 (2): 141–58.

Carter, R. and Nash, W. 1990. *Seeing through Language*. Oxford: Blackwell.

Carter, R. and Simpson, P. (eds). 1989. *Language, Discourse and Literature*. London: Unwin Hyman.

Carter, R. and Simpson, P. 1989. 'Introduction', in Carter, R. and Simpson, P. (eds). *Language, Discourse and Literature*. 1–20. London: Unwin Hyman.

Chambers, C. and Prior, M. 1987. *Playwrights' Progress*. Oxford: Amberlane Press.

Chambers, J.K. and Trudgill, P. 1980/1998. *Dialectology*. 2nd edn. Cambridge: Cambridge University Press.

Chatman, S. (ed.). 1971. *Literary Style*. New York: Oxford University Press.

Cheshire, J. 1978. 'Present Tense Verbs in Reading English', in Trudgill, P. (ed.). *Sociolinguistic Patterns in British English*. 52–68. London: Edward Arnold.

Cheshire, J. (ed.). 1991/1996. *English Around the World: Sociolinguistic Perspectives*. Cambridge: Cambridge University Press.

Coates, J. 1989/1998. 'Gossip Revisited: Language in All-Female Groups', in Coates, J. (ed.). 1998. *Language and Gender: A Reader*. 226–53. Oxford: Blackwell.

Cohen, A. 1996. 'Developing the Ability to Perform Speech Acts'. *Studies in Second Language Acquisition* 18 (2): 252–67.

Cohn, R. 1969. *Currents in Contemporary Drama*. Indiana: Indiana University Press.

Cornish, R. and Ketels, V. 1986. *Landmarks of Modern British Drama: The Plays of the Seventies*. London: Methuen.

Coulthard, M. (ed.). 1992. *Advances in Spoken Discourse Analysis*. London and New York: Routledge.

Coulthard, M. 1977/1985. *An Introduction to Discourse Analysis*. London: Longman.

Coulthard, M. and Brazil, D. 1979/1992 'Exchange Structure', in Coulthard, M. (ed.). 1992. *Advances in Spoken Discourse Analysis*. 50–78. London and New York: Routledge.

Cowie, A.P. 1988. 'Stable and Creative Aspects of Vocabulary Use', in Carter, R. and McCarthy, M. (eds). 1988. *Vocabulary and Language Teaching*. 126–37. London and New York: Longman.

Crystal, D. 1980/1991. *A Dictionary of Linguistics and Phonetics*. 3rd edn. Oxford: Blackwell.

Crystal, D. and Davy, D. 1969. *Investigating English Style*. London: Longman.

Crystal, D. and Davy, D. 1975. *Advanced Conversational English*. London: Longman.

Cuddon, J.A. 1992. *The Penguin Dictionary of Literary Terms and Literary Theory*. 3rd edn. London: Penguin. 839–48.

Culpeper, J., Short, M. and Verdonk, P. (eds). 1998. *Exploring the Language of Drama*. London and New York: Routledge.

Culpeper, J., Short, M. and Verdonk, P. 1998. 'Introduction', in Culpeper, J., Short, M. and Verdonk, P. (eds). *Exploring the Language of Drama*. 1–5. London and New York: Routledge.

Dalrymple, T. 2000. 'Reticence or Insincerity, Rattigan or Pinter'. *New Criterion*. 19 (3): 12–20.

Davidson, J. 1984. 'Subsequent Versions of Invitations, Offers, Requests, and Proposals Dealing with Potential or Actual Rejection', in Atkinson, J.M. and Heritage, J. (eds). *Structures of Social Action: Studies in Conversation Analysis*. 102–28. Cambridge: Cambridge University Press.

Demastes, W. (ed.). 1996. *British Playwrights 1956–1995*. Westport, CT and London: Greenwood Press.

Demastes, W. and Kelly, K. (eds). 1996. *British Playwrights, 1880–1956: A Research and Production Sourcebook*. Westport, CT and London: Greenwood Press.

Dieth, E. and Orton, H. 1952. *A Questionnaire for a Linguistic Atlas of England*. Leeds: Leeds Philosophical and Literary Society.

Distler, P.A. 1991. 'Ayckbourn's Plays in London', in Dukore, B.F. (ed.). *Alan Ayckbourn: A Casebook*. New York and London: Garland Publishing.

Dornan, R. 1994. *Arnold Wesker Revisited*. New York: Twayne Publishers.

Doumont, G. and van Noppen, J.P. 2002. Review: *Texts and Contexts* by Adrian Beard. *Language and Literature* 11(3): 284.

Drew, P. and Heritage, J. (eds). 1992. *Talk at Work*. Cambridge: Cambridge University Press.

Dukore, B.F. 1966. 'A Woman's Place'. *Quarterly Journal of Speech*. 52(3): 237–41.

Dukore, B.F. 1982. *Harold Pinter*. London and Basinstoke: Macmillan.

Dukore, B.F. 1984. 'Alaskan Perspectives', in Bold, A. (ed.). *Harold Pinter: You Never Heard Such Silence*. 166–77. London: Vision Press.

Dukore, B.F. (ed.). 1991. *Alan Ayckbourn: A Casebook*. New York and London: Garland Publishing.

Dukore, B.F. 1991. 'Ayckbourn's Theatricality', in Dukore, B.F. (ed.). *Alan Ayckbourn: A Casebook*. 71–86. New York and London: Garland Publishing.

Eade, J. 1999. *Chess for Dummies*. Foster City, CA: IDG Books Worldwide.

Eggins, S. and Slade, D. 1997. *Analysing Casual Conversation*. London and Washington: Cassell.

El Khalfi, H. 2000. 'Language and Power in the Dramatic Works of Harold Pinter and Eugene Ionesco'. Unpublished PhD thesis. Department of Literature, University of Essex.

Elsom, J. 1978/1986. 'Family Ties', in Scott, M. (ed.). 1986. *Harold Pinter: The Birthday Party, The Caretaker, The Homecoming: A Casebook*. 198–9. London and Basingstoke: Macmillan. Originally published in *The Listener*, 11 May 1978: 611.

Esslin, M. 1968. *The Theatre of the Absurd*. Revised and enlarged edition. Middlesex: Penguin Books.

Esslin, M. 1970. *The Peopled Wound: The Plays of Harold Pinter*. London: Methuen.

Esslin, M. 2000. *Pinter the Playwright*. 6th rev. edn. London: Methuen.

Evans, G.L. 1977. *The Language of Modern Drama*. London: J.M. Dent and Sons.

Faerch, C. and Kasper, G. 1984. 'Pragmatic Knowledge: Rules And Procedures'. *Applied Linguistics* 5 (3): 214–25.

Findlater, R. (ed.). 1981. *At the Royal Court. 25 Years of the English Stage Company*. Derbyshire: Amber Lane Press.

Findlater, R. 1960. 'Plays and Politics'. *The 20th Century*. 168: 235–42.

Firth, J.R. 1964/1966. *The Tongues of Men* and *Speech*. London. Oxford University Press.

Fish, S. 1973/1996. 'What is Stylistics and Why are They Saying Such Terrible Things about It?', in Weber, J. (ed.). 1996. *The Stylistics Reader*. 94–116. London: Arnold.

Fisher, J. 1966. 'Alan Ayckbourn', in Demastes, W. (ed.). *British Playwrights 1956–1995*. 15–27. Westport, CT and London: Greenwood Press.

Fishman, P. 1983. 'Interaction: The Work Women Do', in Barrie, T., Kramarae, C. and Henley, N. (eds). *Language, Gender and Society*. 89–101. Rowley, MA: Newbury.

Flowerdew, J. 1990. 'Problems of Speech Act Theory from an Applied Perspective. *Language and Learning*. 40: 79–105.

Foulkes, R. 1979. 'Terence Rattigan's Variations on a Theme'. *Modern Drama* 22: 375–82.

Fowler, R. 1986/1996. 'Studying Literature as Language', in Weber, J. (ed.). 1996. *The Stylistics Reader*. 196–203. London: Arnold.

Freeborn, D. with French, P. and Langford, D. 1993. *Varieties of English*. 2nd edn. Hampshire and London: Macmillan.

Freeman, D. (ed.). 1970. *Linguistics and Literary Style*. New York. Holt, Rinehart and Winston.

Gale, S. (ed.). 1986. *Harold Pinter: Critical Approaches*. Madison, NJ: Fairleigh Dickinson University Press.

Gale, S. 1987. 'Character and Motivation in Harold Pinter's *The Homecoming*'. *Journal of Evolutionary Psychology* 8 (3–4): 278–88.

Gallagher, K. 1966. 'Harold Pinter's Dramaturgy'. *Quarterly Journal of Speech* October 1966: 242–8.

Gautam, K. 1987. 'Pinter's *The Caretaker*: A Study in Conversation Analysis'. *Journal of Pragmatics* 11: 49–59.

Goffman, E. 1967. *Interaction Ritual: Essays in Face-to-Face Behaviour*. London: Allen Lane/The Penguin Press.

Goffman, E. 1974. *Frame Analysis*. New York: Harper and Row.

Goffman, E. 1979. 'Footing'. *Semiotica* 25: 1–29.

Goldstone, H. 1969. 'Not So Puzzling Pinter: *The Homecoming*'. *Theatre Annual* 25: 20–27.

Greenbaum, S. and Quirk, R. 1990. *A Student Grammar of the English Language*. Harlow, Essex: Longman.

Grice, H.P. 1975. 'Logic and Conversation', in Cole, P. and Morgan, J. (eds). *Syntax and Semantics Vol. 3: Speech Acts*. 41–58. New York: Academic Press.

Gross, R. 1990. 'Coming Down in the World: Motifs of Benign Descent in Three Plays by Terence Rattigan'. *Modern Drama* 35(3): 394–408.

Gumperz, J.J. and Hymes, D. (eds). 1972. *Directions in Sociolinguistics.* 346–80. New York: Holt, Rinehart and Winston.

Halliday, M.A.K. 1961. 'Categories of the Theory of Grammar'. *Word* 17 (3): 241–92.

Halliday, M.A.K. 1963. 'Class in Relation to the Axis of Chain and Choice in Language'. *Linguistics* 2: 5–15.

Halliday, M.A.K. 1970. 'Language Structure and Language Function', in Lyons, J. (ed.). 1970. *New Horizons in Linguistics.* Middlesex: Penguin.

Halliday, M.A.K. 1971. 'Linguistic Function and Literary Style', in Chatman, S. (ed.). *Literary Style: A Symposium.* New York: Oxford University Press.

Halliday, M.A.K. and Hasan, R. 1976. *Cohesion in English.* London: Longman.

Halsey, A.H., Heath, A.F., and Ridge, J.M. 1980. *Origins and Destinations: Family, Class and Education in Modern Britain.* Oxford: Oxford University Press.

Harwood, G. 1975. *Caisssa's Web: The Chess Bedside Book.* London: Latimer.

Hayman, R. 1977. *How to Read a Play.* London: Methuen.

Hayman, R. 1970/1979. *Contemporary Playwrights: Arnold Wesker.* 3rd edn. London: Heineman.

Heritage, J. 1984. *Garfinkel and Ethnomethodology.* Cambridge: Polity Press.

Heritage, J. and Sefi, S. 1992. 'Dilemmas of Advice: Aspects of the Delivery and Reception of Advice in Interactions between Health Visitors and First-time Mothers', in Drew, P. and Heritage, J. (eds). *Talk at Work.* 359–417. Cambridge: Cambridge University Press.

Herman, V. 1998. 'Turn Management in Drama', in Culpeper, J., Short, M. and Verdonk, P. (eds). *Exploring the Language of Drama.* 19–33. London and New York: Routledge.

Herman, V. 1995. *Dramatic Discourse.* London: Routledge.

Hill, H. 1982. 'Rattigan's Renaissance'. *Contemporary Review* 240 (1392): 37–42.

Hinchliffe, A. 1986. 'After No Man's Land: A Progress Report', in Gale, S.H. (ed.). 1986. *Harold Pinter: Critical Approaches.* 153–63. Madison, NJ: Fairleigh Dickinson University Press.

Hollis, J.R. 1970. *Harold Pinter: The Poetics of Silence.* Illinois: Southern Illinois Press.

Holt, M. 1999. *Alan Ayckbourn.* Plymouth: Northcote House.

Hope-Wallace, P. 1965/1986. 'Feeling Cheated', in Scott, M. (ed.). 1986. *Harold Pinter: The Birthday Party, The Caretaker, The Homecoming: A Casebook.* 196–7. London and Basinstoke: Macmillan. Originally published in *The Guardian*, 4 June 1965.

Hornby, R. 1991. 'Ayckbourn's Men', in Dukore, B.F. (ed.). *Alan Ayckbourn: A Casebook.* 103–13. New York and London: Garland Publishing.

Hudgins, C. 1986. 'Intended Audience Response: *The Homecoming* and the "Ironic Mode of Identification"', in Gale, S. (ed.). 1986. *Harold Pinter: Critical Approaches.* 102–17. Madison, NJ: Fairleigh Dickinson University Press.

Hunt, A. 1960. '*Roots* in Norfolk'. *Encore-London*. May/June: 30–31.

Hutchby, I. and Wooffitt, R. 1998. *Conversation Analysis*. Cambridge: Polity Press.

Hymes, D. 1967/1972. 'Models of The Interaction of Language and Social Life', in Gumperz, J.J. and Hymes, D. (eds). *Directions in Sociolinguistics*. New York: Holt, Rinehart and Winston: 35–71. Revised version of Hymes, D. 1967. 'Models of the Interaction of Language and Social Life'. *Journal of Social Issues* 23 (2): 8–28.

Innes, C. 1992. *Modern British Drama: 1890–1990*. Cambridge: Cambridge University Press.

Itzin, C. 1980. *Stages in the Revolution*. London: Methuen.

Jackson, P. 1959. 'Review of *Roots*'. *Plays and Players*. August 1959: 15.

Jakobson, R. 1960/1996. 'Closing Statement: Linguistics and Poetics', in Weber, J. (ed.). 1996. *The Stylistics Reader*. 10–35. London: Arnold. Delivered at the 1958 Conference on Style held at Indiana University, Bloomington, IN, 17–19 April and originally published in Sebeok, T.A. (ed.). 1960. *Style in Language*. Cambridge, MA: MIT Press.

Jefferson, G. and Lee, J.R.E. 1981. 'The Rejection of Advice: Managing the Problematic Convergence of a "Troubles-telling" and a "Service Encounter"'. *Journal of Pragmatics* 5 (4): 399–422.

Kasper, G. (ed.). 1986. *Learning, Teaching and Communication in the Foreign Language Classroom*. Aarhus: Aarhus University Press.

Kennedy, A. 1975. *Six Dramatists in Search of a Language*. Cambridge: Cambridge University Press.

Kermode, F. 2000. *Shakespeare's Language*. London: Allen Lane.

Knowles, R. 1984. 'Names and Naming in the Plays of Harold Pinter', in Bold, A. (ed.). *Harold Pinter: You Never Heard Such Silence*. 113–30. London: Vision Press.

Labov, W. 1972. *Sociolinguistic Patterns*. Pennsylvania: University of Pennsylvania Press.

Labov, W. and Fanshell, D. 1977. *Therapeutic Discourse: Psychotherapy as Conversation*. New York: Academic Press.

Lahr, J. (ed.). 1971. *A Casebook on Harold Pinter's* The Homecoming. New York: Grove Press.

Lahr, J. 1971. 'Pinter's Language', in Lahr, J. (ed.). *A Casebook on Harold Pinter's* The Homecoming. 123–36. New York: Grove Press.

Latham, J. 1965. '*Roots*: A Reassessment'. *Modern Drama* 8: 192–7.

Laver, J. 1981. 'Linguistic Routines and Politeness in Greeting and Parting', in Coulmas, F. (ed.). *Conversational Routine*. 289–304. The Hague: Mouton.

Leech, G. 1983. *Principles of Pragmatics*. London and New York: Longman.

Leech, G. and Short, M. 1981. *Style in Fiction*. London: Longman.

Leeming, G. 1983. *Wesker The Playwright*. London: Methuen.

Leeming, G. (comp.). 1985. *Wesker on File*. London: Methuen.

Leeming, G. and Trussler, S. 1971. *The Plays of Arnold Wesker: An Assessment*. London: Gollancz.

Lennard, J. and Luckhurst, M. 2002. *The Drama Handbook*. Oxford: Oxford University Press.

Levinson, S.C. 1979. 'Activity Types and Language'. *Linguistics* 17: (5,6). Reprinted in Drew, P. and Heritage, J. (eds). *Talk at Work*. 66–100. Cambridge: Cambridge University Press.

Levinson, S.C. 1983. *Pragmatics*. Cambridge: Cambridge University Press.

Levinson, S.C. 1988. 'Putting Linguistics on a Proper Footing: Explorations in Goffman's Concepts of Participation', in Drew P. and Wooton, A. (eds). 1988. *Erving Goffman: Exploring the Interaction Order*. 161–227. Cambridge: Polity.

Londré, F.H. 1991. 'Ayckbourn's Women', in Dukore, B.F. (ed.). *Alan Ayckbourn: A Casebook*. 87–101. New York and London: Garland Publishing.

Lyons, J. 1970. *New Horizons in Linguistics*. Middlesex: Penguin.

Malkin, J. 1992. *Verbal Violence in Contemporary Drama*. Cambridge: Cambridge University Press.

Mandala, S. 2002. 'The Pragmatics of Advice in Natural Talk and Textbook Dialogues'. Unpublished PhD thesis, University of Cambridge, Cambridge.

McGrath, J. 1970. 'Friends and Enemies'. *Black Dwarf* 12 June.

Mills, S. 1992/1996. 'Knowing Your Place: A Marxist Feminist Stylistic Analysis', in Weber, J. (ed.). 1996. *The Stylistics Reader*. 241–57. London: Arnold.

Mey, J. 1993. *Pragmatics*. Oxford: Blackwell.

Meyers, W. 1980. *Aliens and Linguists*. Athens: University of Georgia Press.

Mutalik-Desai, A. 1987. 'The Wesker Trilogy: Propaganda or Allegory?' *Indian Journal of English Studies*. 26: 5–13.

Nash, W. 1989. 'Changing the Guard at Elsinore', in Carter, R. and Simpson, P. (eds) 1989. *Language, Discourse and Literature*. 23–41. London: Unwin Hyman.

Nattinger, J. 1988. 'Some Current Trends in Vocabulary Teaching', in Carter, R. and McCarthy, M. (eds). *Vocabulary and Language Teaching*. London and New York: Longman, 1988. 62–82.

Nelson, H. 1967. '*The Homecoming*: Kith and Kin', in Brown, J.R. (ed.). *Modern British Dramatists*. 145–63. Englewood Cliffs, NJ: Prentice Hall.

Nicoll, A. 1968. 'Dramatic Dialogue', in Calderwood, J.L. and Tolliver, H.E. (eds). *Perspectives on Drama*. 339–71. New York: Oxford University Press.

Nofsinger, R. 1991. *Everyday Conversation*. London: Sage.

Orr, J. 1981/1989. *Tragic Drama and Modern Society: A Sociology of Dramatic Form from 1880 to the Present*. 2nd edn. Basingstoke: Macmillan.

Orton, H. 1962. *Survey of English Dialects: Introduction*. Leeds: E.J. Arnold and Sons (containing the final version of the *Questionnaire*).

Orton, H. and Tilling, P. (eds). 1969. *Survey of English Dialects Volume 3 Part 1: The East Midland Counties and East Anglia*. Leeds: E.J. Arnold and Sons.

Orton, H. and Tilling, P. (eds). 1970. *Survey of English Dialects Volume 3 Part 2: The East Midland Counties and East Anglia*. Leeds: E.J. Arnold and Sons.

Orton, H. and Tilling, P. (eds). 1971. *Survey of English Dialects Volume 3 Part 3: The East Midland Counties and East Anglia*. Leeds: E.J. Arnold and Sons.

Page, M. 1983. 'The Serious Side of Alan Ayckbourn'. *Modern Drama* 26 (1): 36–46.

Patterson, M. 1996. 'Studying Drama', in Bradford, R. (ed.). *Introducing Literary Studies*. 42–58. London: Prentice Hall/Harvester Wheatsheaf.

Pawley, A. and Syder, F. 'Two Puzzles for Linguistic Theory: Nativelike Selection and Nativelike Fluency', in Richards, J.C. and Schmidt, R.W. (eds). *Language and Communication*. London: Longman, 1983. 191–225.

Peacock, D.K. 1997. *Harold Pinter and the New British Theatre*. Westport, CT: Greenwood Press.

Peter, J. 1989. 'Nurturing the Natural Fruits of Comic *Roots*'. *Sunday Times* 12 February: C9.

Piazza, R. 1999. 'Dramatic Discourse Approached from a Conversational Analytic Perspective: Catherine Hayes's *Skirmishes* and Other Contemporary Plays'. *Journal of Pragmatics* 31 (8): 1001–23.

Pilkington, J. 1998. '"Don't Try and Make Out that I'm Nice!" The Different Strategies Women and Men Use when Gossiping', in Coates, J. (ed.). *Language and Gender: A Reader*. 254–69. Oxford: Blackwell.

Pinter, H. 1960/1991. *The Caretaker*. London: Faber and Faber.

Pinter, H. 1962. 'Between the Lines'. *The Sunday Times* 4 March.

Pinter, H. 1965/1991. *The Homecoming*. London: Faber and Faber.

Pinter, H. 1966. *The Birthday Party.* London: Methuen.

Pomerantz, A. 1978. 'Compliment Responses: Notes on the Co-operation of Multiple Constraints', in Schenkein, J. (ed.). *Studies in the Organisation of Conversational Interaction*. New York: Academic Press.

Pomerantz, A. 1984. 'Agreeing and Disagreeing with Assessments: Some Features of Preferred/Dispreferred Turn Shapes', in Atkinson, J.M. and Heritage, J. (eds). *Structures of Social Action: Studies in Conversation Analysis*. Cambridge: Cambridge University Press.

Postlewait, T. 1991. 'Breaking Traditional Modes: Ayckbourn's Drama and Our Critical Understanding', in Dukore, B.F. (ed.). *Alan Ayckbourn: A Casebook*. 57–70. New York and London: Garland Press.

Quigley, A. 1975. *The Pinter Problem*. Princeton, New Jersey: Princeton University Press.

Quirk, R. (ed.). 1968a. *Essays on the English Language: Medieval and Modern*. London: Longman.

Quirk, R. 1968b. 'Relative Clauses in Educated Spoken English', in Quirk, R. (ed.). *Essays on the English Language: Medieval and Modern*. London: Longman.

Quirk, R. 1968c. 'The Survey of English Usage', in Quirk, R. (ed.). *Essays on the English Language: Medieval and Modern*. 70–93. London: Longman.

Quirk, P., Greenbaum, S., Leech, G. and Svartvik, J. 1985. *A Comprehensive Grammar of the English Language*. New York: Longman.

Quirk, R. and Svartvik, J. 1966. *Investigating Linguistic Acceptability*. The Hague: Mouton.

Rattigan, T. 1953a. 'Preface', in *The Collected Plays of Terence Rattigan: Volume 1*. London: Hamish Hamilton.

Rattigan, T. 1953b. 'Preface', in *The Collected Plays of Terence Rattigan: Volume 2*. London: Hamish Hamilton.

Rattigan, T. 1973. *In Praise of Love*. London: Samuel French.

Rebellato, D. 2001. 'Introduction', in Rattigan, T. 1973/2001. *In Praise of Love*. v–xi. London: Nick Hern Books.

Richards, I.A. 1967. *Principles of Literary Criticism*. London: Kegan Paul.

Richards, I.A. 1969. *Practical Criticism*. London: Kegan Paul.

Richards, J.C. 1990. *The Language Teaching Matrix*. Cambridge: Cambridge University Press.

Richards, J.C., Platt, J. and Platt, H. 1985/1992. *Longman Dictionary of Language Teaching and Applied Linguistics*. London: Longman.

Rusinko, S. 1991. 'Upsetting the Balance of the English Comic Tradition', in Dukore, B.F. (ed.). *Alan Ayckbourn: A Casebook*. 41–55. New York and London: Garland Press.

Rusinko, S. 1983. *Terence Rattigan*. Boston: Twayne Publishers.

Sacks, H. 1973/1987. 'On the Preference for Agreement and Contiguity in Sequences in Conversation', in Button, G. and Lee, J. (eds). 1987. *Talk and Social Organisation*. 54–69. Clevedon and Philadelphia: Multilingual Matters.

Sacks, H., Schegloff, E. and Jefferson, G. 1974. 'A Simplest Systematics for the Organization of Turn-taking for Conversation'. *Language* 50 (4): 696–735.

Sanger, K. 2001. *The Language of Drama*. London: Routledge.

Schegloff, E. 1972. 'Sequencing in Conversational Openings', in Gumperz, J.J. and Hymes, D. (eds). *Directions in Sociolinguistics*. 346–80. New York: Holt, Rinehart and Winston.

Schegloff, E. and Sacks, H. 1973. 'Opening up Closings'. *Semiotica* 8 (4): 289–327.

Schiffrin, D. 1985. 'Everyday Argument: The Organization of Diversity in Talk', in van Dijk, T.A. (ed.). *Handbook of Discourse Analysis Volume 3: Discourse and Dialogue*. 35–46. London: Academic Press.

Schenkein, J. (ed.). 1978. *Studies in the Organisation of Conversational Interaction*. New York: Academic Press.

Scott, M. (ed.). 1986. '*Harold Pinter:* The Birthday Party, The Caretaker, The Homecoming: *A Casebook*'. London and Basingstoke: Macmillan.

Scott, M. 1986. 'Introduction', in Scott, M. (ed.). 1986. '*Harold Pinter:* The Birthday Party, The Caretaker, The Homecoming: *A Casebook*'. 9–22. London and Basingstoke: Macmillan.

Searle, J.R. 1976. 'A Classification of Illocutionary Acts'. *Language in Society* 5: 1–23.

Searle, J.R. 1969. *Speech Acts: An Essay in the Philosophy of Language*. Cambridge and New York: Cambridge University Press.

Shank, R. and Abelson, R.P. 1977. *Scripts, Plans, Goals, and Understanding*. Hillsdale, NJ: Erlbaum.

Short, M. 1989. 'Discourse Analysis and the Analysis of Drama', in Carter, R. and Simpson, P. (eds). *Language, Discourse and Literature*. 139–68. London: Unwin Hyman.

Short, M. 1996. *Exploring the Language of Poems, Plays and Prose*. London: Longman.

Short, M. 1998. 'From Dramatic Text to Dramatic Performance', in Culpeper, J., Short, M. and Verdonk, P. (eds). *Exploring the Language of Drama*. 6–18. London and New York: Routledge.

Simpson, P. 1997. *Language through Literature*. London and New York: Routledge.

Simpson, P. 1989. 'Politeness Phenomena in Ionesco's *The Lesson*', in Carter, R. and Simpson, P. (eds). *Language, Discourse and Literature*. 171–93. London: Unwin Hyman.

Sinclair, J. 1992. 'Priorities in Discourse Analysis', in Coulthard, M. (ed.). *Advances in Spoken Discourse Analysis*. 79–88. London and New York: Routledge.

Sinclair, J. and Coulthard, M. 1975. *Towards an Analysis of Discourse*. Oxford: Oxford University Press.

Spencer, S. 2002. *The Playwright's Guidebook*. New York and London: Faber and Faber.

Stenström, A.B. 1984. *Questions and Responses in English Conversation*. Lund Studies in English 68. Lund: Lund University Press.

Stenström, A.B. 1994. *An Introduction to Spoken Interaction*. London: Longman.

Sternberg, M. 1982. 'Point of View and the Indirections of Direct Speech'. *Language and Style* 15 (2): 67–117.

Stevenson, R. 1984. 'Harold Pinter – Innovator?', in Bold, A. (ed.). *Harold Pinter: You Never Heard Such Silence*. 29–60. London: Vision Press.

Strunk, V. 1989. *Harold Pinter: Towards a Poetic of His Plays*. New York: Lang.

Styan, J. L. 1981/1998. *Modern Drama in Theory and Practice Volume 2: Symbolism, Surrealism, and the Absurd*. Cambridge: Cambridge University Press.

Styan, J. L. 1960/1976. *The Elements of Drama*. Cambridge: Cambridge University Press.

Tan, P. 1998. 'Advice on Doing Your Stylistics Essay on a Dramatic Text: An Example from Alan Ayckbourn's *The Revengers' Comedies*', in Culpeper, J., Short, M. and Verdonk, P. (eds). *Exploring the Language of Drama*. 161–71. London and New York. Routledge.

Tannen, D. 1984. *Conversational Style: Analyzing Talk Among Friends*. Norwood, NJ: Ablex Publishing Corporation.

Tannen, D. 1989. *Talking Voices: Repetition, Dialogue and Imagery in Conversational Discourse*. Cambridge: Cambridge University Press.

Taylor, J.R. 1981. 'Art and Commerce: The New Drama in the West End Market Place', in Bigsby, C.W.E. (ed.). 1981. *Contemporary English Drama*. 177–88. London: Edward Arnold.

Taylor, J.R. 1962/1969. *Anger and After: A Guide to the New British Drama*. London: Methuen and Co. Ltd.

Taylor, J.R. 1967. *The Rise and Fall of the Well-Made Play*. London and New York: Methuen.

Taylor, J.R. 1971. 'Pinter's Game of Happy Families', in Lahr, J. (ed.). *A Casebook on Harold Pinter's* The Homecoming. 57–65. New York: Grove Press.

Taylor, T.J. and Cameron, D. 1987. *Analysing Conversation*. Oxford: Pergamon.

Taylor, T. and Toolan, M. 1984/1996. 'Recent Trends in Stylistics', in Weber, J. (ed.). 1996. *The Stylistics Reader*. 87–91. London: Arnold.

Tennyson, H. 1960. 'Interview with Harold Pinter'. *BBC General Overseas Service* 7 August.

Thomas, J. 1995. *Meaning in Interaction*. London and New York: Longman.

Toolan, M. 1996. 'Stylistics and its Discontents; Or, Getting off the Fish "Hook"', in Weber, J.J. (ed.). *The Stylistics Reader*. 117–35. London and New York: Arnold.

Toolan, M. 1988. *Narrative: A Critical Linguistic Introduction*. London and New York: Routledge.

Toolan, M. 1990. *The Stylistics of Fiction*. London: Routledge.

Toolan, M. 1998. *Language in Literature*. London: Arnold.

Toolan, M. 2000. '"What Makes You Think You Exist?": A Speech Move Schematic and Its Application to Pinter's *The Birthday Party'*. *Journal of Pragmatics* 32 (2): 177–201.

Trask, R.L. 1997. *A Guide to Punctuation*. London: Penguin.

Trask, R.L.1999. *Key Concepts in Language and Linguistics*. London and New York: Routledge.

Traugott, E.C. and Pratt, M.L. 1980. *Linguistics for Students of Literature*. New York: Harcourt Brace Jovanovich, Inc.

Trudgill, P. 1990. *The Dialects of England*. Cambridge, MA and Oxford: Blackwell.

Trudgill, P. 1974. *The Social Differentiation of English in Norwich*. Cambridge: Cambridge University Press.

Trudgill, P. and Hannah, J. 1982/1994. *International English*. 3rd edn. London: Edward Arnold.

Trussler, S. 1973/1986. 'The Plays of Harold Pinter', in Scott, M. (ed.). 1986. '*Harold Pinter:* The Birthday Party, The Caretaker, The Homecoming: *A Casebook*'. 123–4. London and Basingstoke: Macmillan.

Tsui, A.B.M. 1994. *English Conversation*. Oxford: Oxford University Press.

Tsui, A.B.M. 1993. 'Multi-act Moves in Spoken Discourse', in Baker, M., Francis, G. and Tognini-Bonelli, E. (eds). *Text and Technology*. 75–94. Amsterdam: John Benjamins.

Tucker, S. 2003. 'A Technician in the Wings: Ayckbourn's *Comic Potential'*. *Journal of Dramatic Theory and Criticism* 17 (2): 71–94.

Tynan, K. 1960. 'The Under-Belly of Laughter'. *The Observer* 3 July 1960: 25.

Vuchinich, S. 1990. 'The Sequential Organization of Closing in Verbal Family Conflict', in Grimshaw, A.D. (ed.). *Conflict Talk*. 118–38. Cambridge: Cambridge University Press.

Wallis, M. and Shepherd, S. 1998. *Studying Plays*. London: Arnold.

Wandor, M. 1987. *Look Back in Gender*. London and New York: Methuen.

Wardle, I. 1971. 'The Territorial Struggle', in Lahr, J. (ed.). *A Casebook on Harold Pinter's* The Homecoming. 37–44. New York: Grove Press.

Wellwarth, G. 1996/2001. '*The Dumbwaiter, The Collection, The Lover,* and *The Homecoming*: A Revisionist Approach', in Gordon, L. (ed.). 2001. *Pinter at 70: A Casebook*. New York: Routledge.

Wesker, A. 1959/1976. *The Wesker Trilogy*. Harmondsworth, Middlesex, England: Penguin.

Whyld, K. 1993. *Learn Chess in a Weekend*. London: Dorling Kindersley.

Widdowson, H.G. 1975. *Stylistics and the Teaching of Literature*. Essex: Longman.

Wilcher, R. 1996. 'Arnold Wesker', in Demastes, W. (ed.). *British Playwrights: 1956–1995*. 416–34. Wesport, CT and London: Greenwood Press.

Wilcher, R. 1991. *Understanding Arnold Wesker*. Columbia, South Carolina: University of South Carolina Press.

Williams, R. 1961. *The Long Revolution*. London: Chatto and Windus, Ltd.

Wittgenstein, L. 1969. *Philosophical Investigations*. Trans. G.E.M. Anscome. New York: Macmillan.

Worsley, T.C. 1959. 'Review of *Roots*'. *Financial Times* 31 July.

Worsley, T.C. 1964. 'Terence Rattigan and His Critics'. *London Magazine* 60–72.

Worth, K. 1972. *Revolutions in Modern English Drama*. London: Bell.

Wright, L. and Hope, J. 1996. *Stylistics*. London: Routledge.

Young, B.A. 1978. 'Preface', in *The Collected Plays of Terence Rattigan*. vii–xviii. London: Hamish Hamilton.

Young, B.A. 1986. *The Rattigan Version*. London: Hamish Hamilton.

Index

*For Product Safety Concerns and Information please contact
our EU representative GPSR@taylorandfrancis.com Taylor & Francis
Verlag GmbH, Kaufingerstraße 24, 80331 München, Germany*

T - #0051 - 270225 - C0 - 219/153/8 [10] - CB - 9780754651055 - Gloss Lamination